The
Cost
of
Courage

DOUBLEDAY

New York

London

Toronto

Sydney

Auckland

THE
COST
OF
COURAGE

THE JOURNEY
OF AN
AMERICAN
CONGRESSMAN

CARL ELLIOTT, SR.
& MICHAEL D'ORSO

PUBLISHED BY DOUBLEDAY
a division of
Bantam Doubleday Dell Publishing Group, Inc.
666 Fifth Avenue, New York, New York 10103

DOUBLEDAY and the portrayal of an anchor
with a dolphin are trademarks of Doubleday,
a division of Bantam Doubleday Dell Publishing Group, Inc.

Grateful acknowledgment is made for permission to reprint excerpts
from *House Out of Order* by Richard Bolling. Copyright © 1964, 1965,
1966 by Richard Bolling. Used by permission of the publisher, Dutton,
an imprint of New American Library, a division of Penguin Books
USA Inc.

"The Twilight of a Southern Liberal: Carl Elliott, Flat Broke and
Nearly Forgotten" by Wil Haygood. Reprinted courtesy of the Boston
Globe.

BOOK DESIGN BY ANNE LING

Library of Congress Cataloging-in-Publication Data

Elliott, Carl, 1913–
    The cost of courage : the journey of an American congressman/
Carl Elliott, Sr. and Michael D'Orso. — 1st ed.
        p.   cm.
    Includes index.
    1. Elliott, Carl, 1913– . 2. Legislators—United States—Biog-
raphy. 3. United States. Congress. House—Biography. 4. Afro-
Americans—Civil   rights.   5. Alabama—Politics   and   govern-
ment—1951–   I. D'Orso, Michael.   II. Title.
E748.E39A3   1992
328.73′092—dc20
[B]   91-19921
                                                       CIP

ISBN 0-385-42091-9

To Barbara Weatherford Cashion,
for whom I have great admiration and respect.
—C.E., Sr.

Contents

ACKNOWLEDGMENTS

We would like to thank the many people whose good faith and support meant so much to the making of this book, beginning with three of Carl's longtime political companions and personal friends: Mary Allen Jolley, Julian Butler and Garve Ivey.

Then there are Carl's children—Martha Elliott Russell, Lenora Elliott Cannon and John Elliott—and Carl's brothers and sisters—Jewell Elliott Peters, Gober O. Elliott, Mabel Elliott Carpenter, Hoyt Elliott Sr., Ernie O. Elliott, Willie Mae Elliott McKinney and Martha Jean Elliott Williams.

In addition, we would like to thank the staff at the University of Alabama's W. Stanley Hoole Special Collections Library, particularly head librarian Joyce Lamont and reference archivist Clark Center; the staff at the John F. Kennedy Library, particularly Erica Stern and Carolyn C. Mazzone; the staff at the Carl Elliott Regional Library, especially reference librarian Phoebe Nunnelly; William Barnard, head of the University of Alabama's history department; Mike

Letcher of the University of Alabama's department of communications; Laurie Dean, reference librarian for the Birmingham *News*; Jim Murray, reference archivist for the Birmingham Public Library; Wil Haygood of the Boston *Globe*; and Paul South of the *Daily Mountain Eagle*.

We would also like to thank Robert Schremser, Scotty Kennedy, Liliane McCarthy, Vicki Lewis and John Williams.

At Doubleday, we are indebted to our editorial staff, especially Jacqueline Onassis, Shaye Areheart, Deborah Artman and Bruce Tracy.

And finally, we thank our literary agent, David Black.

. . . therefore despise not the chastening of the Almighty. For he wounds, but he binds up; he smites, but his hands heal. He will deliver you from six troubles; in seven there shall no evil touch you. In famine he will redeem you from death, and in war from the power of the sword. You shall be hid from the scourge of the tongue, and shall not fear destruction when it comes.

—Job: 5:17–21

And when at some future date the high court of history sits in judgment of each one of us—recording whether in our brief span of service we fulfilled our responsibilities to the State—our success or failure in whatever office we may hold, will be measured by the answers to four questions: were we truly men of courage—were we truly men of judgment—were we truly men of integrity—were we truly men of dedication?

John Fitzgerald Kennedy

PROLOGUE

I'm not a man who shows much emotion. I can't remember crying too many times in my life. I cried when my son died, I know that. When my wife died, I cried again. But normally I don't show a lot of personal feelings. That's just the way I was brought up, the way I learned to be from the time I was a boy. So all those folks up in Boston probably didn't know how I felt when they brought me out in front of that crowd on a rainy Tuesday morning in the spring of 1990 to give me the first John F. Kennedy Profile in Courage Award.

It had been a while since I'd been at a gathering like that. There was Ted Kennedy sitting to my right, Jacqueline Kennedy Onassis on my left. I couldn't help thinking back to when I'd first met Jackie, back before she married John Kennedy, back when I was on Capitol Hill and she was a young newspaper reporter who had dropped in to talk to me in my office. Who could have imagined we'd both be here like this nearly forty years later, with her daughter Caroline sitting on the other side of her, a woman herself, grown and married? And the press—there must have been a hundred of them jammed together in front of us, enough television cameras, photographers and reporters to wad the biggest shotgun this side of Red Bay.

How did it feel? they all wanted to know. How did it feel to be old, ill, confined to a wheelchair, living the life of an obscure outcast for the past quarter century? How did it feel to see the man who had so much to do with casting me out now old, ill and confined to a wheelchair himself—how did I feel about George Wallace? A writer back in Birmingham, a fellow named Ted Bryant, had written a column about the two of us, comparing our lives and our legacies, contrasting Wallace's well-being with what has become my own bad fortune. When Ted Kennedy rose to speak at Harvard University that day, he read Ted Bryant's column aloud. And he cried.

I didn't do that. And I didn't really have any answers for all the reporters' questions. At least not the simple answers they might have hoped to hear. There's nothing simple about all of this. Not now. Not back then. Some say I was ahead of my time. Some say this was a long time coming. The Boston *Globe* and the New York *Times*, *People* magazine, "The Today Show"—they all talked about vindication and courage, integrity and sacrifice. Some even used the word "tragedy."

Well, I don't know about all that. But it *has* been a long time.

A long time since I was a boy growing up in a log cabin on a tenant farm in the hills of northwest Alabama, helping my daddy in the cotton fields, getting up long before dawn to tend my traps in the woods and staying up late at night to read books by the living-room firelight, books about America, books that made me dream there could be nothing more noble, no finer thing for a man in this world to become than a United States Congressman.

A long time since my daddy would take me with him to towns like Vina or Red Bay or Russellville, to hear the politicians who came through those hills, to watch them speak, to feel the mightiness of their words as they thundered off those outdoor stages. Men like "Cotton" Tom Heflin, a fire-eater of the first order, raising his fist to the heavens as his gray hair fell to his shoulders. And Hugo

Black, a thin, lawyerly fella from down in Birmingham, running for the Senate the year I first heard him speak, when I was twelve. I didn't know Black had resigned from the Ku Klux Klan just the year before, and I had no idea he would one day become a member of the United States Supreme Court. All I knew was that one day I'd be making speeches like those men, so I went home and practiced night after night, standing on a stump in the field behind our house, talking to cornstalks and the cotton plants and the darkness.

A long time since I turned sixteen, setting off out of those hills on foot, carrying my dreams in a cardboard box, with two dollars and thirty-eight cents in my pocket, headed south to Tuscaloosa, where a man named George Denny, the president of the University of Alabama, was battling the beginning of the Great Depression by announcing that anyone willing to work would still be able and welcome to make his way through that university.

A long time since I took Denny at his word, sleeping in an abandoned campus building, cooking my meals on an open fire, shoveling coal, cutting grass, painting buildings, sweeping floors, doing whatever it took to get myself through both college and law school, watching other students laugh at me when I arrived and watching them eventually elect me student body president, even sending me to Washington and a private meeting with the man who was and who remains a political god to me—Franklin D. Roosevelt.

A long time since I went back to those hills with that law degree, back to my people, hanging out my lawyer's shingle for dirt farmers and coal miners, taking my pay more often in livestock and produce than in hard cash.

A long time since those same farmers and miners sent me to Congress in 1948, where I spent the next sixteen years doing all I could for them—getting dams put up, libraries built, roads cut, mail delivered—and doing as much as I could for the nation itself— working ten years to build and finally give birth to the National Defense Education Act, which opened college doors to millions of students who without it could never have afforded the education that changed their lives, the same sort of education that changed mine.

A long time since I rode the crest of a progressive, liberal wave in Congress, a wave spearheaded by my political contemporaries from Alabama—Senators Lister Hill and John Sparkman, and Congressmen Bob Jones, Albert Rains, Kenneth Roberts, and others—into a spot on the powerful House Rules Committee, working arm in arm with Sam Rayburn and the new President, John F. Kennedy, when the world was in our hands, when so much of it seemed to be changing for the better, when anything seemed possible.

A long time since it all so suddenly came apart: George Wallace elected governor of Alabama in 1962, Kennedy shot in 1963, the tide of segregation and racism cresting, swamping the South in hatred and driving me out of Congress in 1964.

A long time since I gathered myself to make a stand against that tide, to face the forces of Wallace, to fight the Klan and the Birchers, the gunfire and smears and hysteria that all became part of the Alabama governor's race of 1966, a campaign the likes of which my state and this nation had never seen before and I pray will never see again.

That race was twenty-five years ago, a quarter century. It was the last time a man seriously stood up to George Wallace in this state, and I paid for it. I paid in dollars, cashing in my Congressional pension fund to help finance that campaign, then watching debt follow debt in the years to come, losing the house in which I raised my children, the same house in which I now live as a renter, chipping away at my debt the best I can with a Social Security check and an Army pension. Friends would tell me there was a way out, that I could declare bankruptcy. But I couldn't do that. I wasn't raised that way. A fellow's got to take responsibility for himself, whether his bad fortune is his own doing or someone else's.

I paid in dignity, going back to colleges I helped build, asking to be hired to teach politics or history, as I had done decades earlier at the University of Alabama, and having the doors closed. Loyalty's a funny thing with some people. It seems to sort of slip and slide around sometimes, depending on circumstances.

I paid in friendship, seeing so many who had stood by my side before the fall suddenly turn away as they were swept up by the same forces that left me behind.

And I paid in reputation, still hearing people tell me today that

I have purely and simply been a fool, that everything would be fine if I had just played the game, if I had had sense enough not to commit political and financial suicide for a cause that was so clearly hopeless. They say I'm stubborn, and maybe it's so. But I haven't changed. I'm the same man now that I was sixty years ago.

These were higher prices than I ever imagined. I'm seventy-seven years old now, and I'm still paying them. But we *all* paid the price when the walls of segregation began crumbling across America more than thirty years ago. The torment and the pain, the push and the passion on both sides of the civil rights movement nearly tore this country apart. America—especially the South—paid a high price then, and it is still paying it today. The force I faced twenty-five years ago, the intense, pointed power of racial hatred and sullen resistance, is far from dead in this nation. To fail to see this, to neglect to continue to do all we can to resist and rise above it, is to pay a price higher than any of us can afford.

A long time?

Maybe.

But then again, it hasn't been that long at all. . . .

THE
COST
OF
COURAGE

Alabama felt a magic descending, spreading, long ago. Since then it has been a land with a spell on it—not a good spell, always. Moons, red with the dust of barren hills, thin pine trunks barring horizons, festering swamps, restless yellow rivers, are all part of a feeling—a strange certainty that above and around them hovers enchantment—an emanation of malevolence that threatens to destroy men through dark ways of its own.

Carl Carmer, Stars Fell on Alabama

ONE

ALABAMA FEVER

Maybe you've been through a town like Jasper, maybe not. There are places like it all across Alabama, all across the South, all across the country, in fact. They're the parts of America the interstate highways have left behind. Even the older, smaller roadways have found a way with their modern bypasses to swing around places like Jasper. The quick-food drive-throughs, the malls and the motels that tend to sprout up along those roads have a way of slipping the heart right out of a community, turning its old main street, its courthouse square, its small downtown stores and service stations into so many echoing shells.

That's pretty much what's happened to Jasper. The downtown section is nothing like the place it was when I hung up my lawyer's shingle here in 1936, when I married and started my family here in 1940 and when I was first elected to the United States Congress from here in 1948, posing with my wife and children for newspaper pictures on the front porch of the same house where I still live.

There were no Holiday Inns or Exxons or Burger Kings back then, but there was a statue at the center of town, a couple blocks from my door, on the lawn in front of the county courthouse. That statue is still there, three Confederate soldiers carved from stone in 1900, standing sentry for eternity, facing south.

There's a poem etched in that monument's granite base:

> *COMRADES*
> *Furl that Banner*
> *True 'Tis Gory*
> *Yet 'Tis Wreathed Around in Glory,*
> *And 'Twill Live in Song and Story,*
> *Though Its Folds Are in the Dust.*

Some things change and some don't. Young men still roar through this town in their pickup trucks on Friday nights, and often there are still Confederate flags flapping in the cab windows of those trucks. There are still letters to the editor in the local papers pleading for Alabamians to finally put the fear and hatred of racism behind them. And there are still letters warning that the black man had best be kept in his place.

It can get confusing sometimes, looking out my window at the video rental store a block from my yard and at the cable television set in my living room with its thirty channels, then thinking back to the log cabin I was born in, where I read books by the light of the fireplace, the only light we had.

I'll watch the evening news with its images of President George Bush greeting young Congressmen I've never met, and I'll glance over at the photo sitting on my living-room mantel, a picture taken three decades ago, of me flanked by another President, John Kennedy, and his Vice-President, Lyndon Johnson, the three of us with our hands gripped in triumph.

I look at the glass and brick building down the street from my house, the one with the words CARL ELLIOTT REGIONAL LIBRARY mounted above its front door, and I think back to my boyhood, when the books I read came by mail from the Sears, Roebuck company, came by train from Chicago south to these Alabama hills.

I'd wait for that train up at a place called Gober Ridge, the place where I was born, some seventy miles north of Jasper, deep in the hills and piney woods that blanket the southern Tennessee Valley. There are no bypasses up there, no motels. In fact there have been relatively few changes to speak of from the day I came into this life in a Gober Ridge cabin on the twentieth day of December 1913.

It was and still is what you'd call back country up there, a place where people make their living close to the land, on small farms hacked out of stony slopes or in coal mines beneath the red clay and rocks that cover those hillsides. It was and still is hard country up there, at the southern tip of what people today call Appalachia.

This is not the sort of place most folks picture when they think of Alabama. More likely the images that come to mind are of sprawling plantations, pillared mansions, moss-draped oaks and cotton fields to the horizon, women dressed in antebellum hoopskirts dancing with beaus clad in the gray uniforms of the Confederacy.

Maybe the images are of slavery.

Maybe they're of the Klan, of Montgomery and bus boycotts or of Birmingham and bombings. Or of George Wallace planting himself at the entrance to the University of Alabama.

Or maybe people just think of Bear Bryant and 'Bama football.

Those things are all real enough, but they belong to a different Alabama from the one in which I was brought up. They belong to an Alabama I didn't encounter until I came down from those hills to make my way in the world. By then I was already shaped by the soil from which my father and mother drew our family's living, the same dirt on which their fathers and mothers before them made a life for themselves and their children.

It might seem that my story ought to begin with the log cabin in which I was born that winter evening the year before the outbreak of World War I, but really it begins long before then. Basically it begins with Hezekiah Massey, my great-grandfather on my mother's side.

History books in these parts talk a lot about the Indians that originally settled this state, what they called the four "civilized tribes" of this region—the Choctaws, the Chickasaws, the Cherokees and the Creeks. The books talk about how so many of the place names we have down here today—towns like Tuskegee, Tuscaloosa and Chattahoochee, rivers like the Tallapoosa and the Tombigbee, even the name of Alabama itself—came from the Indians. They talk about how the Spanish conquistador Hernando de Soto came through in 1540 with hungry dogs and nearly a thousand armored soldiers and slaughtered what some say were eleven thousand Indians at a village called Maubila in a desperate search for gold.

De Soto didn't find what he was looking for in Alabama, and he eventually moved west. But he left behind a cloud of devastation, confusion and fear among the Indians that would hang over them for the next three centuries, as waves of white men from Spain, France, Britain and finally the new nation of America followed De Soto's lead.

By the turn of the nineteenth century, scattered bands of American pioneers from Georgia, the Carolinas, Virginia and Tennessee were drifting into the Alabama wilderness in oxcarts on rough dirt roads, claiming Indian land as their own in the name of what their leaders back in Washington came to call "manifest destiny." When the Indians finally fought back, massacring some two hundred and forty white men, women and children at a forest stockade near Mobile in 1813, the conflict called the Creek War was begun.

To tell the truth, it wasn't much of a war. Andrew Jackson came in with about three thousand well-armed men and laid waste to the Creeks, annihilating nearly a thousand of them at a place called Horseshoe Bend in 1814 and signing the first of a long line of one-sided treaties that eventually forced most of the Indians out of the state. Jackson's triumph at Horseshoe Bend was his first step toward the White House. By 1829 he had made it to Washington, and the next year he put his presidential signature on what was called the Indian Removal Act.

The government couldn't have been much plainer about its intent to eradicate the Indians, and Jackson was the agitator of every bit of this. He was the hero of this back country, a popular man, so popular that more than a few folks in these parts named their children after him. One of those children happened to be my mother's father, Andrew Jackson Massey.

But what Andrew Jackson did with the Indians around here was, as far as I'm concerned, unforgivable. The Creeks gave him a pretty good fight, and he never forgot it. He and his crowd beat those Indians into a pulp, burned them in their houses, just a horrible slaughter. Then, almost immediately, he began to drive every Indian out of this state, either west to Oklahoma or south to Florida. Drove them like cattle, he did.

What seemed to drive Andrew Jackson himself, as much as ambition—and he had plenty of that—was pure hatred. He was one of the most brutal men that ever graced—or disgraced—the history of this wild country here. But to this day most people around these parts will have none of that. They think as much of him, if not more, than they do of George Wallace—and that's a lot.

By the time of the 1835 "Trail of Tears," a forced march during which four thousand Cherokees died as they were herded off their native soil in these parts to settlements west of the Mississippi River, twenty million choice acres of Indian land in Alabama had been ceded to the whites. Not long after that march, a Creek chief named Eufaula delivered a eulogy of sorts in an address to the Alabama legislature. "The Indian fires are going out," the chief told his white audience.

The Creeks were the last to go. By 1838 most of them had fled to Florida, and Alabama's Indian fires were extinguished.

By then a North Carolina native named Hezekiah Massey had arrived with his parents at a homestead in Pickens County, Alabama, where the Chickasaws once roamed. His parents were among the pioneers who had caught what they called "Alabama fever" after Jackson's victory at Horseshoe Bend. No sooner had that battle ended than white settlers from the East swarmed into what Jackson himself called "the best unsettled country in America."

Actually, the country Jackson was talking about was the rich bottomland in Alabama's north central river valleys and the thirteen-thousand-square-mile crescent of black alluvial soil that sliced through the belly of the state. This central swath was the area that came to be called the "Black Belt," the fertile heartland that would make wealthy men of the cotton farmers who settled there and depended on slave labor to turn the dark, gummy fields white with cotton and to build their owners' fine verandaed homes. By the time of the Civil War, this area of Alabama produced nearly a quarter of the nation's cotton—and its slave population had leaped from 42,000 in 1820 to more than 435,000 in 1860.

There were no verandas where Hezekiah Massey settled once he took a wife and set out on his own in these northwestern hills. And there were hardly any slaves. In fact, when Alabama formed a convention to ratify its constitution prior to becoming a state in 1819, the hill farmers pitched a bitter battle against the central Black Belt planters to keep the landowners from counting their slaves when determining seats in the state's House of Representatives. The hill farmers had no slaves to speak of, and they saw how the scales would be tipped against them if their wealthy counterparts to the south were allowed to count theirs.

After some stormy debate, the convention finally relented and voted to count only whites. But the tone was set for a rift that is still strong today, a rivalry between what the central flatlanders call "hillbillies," "clay eaters," "piney woods folks" and "poor white trash" and what the hill folks consider the haughty, well-heeled Bourbon aristocracy of the Black Belt. It's your basic class conflict is what it is, and it came to color much of my own career, both politically and personally. But that was later.

The Alabama hill country into which I was born was a world unto itself, not much different from the world Hezekiah made for himself after he married a woman named Margaret Bonds in December 1849 and moved to a place called Trace Branch, some twenty miles as the road winds from Gober Ridge.

It was this part of Alabama that a New York architect and landscape artist named Frederick Law Olmsted visited in the 1850s. Olmsted was the man who planned New York City's Central Park. He was an ardent abolitionist. And he wrote in detail of the people and places he came across while roaming the South. Among Olmsted's writings was this entry:

Northern Alabama, June 15th, 1853.—I have to-day reached a more distinctly hilly country—somewhat rocky and rugged, but with inviting dells. The soil is sandy and less frequently fertile; cotton-fields are seen only at long intervals, the crops on the small proportion of cultivated land being chiefly corn and oats. I notice also that white men are more commonly at work in the field than negroes, and this as well in the cultivation of cotton as of corn.

What Olmsted saw was true of Hezekiah Massey and most of the small farmers who settled these highlands: they actually preferred the sandy soil of these hills because they could plow it themselves. The sticky clay of the Black Belt required crews of slaves to till it into workable fields. The hill people, on the other hand, worked their own fields, proud of their self-reliance, preferring to raise food crops to feed and support their families rather than grow cotton to trade at market. But to outsiders, especially the wealthier lowlanders, the mountain folk were looked on with scorn. Even the blacks ridiculed them with a rhyme of the time: "You can't raise cotton on sandy lan'; I'd ruther be a nigger than a po' white man." These homesteads did indeed look poor to outside eyes, eyes like Olmsted's:

The large number of the dwellings are rude log huts, of only one room, and that unwholesomely crowded. I saw in and about one of them, not more than fifteen feet square, five grown persons, and as many children.

An Alabama historian named Albert Burton Moore—who became dean of graduate studies in history at the University of Alabama and was one of my professors during my studies at the university—was more specific about these "huts":

A single cabin was usually provided with just one door and one window. The window gave light and ventilation was supplied by the cracks in the walls and the floor. A shutter was put on both the window and the door, which was made of rough

clapboards fastened together by wooden pegs driven into auger
holes. Glass windows were unknown. The clumsy old shutters
swung and creaked upon wooden hinges, for steel hinges were
unknown. . . .

The interior of the early cabin was as humble as the exte-
rior. With an axe saw, drawing knife, plane, augers and chisels,
the master of the household made his rough bedsteads, stools,
chairs, benches and cradles from the timber that grew on the
sides of the hills. A description of the cradle, which was common to every household, will suffice to give some idea of the
utter crudeness of the furniture of the household. It was simply
half of a hollow log with a bit of rocker-shaped clapboard fastened on each end. In such a cradle . . . young hopefuls,
wrapped in quilts or the fur skins of wild animals, were lulled
to sleep.

That description doesn't sound much different from the cabin I
was born in. And neither does Olmsted's impression of the simple
honesty, hospitality and earnestness of the hill folk he found in 1853
differ much from that of the neighbors I grew up with, the sort of
people who taught me that, as valuable as a formal education is,
there are some things a man can't learn from a book.

An Alabama planter of that era, a man named D. R. Hundley,
described his hill-country counterparts as "lank, lean, angular, and
bony, with . . . sallow complexion, awkward manners, and a natural stupidity or dullness of the intellect that surpasses belief." When
you read words like that, it's best to consider the source. Olmsted,
for instance, saw things differently. Here's what he learned while
watching an Alabama hill family work their field on a sleepy summer
afternoon nearly a century and a half ago:

. . . I found a good spot for nooning. I roped my horse out to
graze and spread my blanket in a deep shade. I noticed that the
noise of their work had ceased, and about fifteen minutes after-
wards, Jude suddenly barking, I saw one of the men peering at
me through the trees, several rods distant. I called to him to
come up. He approached rather slowly and timidly, examined

the rope with which my horse was fastened, eyed me vigilantly, and at length asked if I was resting myself. I replied that I was; and he said he did not know but I might be sick, and had come to see me. I thanked him and offered him a seat upon my blanket, which he declined. Presently he took up a newspaper that I had been reading, looked at it for a moment, then he told me he couldn't read. "Folks don't care much for education round here; it would be better for 'em I expect, if they did." He began then to question me closely about my circumstances —where I came from, whither I was going, etc. . . . .

He asked if I had not found the people "more friendly like" up in this country to what they were down below, and assured me that I would find them grow more friendly as I went further North, so at least he had heard, and he knew where he first came from (Tennessee) the people were more friendly than they were here. "The richer the man is," he continued, pursuing a natural association of ideas, "and the more niggers he's got, the poorer he is . . . these yer big planters they don' care for nothing but to save. Now, I never calculate to save anything: I tell my wife I work hard, and I mean to enjoy what I earn as fast as it comes."

Of all the "more friendly like" people up in those hills, there were apparently few any more friendly or well liked than my great-grandfather Hezekiah Massey, or "Uncle Hezzie," as most folks in these parts called him. He's mentioned in more than one Alabama history text as the quintessential Alabama pioneer, a poor farmer, but a proud one. My forebears were known for their large families, and Uncle Hezzie was no exception—he had 12 children, 88 grandchildren, including my mother Nora, and more than 200 great-grandchildren, including me.

In 1910 a schoolteacher and state senator from these parts named Charley Ross West, who later became a good friend of mine, wrote a profile of my great-grandfather that was published in the county newspaper. The piece was titled "A Pioneer Citizen: A Brief Sketch of *Hezekiah Massey,* one of Franklin County's Grand Old Citizens, and his Queenly Wife":

"Uncle Hezekiah" Massey, as he is lovingly called by all who know him, and who lives on Trace branch near old Nauvoo, below Belgreen, is perhaps one of the most widely known men in the county. . . .

He was born in North Carolina but moved to Alabama with his parents when he was only nine years old and settled with them in Pickens county. . . . "Uncle Hezzie" says that neither his father nor his mother knew a letter in the book; neither did either of them ever see a train. . . . "Uncle Hezzie" says that he never rode on a train in all his life and was never out of the state since he came here except twice. . . .

On the 12th of next December "Uncle Hezzie" will be 88 years old and has made farming his life long occupation. He has made a crop every year since coming to the state, till two years ago, when old age caused him to turn loose the plow handles—never more, perhaps, to plough a furrow. He is now in feeble health and realizes that e'er long he will have to lay down for all time, the working tools of life. His whole life has been simple but well spent. . . .

Mrs. Massey, wife of "Uncle Hezzie," was 82 years old the 12th of this past August. While she shows her age to a great extent, yet she is holding up well. She walked four miles not long since to visit her son David, on Little Bear Creek. . . .

Now since his boys and girls have married, his home has been greatly changed. It has been transformed, so to speak, into a quiet, peaceful country home, surrounded by some of nature's most beautiful scenes of cliffs and glades.

I spent this day at this home and what a great pleasure it was to talk with these old people who have been here more than four score of years. . . . If all people would live such lives as these good old people have lived, we would have little use for laws, such as are now on our statute books.

Hezekiah Massey died the month after those words were printed. Three years later, I was born.

———

What I know of my great-grandfather came from my family's stories and from friends like Charley West. But what I know of Hezekiah's wife Margaret, I saw for myself. She lived until I was thirteen, and if her husband typified the hill farmer—working his fields single-handedly for half a century and refusing to padlock his crib or smokehouse because he felt that would be "a reflection" on his neighbors—Margaret Bonds Massey epitomized the kind of woman who shared that life and shouldered her load.

She was a tough woman; my God, she was tough. She buckled up to this wilderness just like she was made for it. Helped her husband conquer their little piece of it and in doing that raised a dozen children as well. As I was growing up, she was still making those four-mile walks to see her boys. She hiked the same distance to and from church every Sunday. I've got a photo of her fresh from one of those Sunday strolls, and she looks like she could kill the Devil himself, if he was foolish enough to get in her way.

Every so often Grandma Massey would go back to see "her people," as she called them, down in Pickens County, some ninety miles to the south. She'd get on a horse up there on the farm, and, riding sidesaddle, it'd take her four or five days of good riding, twenty miles a day through woods with no roads. No roads, no bridges. This was *real* wilderness. When night overtook her, she'd stay right there in the woods, no problem. If the wilderness had anything to do with Grandma Massey, it was welcome to do it. She was not one to back down.

And she knew the Civil War first hand. Four of her brothers died fighting it. They were Confederate soldiers, but the decision to take arms against the North was not easy for men in this part of Alabama. By no means was it all one way up here. There was a lot of Union sentiment in this area. A large number of men in this back country were what they called Unionists. The figures on the number of Alabamians in the Confederate Army are sketchy, but the best estimates are that some 130,000 served under the Stars and Bars. Another 3,000 joined the Union Army, and almost all of them were from these hills. It was hard for the men up here to see the Southern cause the way the Black Belters looked at it.

It says something that in 1860, when cotton planters made up less than one third of one percent of Alabama's white population and were nearly eighteen times as wealthy as the average white Alabamian, they held one fourth of the seats in the state legislature. Theirs were some of the loudest voices calling for secession from the Union on the basis of states' rights and the protection of an economic system based on slavery—issues not too different from the basis of segregationism throughout the South a century later.

The ordinary fellow up in this area back then called it a rich man's war and a poor man's fight. They felt their forebears had fought for the independence of this country from England, and they weren't going to help tear it up. Remember, it had only been eighty years since the first war, the Revolutionary War. A lot of folks up here still remembered that. They were more loyal to what they called "the flag of our fathers" than to this new Stars and Bars.

There was talk for a time among north Alabamians of seceding from the state and joining mountain sections of Georgia and Tennessee to form a new state called Nickajack. Nothing came of it, but there was one county, Winston County, that actually did vote to secede from Alabama. People around these parts today still tell stories about the "Free State" of Winston County.

Which all goes to show that these people up here, the common people, never were convinced, by and large, that the Civil War was a good idea. They didn't think a lot of Lincoln and what he was doing in Washington, but they weren't for cutting themselves off from their country either. When the Confederacy passed a conscription act in 1862, hundreds of north Alabama Unionists hid in mountain hollows and caves rather than become part of the Rebel Army. Folks called them "mossbacks," because of the moss that supposedly grew on their clothing in the damp, clammy gullies where they huddled. In 1862, one Confederate general guessed there were as many as ten thousand "Tories" and deserters scattered among Alabama's northern mountains.

Hezekiah Massey was not among them. He joined the Confederate Army in 1862 and went away to fight for three years. While he was gone, his home and family, like so many in these hills, were left unprotected against the vagrants, raiders and renegade troops on both sides that passed through these mountains. There was plenty of fighting going on among neighbors themselves as well. Men, and even women and children, suspected of being traitors to the South, were beaten, tortured and in some cases even hanged. It is said that Confederate soldiers off at war sat around their campfires at night, making up lists of those they would "attend to" when they got back home. To this day there are people in these parts whose bitterest memories of the Civil War are not of any battles with soldiers in blue but of feuds with the family down the road. One of the people who lived with that kind of memory was Hezekiah Massey.

While he was away, a gang of partisan rangers, a home guard of sorts, had taken it on themselves to roam the countryside. Bullies is what they were, busybodies. One day some of them came by Hezekiah's farm and asked for his oldest son, my grandfather, Andrew Jackson Massey. The boy was about thirteen years old at the time. This gang of men said something about him being a Unionist and the next thing he knew they were giving him a whipping. Family legend is they tied him to a tree and beat him pretty bad with a rope, for no reason other than pure meanness.

When Hezekiah came home from the war and heard about that, he was enraged, absolutely infuriated. He couldn't hunt these men down. He didn't know who they were. But he did know that everyone in this area was a Democrat in those days, including those rangers, whoever they were. So Uncle Hezzie turned to being a Republican, and he voted Republican the rest of his life.

Hezekiah Massey's Republicanism ran through my mother's side of the family, but my father's people, they were dyed-in-the-wool Democrats. It was his people—actually his mother's family—who founded Gober Ridge. And it was they who produced the person who first directly shaped my life: my grandmother, Penelope Emma (Gober) Elliott.

Her father was a blacksmith and Primitive Baptist preacher named James Gober. "Hardshells" is what some people called the Primitive Baptists, but whatever term you used, a man like James Gober was who you were talking about. The smithing is how Gober fed his family, but the preaching is what meant most to him. And his preaching is what his daughter Penelope clutched to her soul when she left home at eighteen to marry a fellow named John Elliott in 1873.

Now this John Elliott, he was a rarity in these hills, a well-educated man. He taught school, and he was said to be the best mathematician in the county. He married Penelope Gober and had eight children by her, including my father Will, their youngest son. But there's not much more that I know about my grandfather, because in 1900, when my father was eleven, John Elliott left. Just up and went to Texas. There was a saying in those days in Alabama if a fellow got into any kind of trouble and couldn't be found—people would say he'd "gone to Texas." Well, John Elliott actually went.

Of course that put Grandma Elliott in a particular viewpoint about him and all his people from then on. She would go into an absolute rage if his name was brought up. She was left with her children to raise by herself, and when my father, her favorite, started his own family, she moved in with him. It was understood in our house that we didn't ask about the Elliott family history at all. I knew my father was their youngest son, but that's about all I knew.

I also knew my father had typhoid when he was about eight and again when he was eleven. Back then they called it the "slow fever," and it settled in his left leg, leaving it badly crippled, almost useless. It never grew to more than about half the size of his right. Still, he managed to farm, which is how he was making his living when he married my mother in 1913. He didn't have his own place, he couldn't afford that. So he worked another man's land, tenant farming on a relative's property up on the Ridge, which is where he and my mother lived when I was born at the end of their first year of marriage.

As hard as my father worked, and, Lord, I've never seen a harder-working man in my life, he needed my mother to help in the fields. He'd plow a row, swinging his bad leg out to the left side of the furrow as he went, then he'd have to rest under a tree while my mother did a row herself. With both of them out in the fields, it was left to Grandma Elliott to raise me until I was big enough to join them.

One thing I've been blessed with in my life is a pretty good memory. It helped me when it came to counting votes in Congress. And it's helped me understand how I grew up, what parts of myself came from the people who raised me.

I remember, for instance, playing around an uncle's beehives when I was two years old. Of course I wound up turning one of the hives over, and what seemed like a million angry insects came swarming out, stinging every part of my body. I was in pretty bad shape. My father took a mule and beat it away to town, about five miles, to look me up a doctor. When that doctor arrived, he mixed up a vast amount of some sort of goo, took a paddle and spread that stuff on the stung places, which was basically all over my body. Then they put me to bed for what I still recall as the longest night of my life.

But what I recall most was my father standing over me and saying, "Now, you'll get well a lot faster if you don't cry."

Don't cry.

A child hears something like that, and he takes it to heart. He fully and totally believes it. That was one lesson that stayed with me all my life. My father just didn't believe in crying. None of my family did. They were strong and honest, but they were not very emotional people. Sometimes I've wished they had been more so, but they weren't.

Another thing I remember is Grandma Elliott riding to church every weekend. If she was there, I was there. And those church doors didn't open but she was there. Church was at the very core of Grandma Elliott's life, especially after her husband quit her.

She drove a buggy, sort of a surrey with fringe around the top, with a white horse my father had given her to pull it. She'd load me into that buggy and off we'd go for the three-mile ride to the church. And this was no mere morning affair. It was a three-day meeting. We'd leave Friday morning, stop at Grandma's niece's place about halfway there, to visit and maybe have a bite to eat. Then on to the church, where we arrived early Friday afternoon, which is when everything began. Grandma insisted on being one of the first people to get there. If she couldn't be on time, she'd just turn around and go home. She had absolutely no patience with somebody who wouldn't be on time.

We'd get there and sing those old hymns, just voices, no instruments whatsoever. As far as the Primitive Baptists were concerned, musical instruments were the Devil's business. When it came to singing, the Lord's instrument was the human voice, and that was enough. Everything was a cappella. We had a hymnbook a couple of inches thick and there were no musical notes in it at all. Just the words.

We would sing, and there would be foot washings as well, good old-fashioned back-country Baptist foot washings. Grandma Elliott would have her feet washed, but she wouldn't let a man do it. Her feet always had to be washed by a woman.

There was always a preliminary to the preaching, a warm-up, so to speak, for the sermon. The people who could read were called on to recite a verse or two from the Bible. Not half the people in that church could read, and fewer women than men, but Grandma Elliott could read. She was a fine reader, one of the best, and it seemed to me that her mission in life may have been to teach me to read too.

By the time I was three, she was sitting me down at home with the Bible, reading it aloud to me and having me summarize each chapter as we went. By the time I was four, we'd worked our way through the entire book that way, and I figured we were finished. But then we began all over again, this time with *me* doing the reading.

Apparently this was something special in those parts, a boy reading at that age. The word went out across the countryside, and people started coming around just to listen to me read. They'd come and sit on the porch, and I'd read and they'd discuss it sometimes. Of course all this country down here was and is still known as the Bible Belt, and reading the good book was a pretty common form of entertainment. A fellow might not have anything in the cupboard, but he'd sure as hell have a King James version of the Bible around his house somewhere. That just went with the territory. And when folks got together, as often as not they'd bring the Bible out.

A little later, when I was big enough to get around some on my own, I was hungry to find books any way I could. I'd never heard of a library. There was no such thing in those parts, and wouldn't be for another thirty years, until Congress finally passed the Library

Services Act in 1956, which would build libraries and bring books to rural people across America. I'm proud to say I was one of the sponsors of that act and of subsequent legislation that kept the program going in the years that followed.

But back in the 1920s there was no such help for a book-hungry boy like me. There were, however, men like my uncle Bob Rea, who lived down the road from our farm. Uncle Bob was a missionary Baptist preacher, more well off than most folks in our area, but far from wealthy. What he had, though, was a huge wooden box in the back of one of his rooms. And in that box were books, about a hundred of them. He kept a lock and key on that box; that's how precious those books were to him. And he wouldn't just hand them out to anybody. You had to show you were *serious* about this book business if you wanted to borrow them from Uncle Bob. What he'd do is let you take two. When you brought them back, you had to show him you'd actually read them. Then you could take two more.

What Uncle Bob had going there was a primitive library. And I took to it like nobody's business. I read two books a week. A series on the continents. Another on English literature. Classics. Politics. Within a year, I'd worked my way through every book in Uncle Bob's box. Thirty years later, when I stepped on the floor of Congress to convince my colleagues that there were boys and girls throughout this nation as hungry for books as I had been, I looked back to Uncle Bob with more gratitude than I can put into words.

Before I was four, Grandma Elliott had taught me to write as well. Letters were a large part of her life—not just her own letters, but other people's as well. There were so many people in the county who couldn't read, and her reputation for reading was so wide-spread, that folks would actually come from miles around to bring their mail to her so she could read them their letters aloud. This happened often once World War I started and letters began coming home from overseas. Grandma Elliott would read people their mail, and she'd answer the letters for them as well, writing what the neighbors dictated to her.

That was something so important to her, that letters were made to be answered. You didn't get a letter and just toss it on the table and say, "Well, I'll get to that sometime." You sat down and wrote a letter right back, right away. It was a pleasure. She taught me that, and I must say I still have the same habit today. I use the telephone as much as the next fellow, but I'm afraid it's killed the art of letter writing, and that's not just nostalgia talking. You have to think about what you want to say, and you have to find the right words to say it, when you are forced to put it down on paper. I think one thing that enabled us to become a fairly educated nation was the fact that we once put so much time and thought—and feeling—into letters.

Grandma Elliott had me read the mail the same way she had me read the Bible. She'd send me out every afternoon to meet the postman, coming by on his horse. That was a real highlight for both of us. That's one way I learned so much about our kin throughout this country, by reading the letters they wrote to her. And she'd have me write back as well, critiquing each one before putting it in the mail, checking it over for spelling and such.

I don't recall much strain between my mother and my grandmother, as you might expect there'd be. No struggling for control of the household. A big reason for that was the simple fact that my mother was one of the most easygoing people on this earth. She was a big strong lady, muscular. But she was gentle as well, and she was real good at letting other people feel their importance. She never seemed to have any problem with the fact that every meal in our house saw my father seated at one end of the table and his mother seated at the other.

About the only time I saw anger between the two was over a book. Every Christmas Grandma Elliott would tell my mother I ought to have a book. There were two ways to get books in this area of the country at that time. You could buy them from a fellow who occasionally came around in his buggy. If you didn't have any money, he'd take a couple of chickens and tie them to his wagon, or he'd settle for something else of like value. Or you could order a book from the Sears, Roebuck catalogue from the company's headquarters in Chicago.

Now this particular Christmas it just slipped my mother's mind that she was supposed to order a book for me from Sears. It got close to the holiday, and Grandma Elliott found out it hadn't happened. She didn't say a word. She just set her jaw and reached for the pocketbook she kept in her bosom. It never had very much in it, sometimes six or eight dollars, always silver dollars. The silver issue was a big political question at that time, and the words of William Jennings Bryan were gospel throughout this part of the country. It was in 1896 that Bryan pronounced: "You shall not press down upon the brow of labor this crown of thorns. You shall not crucify mankind upon a cross of gold." Twenty years later Grandma Elliott still took those words to heart.

It didn't take but one of her silver dollars to buy a money order from the mailman for a fifty-cent book from Chicago. That's how a lot of business was done in those days, by money order. Rural people didn't have much to do with banks. Grandma sent me out to meet him with a letter and the money, and in two weeks, just in time for Christmas, my book arrived on the Illinois Central Railroad.

That railroad ran right through our farm, its trains stopping at a little spot called Coker Spur, about one mile from our house. That's where I'd go three days a week to pick up the Atlanta newspaper for Grandma Elliott. It was World War I she wanted to read about—and the neighbors had her read the headlines to them as well. But the only war that really mattered to her was the one that had been fought fifty years earlier. If there's one person who taught me what the Civil War can mean to a person from the South, how it can simmer in the soul, it was Grandma Elliott.

The Gobers had all been Confederates, Dixie through and through, and Grandma Elliott was a war girl if ever there was one. There wasn't one battle she couldn't talk about as if she had been there—Shiloh, Bull Run, Vicksburg—and the way she told it, we won them all. She *never* would acknowledge that we got whipped. Whenever she talked about the surrender, it took her maybe thirty seconds to say the word. *Sur—ren—der.* She'd date things by the year of the surrender. This happened the first year after the surrender, that happened the year before the surrender. There was no calendar to mix her up, no birth of Christ. It was simple. The surrender, that was the dividing point. And the way she said that word, she made it sound proud. In fact, I got the impression in my mind, being young and not knowing much, that surrender meant we had *won*. For a long time, until I was six or seven years old, I thought the South had won the Civil War.

Her stories never totally convinced me that the South was a state unto itself—the way so many folks down here still think of it. But hearing Grandma Elliott talk about the war prepared me for the diehard Confederates I'd meet throughout my career, men like the old fellow I came across at a political rally in 1938, in a small Alabama town called Oakman.

I was on the speaker's committee for the Democratic campaign that fall, and we had a rally over at Oakman, about sixteen miles down the road from Jasper. Those rallies usually brought out a considerable amount of excitement, especially in those days, when there wasn't much else going on in the way of entertainment. This particular night the place got pretty heated. Lots of speeches, lots of blood running pretty hot. And suddenly this old fellow jumped up in the back of the room, Courenton was his name. He jumped up clear out of the blue, it seemed to me, and announced to that crowd, "If those damn Yankees come down here again, we'll *whip* 'em again!" That old fella was not about to admit that this thing was over.

Neither was the wealthy Virginian I visited in the mid-1950s with my friend Pat Jennings, when Pat was running for reelection to Congress up there. We were campaigning down in the western part of Virginia, around the Shenandoah Valley, and Pat decided there was this fellow we had to stop and see, "a real crackerjack about the Civil War," Pat said.

As soon as we got in the front door of this man's hillside mansion, I saw what Pat meant. There in the drawing room, covering almost an entire wall, was a painting of old Jeb Stuart astride a horse, looking defiant and strong, maybe a little mean, looking like he was set to ride right out of that frame. All it took was a mention of Jeb, which of course couldn't be avoided, and this fellow not only got off to talking about how he was a direct descendant of Stuart, but he insisted that we drink a toast to the man and to the mighty hosts of the Virginia Army.

Well, one toast followed another, and this old fellow got to talking about how we whipped 'em at this place and we ran 'em off that place. And pretty soon the afternoon had come and gone. When we finally got back outside, I told Pat there was no need for us to go campaigning anymore that day. "What we need to do," I told him, "is get ourselves entirely sober."

This Confederacy thing still hovers over the South like a fog that refuses to lift. It wrapped Grandma Elliott like a shroud. Even in the waning days of World War I, when her eyes were failing and she had me read aloud the newspaper accounts of Kaiser Wilhelm II and the new railroad gun the Germans had developed—Grandma Elliott was always fascinated by the details of weaponry—she would still talk about the War Between the States, still making sure I understood the details of the cause.

As World War I wound to a close in the winter of 1918, Grandma Elliott lay on her sickbed, fighting to stay alive through Armistice Day. Come November the word was the treaty would be signed any day, so Grandma Elliott started sending me down to the tracks where the trains passed through our farm. If the war was over, she said, those trains would have an American flag hung on their engine, signaling victory. Finally, on November 11, the flag was there. I ran home and told Grandma Elliott, and she laid back with a smile. Our side had won another one.

A month later, I turned five years old.

A month after that, on January 21, 1919, Grandma Elliott passed away. There were eight brothers and sisters born after me, nine of Penelope Elliott's grandchildren in our house, but I was her first and her favorite.

She died with her hand on my head.

All over Alabama, the lamps are out. Every leaf drenches the touch; the spider's net is heavy. The roads lie there, with nothing to use them. The fields lie there, with nothing at work in them, neither man nor beast. The plow handles are wet, and the rails and the frogplates and the weeds between the ties: and not even the hurryings and hoarse sorrows of a distant train, on other roads, is heard.

James Agee, Let Us Now Praise Famous Men

Two

GOBER RIDGE

With Grandma Elliott gone, my father stepped into my life in a way he hadn't been there before. I was his oldest child, and I guess he saw in me the boy he had once been as well as the man I could become. So he shared more with me, it seemed, than with my brothers and sisters. Not all that he shared was pleasant.

I remember we were riding home from the little town of Vina one afternoon, after delivering a bale of cotton to the gin there. I was four, but already my father had started taking me with him on trips like that, getting me ready for the time when I'd be carrying my weight on the farm. This day he suddenly pulled the wagon off to the side of the road, dropped the reins, took a deep breath, reached in his pocket and brought out a slip of paper.

"Can you read that?" he asked, handing the paper to me. It was a paycheck. On one side was printed a big arm and hammer, the sign of the baking soda company, and on the other side was a number: three dollars and thirty cents. That was what my father had cleared on that year's crop.

"Carl," he asked, looking off into the woods, "can you tell me how a man is supposed to make a living for his family on a total income of three dollars and thirty cents?"

"I don't see how you can do it, Pa," I said.

I could see his heart and spirit were damn near broken, but I didn't know what to do. He sat there a minute or two, studying that piece of paper. Then he turned and looked me straight in the eye. A four-year-old pays attention when his father looks at him that way.

"You've got to use your head, boy," he said. "You've got to have a better break in this life than I've had, and you're going to have to make that break yourself."

Will Elliott didn't get many breaks in this life. It seemed the scales were always tipped against him, beginning with his bad leg. It never grew larger around than his forearm, and he spent his entire life compensating for it, throwing it off to the side as he walked. He had to constantly be careful about where he went and what he did, but he was absolutely determined that everything he did, he did on his own. He was not a small man—six feet tall, two hundred pounds —and if anyone insulted him, he took immediate retribution. And it was easy for him to see an insult where his leg was concerned. Sometimes he gave a whippin' and sometimes he got one.

Even in his last days he was that way, even with the people closest to him. Early in 1963, the year he died, I came home from a political trip. I'd been a Congressman fifteen years by then. I went by the house where he and my mother were living, the house I'd built for them back in 1948, the year I first went to Washington. My father was pretty crippled by then, worse than ever. So I took him by the arm to go up the steps, and he jerked that arm away from me with more strength than I knew he had.

"I don't allow myself to lean on *anybody*," he said. And he moved on into the house by himself.

My father never leaned on anyone in any sense of the word. In the early days of the Depression, about 1930, the Hoover administration began giving away free bags of flour across the country, through the Red Cross. When a trainload arrived at the town of Red

Bay, my mother sent my father over to pick up the two forty-eight-pound sacks each family was alotted. He was reluctant, but I can hear her telling him that we were in terrible shape and we had all these children here and we were facing starvation. So he went, but he came back empty-handed. He claimed that just as they got to his name on the list they ran out. I don't know how true this was, but I never saw a fellow who looked as relieved as my father did when he came home without that flour.

He was a proud man, and he had a hair trigger about his leg. But other than that, the only fighting my father ever did was to stand up for what he thought was fair. As a poor man dealing with merchants and businessmen who were not always completely honest, he had to take a stand more than once. One of those stands was over at Coker Spur.

We had hauled a load of wooden staves to a mill by the railroad, where a man from Chicago was waiting to count them. I was five then, and I decided I'd count them too.

I was up on the wagon with my father, and this man from Chicago, a big Irish fellow, he finished and said there were seven hundred and twenty staves on this load. And I said to my father right quick, I said no, that was not right, that I'd counted seven hundred and *sixty-two*.

Well, this big Irishman looked up and said, "Now who in the hell employed *you*, boy, to count these staves?" I said I was not calling him a fraud but that he was wrong, that we had forty-two more staves on that wagon than he'd said.

He started fussing at me again, and my father just jumped off the wagon, leaped right on top of that big Irishman, and they started rolling in the dirt. Pretty soon they were both bloody all over, just as bloody as fresh-killed hogs. I sat there with my mouth hanging open, not knowing what to make of it. But I knew one thing: there was nothing in this world, not in heaven or hell or anywhere in between, that my father was afraid of.

He wanted me to be that way too. From an early age he took me hunting with him at night, for possum or anything else a dog might tree in that part of the country. He wouldn't carry a lantern. It was just us and the woods and the night.

This one night he brought us to a cemetery, one of those small overgrown cemeteries you sometimes come across in country like this, seemingly in the middle of nowhere. This one had a built-up brick tomb in it, and we sat down there, in the blackness, listening to the night sounds—and to all the other sounds a seven-year-old hears in a place like that. After a few minutes my father turned to me.

"Do you hear any ghosts, or haints or hobgoblins of any kind?" he asked.

I said no, and he nodded his head. After a couple more minutes of silence, he spoke again.

"The reason you don't hear none of those things," he said, "is 'cause they ain't *out* there."

My father wanted to teach me fearlessness. And he taught me fairness, too. People looked on him as being totally honest, a fellow you could count on in a pinch, someone you could go to the well with if you needed the water. He didn't have a lot to do with other people, preferring to go his own way and tend to his own business. But there were times when he was looked to as a leader. One of those times was during the tick epidemic of 1921.

The state was invaded that year by cattle ticks, bad enough that a law was passed requiring every cow to be washed in a concoction to kill and keep away the insects. Dipping vats were set up all across the state, but when they put one up on Gober Ridge, there was trouble. People tend to get frightened of things they don't know about, and they didn't know a lot about this stuff the state was telling them would get rid of those ticks. Rumors started spreading that this liquid got rid of the ticks all right, but that it got rid of the cattle too. When the day came for the dipping to take place, a crowd of farmers collected around the vat—a huge concrete tub, big enough to put a cow in up to its shoulders—and a spokesman for the group stepped forward and faced the government representative.

"We ain't gonna dip no cattle," he said.

Will Elliott was among that group, but he was not one to let

another man speak for him. My father had studied the situation on
his own, and he had decided that this dipping business made sense.
The government representative, my uncle Bob Rea, he recognized a
showdown when he saw one. And he knew where to turn to play his
trump card. He climbed up on a tree stump and looked down at the
crowd.

"Now we're gonna start to commence the dipping here," he
said, "and the first man that's gonna take his cow through is Will
Elliott over there."

My father didn't hesitate. He led the animal up a ramp and
down into that tub, the cow growling and bawling as she went
through the wash. When she came out the other end, every other
man there fell in line and followed suit. Uncle Bob knew what he
was doing when he chose my father to lead the way.

Something I never got from my father was his love of animals.
He liked being around them as much as people. Goats, sheep,
horses, mules, cows, dogs, he had a way with them all, and you
could see they took to him. If my father had been as good with
people as he was with animals, there's no telling where he could
have gone. He could do anything with a creature. They were just
drawn to him. When we'd go looking for one of the horses, he'd
make a sound between his teeth—I could never do it—and that
horse would come in from as far as a mile away. My father milked
the cows and cared for them like they were his children. He was the
finest hog raiser you ever saw. And dogs, he always had two or three
dogs.

Me, I'd rather read a book than be messing around with animals. Feeding and cooling and watering those beasts was something
I had to do, but my father respected my need to read as well. Maybe
it was Grandma Elliott's influence or maybe my father recognized
that it might be books that would propel me off the land that sometimes seemed to trap us all.

For whatever reason, my father encouraged me to read, picking
up where Grandma Elliott left off. He had me read aloud to him in
the evening, particularly from the Bible, which he studied as closely
as any country preacher. In fact, those preachers would come
through and they'd just get chewed up by my father. I'd sit there

and marvel that he could tell them exactly where to find all sorts of strange things in the Bible, and could tell them when they'd misquoted something. He'd call their hand every time. He really got into the business of straightening out the preacher who didn't get it right.

He had a hunger to simply know things. I think that was another burden in my father's life, that there was so much he wanted to know and simply didn't. He had a fifth-grade education, which was about standard for men in those parts at that time. But he was absolutely spellbound by anything that had to do with facts and figuring. He was fascinated by mathematicians—who knows how much of that had to do with the fact that the father who had left him as a boy had been one? If somebody came through the countryside, selling animals or goods or what have you, and word got around that this person was good with numbers, my father would hook up with him and just hover, asking one question after another. He'd think up problems for the man to do, and he'd have the fellow figure it out on a stick or a piece of lumber, whatever was handy. My father used to say mathematics was the language of the gods, and that affected me. I told myself early on, If this stuff is the language of the gods, I better get right down and start learning to speak that tongue.

But nothing compared to the beauty of words for me. Their rhythm, the way they sounded when you spoke them, even the very shape of the letters on the page, I fell in love with those things from an early age. I read the Bible a lot, but it wasn't the content I cared about so much as the lyricism of the language. It was like music to me. And somehow I knew that music was going to eventually lead to something better than the life I saw around me, although I loved and respected that life.

Long before I went to school, the foundation of my education had been laid, and my lessons went beyond reading and writing and arithmetic. I watched the way my parents were with each other, and I learned about quiet dignity. Theirs was a relationship that was based pretty much on strength and quiet understanding. They were both from what you would call good country stock. There was not a lot of open emotion, but there was a comfort between them. To raise nine children without any conveniences whatsoever, no run-

ning water and no refrigeration, no electricity, no automobile—
there were times when irritations would develop between them, but
that was rare. And my father never struck my mother in his entire
life.

Nora Massey Elliott was a strong woman, which almost goes
without saying up in those hills. She loved all nine of her children,
but she wasn't one to fawn. And she wasn't one to mince words.
One day she had all five of us boys clearing off the hillside that ran
to the southeast of the house. It was stacked with piles of brush left
from the autumn before. One pile was so big I couldn't move it. My
next brother, Gober, he couldn't budge it either. Neither could
Hoyt. And neither could the twins, Ernie and Ernest. So I went to
tell Mama we'd have to burn it, just set fire to it and remove the
whole thing from the face of the earth.

She didn't say a word. She just stepped off the porch, walked
out to where that brush pile was lying, picked the whole damn thing
up over her head and moved it to where she wanted it. Then she
went right back in the house and about her business. Didn't say a
word.

Mama wasn't what you would call either outspoken or political,
but if something mattered to her, she wasn't shy about pursuing the
issue. Women's suffrage was an example. Mama believed in it, and
when some organizers came looking for someone to represent the
cause in our community, she accepted the job. I remember going
door to door with her that summer, carrying campaign literature
and being met as often as not by the not too friendly man of the
house. Word got around pretty quickly about what my mama was
doing, and people began to make fun of us. Of course that neither
bothered nor deterred my mama one bit.

I remember one old fellow answering his door and telling my
mama that as long as he wore the pants in that house *he'd* take care
of the voting. Years later, when I came to Washington as a Congressman, I saw plenty of women walking around wearing pants,
and I couldn't help but think back to that old boy and wonder what
he'd have to say now.

My mother's suffrage support came back to me in another way
after I was in Congress. One of the first issues I faced in the House

of Representatives was a bill giving women the right to serve on federal juries. There was a lot of opposition to that bill. It was passed with a very close vote, and one of those votes for it was mine. I got a lot of angry—downright *mean*—letters from all over the country and especially from Gober Ridge about what a terrible mistake I'd made. Of course those letters made no more difference to me than our neighbors' ridicule back on Gober Ridge made to my mama. I'd done what I believed was right, and so had she.

We were poor people, there was no doubt about that, but I never felt particularly poor. Up in those hills, you see, people were kind of short on comparisons. Everybody was in the same boat, living the same way, and, for a child, a lot of that living was just plain fun. We'd get up in the morning sometimes, for instance, and go out and hunt rabbits for breakfast. We didn't have any money for shells, so my brothers, they'd run those rabbits down and catch them with their bare hands, throw them in a sack and take them home for dressing and cooking.

Me, I was a trapper. From November through February, I'd run my lines deep in the woods, looking for mink, muskrat, possum, red fox, gray fox, raccoon and skunk. I'd get pretty good money for the furs: ten dollars for a mink, five for a red fox. Muskrats only brought a dollar apiece, but every little bit counted. When you added it all up, I could earn about a hundred dollars during the trapping season.

I started trapping when I was ten and didn't stop until six years later when I left for college. Every morning I was up at two o'clock and out to run my lines. There was something almost magical about being out in those woods, following the streams, breathing the cool, clean night air. Some days there'd be nothing on the line. Every trap would be bare. Other days you'd hit the jackpot. One season I remember catching nine possums in a single line. That was a feat any man would be proud of.

The fur money all went to my family, with my mother giving me a little back for myself. There was no question about it. Everything was for the family. Everything we pulled in was shared by us all, and almost everything we pulled in came off the land. We lived off the fields and woods. We gathered wild huckleberries, wild blackberries. We killed squirrels in squirrel season, occasionally shooting them but most of the time just knocking them out of trees with rocks. We'd take them home and Mama would fry them up for breakfast. A typical breakfast would be that and some biscuits and maybe some lean meat, which is what people up there have been calling bacon since pioneer times.

We grew all our own vegetables, a garden for every season of the year. My father was a good man with food, and to him vegetables meant more than anything else. That and good sweet milk. We all had our chores to do, but he always looked after the milk himself, carrying it down to a spring he'd built up into a pool with rocks around it, a place to keep that milk good and cool.

Something my father enjoyed eating is what they used to call johnny cakes, which is basically corn bread. That was something Alabamians learned to cook from the Indians, and you'll still find it on most any country dinner table in these parts. We ate plenty of johnny cakes when I was growing up, maybe a little too many. I remember my son John asking me one day what I'd like to have carved on my tombstone when I was gone. It didn't take me long to come up with the answer.

"One sentence," I said. *"I'm through eating corn bread for breakfast."*

It was only three miles from Gober Ridge to the town of Vina, but when I began attending school there in the third grade, it was as if I'd stepped into another world, one beyond my brothers and sisters, my mother and father and the farm. It was a town of only three hundred, about the same size as it is today, but Vina had a ten-room schoolhouse (nine more than the rural church I'd gone to for first and second grades) with eight teachers (six more than the church school) and one hundred students (compared to forty at the church).

But even better than all that, Vina had politicians.

With no television and hardly any radios to speak of in those days, and with newspapers spread nowhere near as far and wide as they are today, political candidates had to come to the people to get their votes. Anywhere a train stopped, that's where the candidates would step off and make a speech. And the train stopped in Vina.

This was the 1920s, and they didn't have any of this business of all the candidates getting together for what they call a debate, seesawing around with everything, taking turns and giving everyone equal time. Back then it was one man and the crowd. If you were the speaker, you were the speaker. That was it. It was your show, sink or swim.

And those speeches were an event the whole town turned out for, as well as everyone within horse riding or walking distance from the surrounding countryside. It was a festive scene, pretty near a daylong party. The speaking might start at ten o'clock and last until noon—any speaker worth his salt was good for at least two hours. Following that, everyone would have lunch. The women in the community would kill a goat or cook a pig, and everybody would eat until they were full. By then most of the afternoon was gone.

As with so many things beyond his reach, my father was fascinated with politicians. Each time one came through, he made a point of taking me with him to see the show. And in the 1920s in Alabama, politicking was one hell of a show.

In the years following the Civil War, the voices of the farmers had become loud ones. A man could still wave a bloody gray Confederate shirt or make jokes about the "niggers" and win plenty of votes, but there was a wave of discontent rising among the white lower classes, focused on what they considered the "Big Mules," the "rich and powerful sons" who ruled Alabama politics. The same class conflict that was in place when Alabama first became a state was sharpened by the economic hard times that followed the War Between the States.

Rebelling against the "furnishing merchants" who kept them in debt by advancing them seeds and supplies at high prices and exorbitant interest rates, small farmers banded together and joined the national association of farmers called the Grange, replacing many of those merchants with cooperative stores run by themselves. They pushed for tenant farmers to be paid with wages rather than a share of the crop. And they fought to fill the legislature with more farmers and fewer of the Black Belt planters and industrialists who lorded over the state.

There's a word for the suspenders that hold up a pair of farmer's overalls—they're called galluses. A man who works his land by himself, a man like my father, would often unhook one of those suspenders, leaving one arm free to steady a plow while the other steered his mule. A man like that was called a "one-gallused" farmer. And that late nineteenth-century movement spearheaded by groups like the Grange, they called that the One-Gallused Rebellion. Some called it the Redneck Rebellion.

Any way you put it, there was a lot of fear among Alabama's landed gentry that this revolt among plain white farmers and coal miners might pull in blacks as well, creating an unheard-of political alliance, one that gave most white Alabamians nightmares. It was the fear sparked by this turn-of-the-century Populism that moved the Alabama legislature to rewrite the state constitution in 1901, making it virtually impossible for blacks to vote and making it mighty tough for poor whites to get to the polls.

Although both the Grange and similar successors—the Farmers' Alliance and Agricultural Wheel and the Colored Farmers' Alliance—were defunct by the beginning of the twentieth century, Populism remained a force to be reckoned with in Alabama politics. When candidates came to these northern hills looking for votes, they knew they were stepping into the heart of Populist territory.

One of the first politicians I saw was William B. Bankhead, who was a U. S. Congressman from Jasper. Bankhead had a pretty famous father, John, who was a U. S. Senator from 1907 to 1920. And he had a daughter named Tallulah, who would make her own worldwide name after she moved from the local stages around Jasper and broke through to theater stardom over in London. Will Bankhead did well for himself, eventually becoming Speaker of the House in 1936 and briefly contending for the Democratic presidential nomination in 1940.

But on a wet November afternoon in 1922, Will Bankhead was

in Vina, contending for the votes of farmers like my father. I left school early that afternoon to join my father at Fred Massey's store, where Bankhead was scheduled to make his speech. Massey was a Republican, but that didn't matter. This was a big deal, and he was happy to host it.

The place was lined with folding chairs, mostly taken by the ladies. Men and boys, including my father and me, stood in the back and along the sides. You could hear the train arrive, and when Bankhead walked in that room, you could see he was cut from a different cloth. His suit, even with splotches of rain on it, spelled prestige. I hardly remember what he said—it was a long, hot speech in that crowded, steamy general store. But when he was done, my father carried me up to meet him.

"Well, young man," said the Congressman, "what do you plan to be when you grow up?"

I didn't hesitate. A year earlier my father had bought a book for me titled *Lives of the Presidents,* and I devoured that book by the light of our fireplace. It had a chapter on every President, and I knew each one inside out. I couldn't imagine being a President myself. I never had that fantasy. But after watching and listening to Bankhead, I saw something I did want to be.

"I'd like to have a political career," I said, "just like yours."

Bankhead didn't miss a beat.

"Well now," he said, leaning down toward me, "I'm getting up there in service myself now, and there's no reason why you shouldn't succeed me about the time I'm ready to step aside."

I said to myself, My God, this fellow's right. There's no reason I shouldn't take his place.

It wasn't till I came to school the next week that I found out he'd been telling every eight-year-old in the county the same thing.

There were plenty of other politicians who came through these hills like that. Hugo Black stopped by Vina in 1926, the year he made his first run for the U. S. Senate. Few people knew that Black was a member of the Ku Klux Klan at that time, indeed that it was largely the support of the Klan that helped him make that campaign. It was

only after he became a U. S. Supreme Court justice in 1937 that this
fact became known by the general public. But by then Black's brief
membership in the Klan was completely overshadowed by his years
of work in the Senate, none of which indicated any prejudice in
terms of race or religion. Of course he went on to be hailed as one
of the finest, fairest and, yes, most liberal jurists ever to sit on the
nation's highest court.

But all that was far in the future when Black arrived in Vina
that afternoon in 1926. He came alone, at the wheel of a 1926 Ford
roadster. Parked it across the street from P. P. Hopkins' barbershop. He stepped out dressed all in white—white linen suit, white
necktie, white shoes with a little streak of black around the toes. He
just stood there by his car, completely at ease, as an audience of
about a hundred circled around him. I'd seen his picture in the
newspapers, but still I was struck by how slight he was. Maybe that's
because I was reared in a family of fairly big men.

Black was log-cabin born, like me. His father ran a rural farm
supply store over on the eastern side of the state. Hugo Black knew
how to talk to farm people, and he knew what issues counted most.
The issue that eclipsed all others up here at that time was electric
power. The Muscle Shoals Dam, which would become the heart of
the Tennessee Valley Authority project in the 1930s, was not far
away, but at that time it was a monument to inertia, a sleeping giant
built at the close of World War I but never put into operation. The
federal government was just letting it sit, while the homes throughout those hills continued to depend on coal, matches and wood in
the same ways as their pioneer ancestors.

To understand what it meant to live in a rural home without
electricity, listen to what a woman named Sally West, from Winston
County, just south of Gober Ridge, had to say in an essay titled
"What Rural Electrification Means to Alabama," published in 1956:

> . . . In those days the rural housewife rose very early in the
> mornings, as a matter of course, and prepared breakfast while
> her stove slowly, and most times sulkily, responded to the fluc-
> tuating heat produced by wood the menfolk had grudgingly

prepared. . . . If coal was used it meant more soot and grime, and therefore extra work for the housewife. . . .

Before electricity washday in rural districts was something no modern woman will ever understand. It was practically an all day job, backbreaking and steamy hot in summer; and no more pleasant in winter, when the dirt was wrested from clothes by main strength and strong suds. And when the clothes were dry, the ironing was done with heavy, sad irons (appropriate word!), heated with variable success. Each iron held heat only a few minutes and had to be changed accordingly. . . .

Besides the electrical appliances and "gadgets" that have to do with saving the housewife time and work, there are those two pleasure-producing and educational machines, the radio and television. Now, *the country woman is no longer shut away from the rest of the world. . . .* She knows, almost as it happens, what is going on everywhere. . . .

To have a home lighted so that the family may read or study, without eye strain, is such a boon that mere words cannot truly express what it means to emerge from darkness into light. . . .

. . . wonder of all wonders, this delivery from the prison of isolation and darkness and drudgery.

This was what Black spoke of that day: of the promise of rural electrification to light the homes and make fertilizer for the fields. His speaking style was more conversational than any I'd heard, but he knew exactly what he was doing, working the crowd with care, every sentence with a strategy to it. When he was done, I felt I'd seen a smart man, a real smart man. Almost a scientist. More than twenty years later, when I arrived in Washington as a freshman Congressman, I found out just how politically meticulous he was.

It was January 1949, my first month in Washington, and I was feeling my way around the capital, getting my feet on the ground. One of the first people I stopped in to see was Hugo Black, who by then had been a Supreme Court justice for twelve years. I'd seen him once since that speech in Vina, when he arranged a meeting for me with President Franklin Roosevelt while I was a student at the University of Alabama. But I didn't expect him to remember that. I'm sure he arranged more of those sorts of meetings than any man could remember. In any case, now I had come to pay my respects.

I began to introduce myself, and he cut me off.

"Who are you?" he asked, peering at me through squinted eyes.

I started to tell him I'd just been elected to the House of Representatives, but he waved me off.

"I *know* you're a member of Congress and all that," he said. "But who *are* you? What's your *background?*"

So I began to tell him about Gober Ridge and about my father, and without saying a word, he reached into his desk drawer and pulled out a little black book. He started leafing through it, then stopped at a particular page, with his finger on one of the handwritten lines. He looked up and said, "Is your father G. W. Elliott?"

I said, "That's him, all right."

A pause.

"And you're Carl Elliott?"

"That's right."

He looked back down at his little book.

"Now did I have any other supporters on Gober Ridge that you know about?"

I told him, and they were all there, on this page he'd written in 1926.

"Well," he finally said, pushing the book back in the drawer, "you qualify."

Hugo Black was an impressive man, but as far as I was concerned, when it came to pure power in front of an audience, when it came to the magic of manipulating a crowd and whipping them into a state where they were ready to do damn near anything you told them to do, when it came to transforming a political stage into a theater that outdazzled anything mere actors and actresses could create, there was not a man on this earth who could hold a candle to "Cotton" Tom Heflin.

J. Thomas Heflin, son of a hill-country doctor, eight times elected to Congress, twice to the Senate, and one of the most audaciously flamboyant characters ever to step onto the political scene, in this state or any other. I had heard all about Tom Heflin before I ever saw him. I had heard tell of the striped trousers he favored, and the double-breasted waistcoats and bow ties he wore. I knew he was supposed to be a spellbinder with words, whether he was talking about the crop that gave him his nickname ("Cotton is a child of the sun. It is kissed by the silvery beams of a Southern moon and bathed in the crystal dewdrops that fall in the silent watches of the night."), or about the "nigras" he'd ridicule in his homespun way ("I believe . . . that God almighty intended the nigra to be a servant to the white man"), or about the Catholics he swore were plotting to take over the nation.

I'd heard about all that, and when I heard he was coming through Russellville in that same 1926 Senate campaign as Black's, I wasn't about to miss it. Russellville was thirty miles away, over bad roads, a long way to go for a twelve-year-old. But I slipped a horse out and made the trip. And I would have ridden ten times that distance to see what I saw that day.

He was fire and brimstone from the word "go," giving Wall Street hell, telling the farmers how the thieves in New York had stolen the value of their cotton. But he didn't stop with the bankers. He went after the blacks and gave them a good cleaning up, then the Jews, then the Catholics, playing them all like keys on an organ, raising that big fist of his to the heavens and shaking his long gray hair.

I'd never heard a speaker like that in my life. His timing was absolutely the best I'd seen, before or since. He had just one story after the other, and he told them all beautifully. God, he'd latch onto the King James version of the Bible and I swear he could tell it to you as well as any religious man anywhere. The crowd was spellbound, absolutely entranced. The faces around me looked hypnotized. Time and again that afternoon I said to myself, God give me the power to speak like this man.

But the one thing I could not do that Cotton Tom would do—the thing that when I look back on it I can see was the source of his power—was I could not hate like he could. Hate is a powerful force, and a man who knows how to tap it, well, he can go a long way with it, a frighteningly long way. That was something else I saw in the faces of the crowd that day—the frenzy of hate—and that shook me a bit. I thought about that all the way home.

Hate isn't always out in the open like that. Sometimes it sits back a little, couching itself in ridicule, in meanness and laughter at someone else's expense. That's the sort of hatred I saw with "Nigger Shorty."

I never saw a black man until Shorty Jones. He worked as a cook and a janitor at J. W. Rogers' general store in Vina. Nigger Shorty, they called him, the only black man many of them had ever seen. As the name implies, he was a little fellow, hardly more than five feet tall, weighed maybe a hundred and twenty pounds. People were always making jokes about Nigger Shorty, but I couldn't understand why. People would start to snickering about him, and I'd say, "Now what's wrong with Shorty?" I thank the good Lord I never did get swallowed up in that sort of scorn.

As time went on, I became regarded as a fellow who didn't necessarily go along with the crowd. When somebody said to me that everybody in town is saying so and so, I'd say, "Well, what the hell, what difference does it make what everybody says?" I always tried to keep an open mind, to listen to what people had to say, to hear them through at least once before making up my own mind. But, by God, I didn't believe that anybody had the right to think for me. Not about race, not about religion, not about schools, not about anything. That's the way I was then, that's the way I was in Congress, that's the way I am today. I know that doesn't sound much like a politician, but there it is.

The only hint of racism I ever had at home was left behind by Grandma Elliott. It was another of those seemingly small things an adult doesn't think twice about but a child remembers forever.

Grandma Elliott was strongly against coffee drinking, and she told me time and again not to touch it. Still, I'd try to sneak a sip here and there. Well, one day she played a trump card on me.

"You've heard about Nigger Shorty, haven't you?" she asked me.

I said yes, I had.

"Well," she said, "you'll look just exactly like him if you keep drinking this coffee. You'll turn as black as Nigger Shorty."

I didn't think that affected me much at the time. I was only five. I certainly had no bad feelings toward Shorty, and I don't think I believed Grandma Elliott about this business of turning black. But somewhere inside me those words did something, because from that day on I never drank a single cup of coffee, not even when I was in the Army infantry during World War II. I'm pretty sure I was the only man in my battalion who did not drink coffee.

No, I don't believe there was any hate inside me, but there was something else burning in there, a flame lit by the words, ideas and feelings I'd absorbed in my home and fanned by the spectacle of these men who could take a crowd of people and, through the sheer power of their words, roll those people in their hands like putty. I wanted to be a word master like that, to be able to thrill crowds, to raise their expectations and hopes, and then be able to *do* something about it.

I wanted to be a Congressman. I wanted to speak like Cotton Tom, and the night after I first saw him, I began practicing.

We had a big stump out behind our house, where we'd set stove wood to cut it. I started going out there, late at night, sometimes as late as midnight, climbing up on that stump and making speeches. My only audience was the crickets. My light came from the moon.

One night I remember my daddy heard me out there. He had no idea what I was up to, so he jumped in his overalls to go out and see. I don't know what he thought when he got out there and saw what I was doing, but he listened awhile before he let me know he was there. And I heard him when he went back in the house and said to my mama, "That boy's a fine speaker."

Throughout my school years, I split the seasons between work on the farm and classes in Vina. From March through November, I worked full time in my father's fields. Then, during those five winter months, I tasted the life of a small-town boy, even playing a little basketball and football for the Vina Red Devils. I was a tall, kind of gangly boy, hardly built for a game like football. In fact, I probably would have never taken up that sport if not for my father.

He'd never seen a football game as far as I knew, but along about the tenth grade I noticed that he had started coming up with football phrases in some of his talk. I was downtown one day and met a fellow who lived near the pasture where the football team practiced, which was about a mile from the school. That pasture was the only piece of level land around. Part of every day's practice was running the mile to and from that field.

This fellow told me he'd been seeing my daddy hauling lumber past that area lately, and that my daddy had taken to parking up there at the end of the football field.

I said, "What's he doing up there?"

And this fellow said, "I'll tell you what he's doing. He's studying that football harder than you're studying your lessons."

The next two seasons I put on the pads of a Red Devils offensive guard. It was around that same time that girls started becoming a part of my life. I began dating when I was fourteen, courting on my feet. I had to walk two or three miles to a girl's house. We'd meet in the parlor, sit there and talk, and if she had a radio we'd listen to that. I remember this one girl who didn't want to disturb her parents, so she had us both wear these earphones that had just come out. They were the newest thing. There we sat, both wearing these big earphones, listening real hard to this awful, faded big band music coming from Chicago.

Sometimes my date and I might take a ride in the rumble seat of an older friend's car. And there were movies. The night the Red Bay movie house premiered *Wings* with Clara Bow in 1928, I was there, fourteen years old, with a sixteen-year-old date. She was getting ready to move on to better pickings, but I was happy that night.

More than anything else, though, all through high school, I worked. Besides my chores on the farm, I had my traps to run every morning. And when I was fourteen I took a job as the Vina school's janitor. Every morning I'd arrive at the schoolhouse early and fire up the building's eleven coal-burning stoves. Late in the afternoon, I oiled the floors with used motor oil to keep the next day's dust down.

It made for a long day, getting up at 3 A.M., slogging through the woods, running my trap line on the way in to work at the school. Pretty often I'd catch a skunk along there, and that made for some problems later in the day. You see, a skunk will use every means at his lowly command to continue existing. On first contact he'll spew the whole place around him with that horrible skunk smell. Then, when that fails and you're in the process of getting him out of the trap, he'll pee on you. Finally, when you're in the process of skinning him, he's got a tiny sack under his belly and he just lets go of that. It's his last gasp, but it's enough.

By the time the other kids would arrive at school, I'd have those stoves going solid, fired white hot from the top down, and everybody would rush to crowd around them—around all but the one I was next to. There was actually a movement among my classmates for a while to get a new janitor, one that didn't catch skunks.

That uprising passed once I was able to hunt down an old woman named Mrs. Harbin, who lived near my home. She was what they called an herb doctor, and after I described my problem, she boiled up a bunch of assorted plants into a kind of paste, spread some of that paste on me with a piece of wood, then told me to come back the next day. She did that with me for about a week, and that was it. Somehow that treatment worked as a shield of sorts. I kept on catching skunks, but I no longer caught hell from my schoolmates.

By the time I was grown and looking to leave for college, the walls were really closing in on our life up there. The Depression that hit the whole country in 1929 had already swept through this part of the country about ten years earlier. We'd moved on and off several farms, even owning one of our own for a short time. But things never looked as bleak as they did when I was getting set to go off to school.

There is no feeling like having your farm foreclosed, being put out, feeling like you're at the absolute end of the road. There was no place to turn unless you were lucky enough to have a kinsman who had a little land and could take you in and let you work it. Even then you were always behind, with no hope of getting ahead. Once a farmer was in that situation, just about all hope was lost. And yet my parents never lost theirs. They never stopped fighting back, and I never felt better than the day I was able to buy them a farm of their own.

Actually, there was one day that made me feel even better than that. It was in 1963, the year before I lost the seat I had held in Congress for sixteen years. The opposition to me had begun to build pretty good. George Wallace and his people were closing in, getting ready. And there was this one old boy from down in Lamar County, an aggravating son of a bitch if I ever saw one. He came up here and stopped in to see my father, telling him how they were going to beat me this time. This fellow wasn't worth a damn, to tell the truth, but he liked to stir up trouble.

Well, my father cut him off and said, "Now listen to me. I don't know a thing about politics, and I've got no desire to learn anything more than I need to know as a citizen.

"But I do know this, by God. I know that you may be right, you may defeat my boy. But, by God, you won't *scare* him, because I taught him not to be afraid."

When I graduated in the spring of 1930 as the Vina school's valedictorian, I became the first person in my family ever to go through high school. By then I was thinking every minute about college. Sometimes I'd wonder about making my way to a place like Harvard, but I realized that was out of the question in terms of money. Even the University of Alabama, one hundred miles to the south, in Tuscaloosa, seemed too far away as that spring turned to summer.

It was the hardest year we'd had since I was born. A drought set in that spring and never did let up. That summer was the first time I ever saw cornstalks just die in the fields. Normally the deep taproots could draw at least enough water to keep the plants alive, but not that year.

And my mother was in bed for eight weeks with a blood disease, a vein fever, they called it. My father found work hauling lumber, and I worked with him doing that. This was the year after the Depression began, and work of any sort was awfully hard to find, so I considered myself lucky when I got a job shooting gravel.

The state didn't pave country roads in those days. They just covered them with gravel. And the way they got the gravel was to dynamite it out of rocky hillsides. Just blow a part of the hill to pieces and haul those pieces away to cover a road.

They called it shooting gravel, and it was dangerous work. A man had to know his way around dynamite to get that job, and it just so happened that I'd learned how to shoot dynamite through the 4-H club. We used to clear stumps out of fresh land. When I heard that the regular shooter over at a nearby gravel site had gotten sick, I went over, talked to the boss and next thing you know I was the youngest gravel shooter they'd heard of in those parts, sixteen years old.

It paid well, a dollar a day, which was more than the poor fellows loading the wagons down below were making. And they had to work a lot harder than I did. All I had to do was keep enough gravel shot down to keep them busy. I was never worried about blowing myself up with that dynamite—I was pretty careful. But I remember thinking, God save me if all this stuff doesn't go off and some kid comes pecking around here later and winds up blowing himself to kingdom come.

At the end of that summer, after using most of my pay to help the family, I had about twelve dollars on hand. If I was going to college, I had to have a pair of shoes and a new shirt or two. When I went down to J. W. Rogers' store to buy those things, he started talking to me about his own college education, the one he never got. He told me how he'd had to drop out of school, how someone had promised to pay his way, then had to back out after the first year, and he never was able to finish. He said if he'd been able to go he'd be a doctor instead of a merchant now.

Then he asked me how much money I had. I told him I had two dollars and thirty-eight cents.

"Two dollars and thirty-eight *cents?*" he said. "You're wasting your time, boy."

I told him I didn't see the waste at all. "I may not have any money," I told him, "but all I need to do is get down there, then I'll make it by wit or whatever."

"That's not the way to get a college education," he said. Then he studied me for a minute and pulled out his checkbook.

"I'm going to write you a check for twenty-five dollars here," he said. "If you can get yourself started down there on that, there might be another one like it I can send to you later on in the year."

Two days later, in September of 1930, with my best friend Oscar Nix by my side, with everything I owned in a cardboard box under my arm, with two dollars and thirty-eight cents in cash in one pocket and a check for twenty-five dollars in the other, I began walking to Tuscaloosa.

The University of Alabama is the capstone of the public school system of the state. . . . the University is within easy reach of every youth of Alabama.

Dr. George H. Denny, president of the
University of Alabama, 1912–35

THREE

〰

UNIVERSITY YEARS

In 1930, Tuscaloosa was a city of about fifteen thousand people, built on the banks of the Black Warrior River, at the middle of the western side of the state. Its name came from two Choctaw Indian words—*tusko,* meaning warrior, and *loosa,* meaning black. But it was the Creeks who built it into what the early white settlers called Black Warrior Town, and when the Creeks revolted in 1813, American troops captured and burned the place to the ground. It was "wiped from the face of the earth," wrote a frontier scout riding with those troops, a scout named Davy Crockett.

The town was rebuilt by the white settlers who came after the Creek War, most of them planters who brought in slaves to clear the canebrakes from the riverside fields and to fill those fields with corn and cotton. By 1825 these planters, along with local merchants bolstered by the cotton trade, were powerful enough to have the state capital moved from its original site at a place called Cahaba to Tuscaloosa. Cotton money built huge columned mansions around the city. Rows of majestic water oaks were planted along Tuscaloosa's streets. People began calling it the Druid City.

But the most significant achievement during Tuscaloosa's twenty-years as the capital city of Alabama was the opening of the University of Alabama. Built on forty-six thousand acres of land given the state by the federal government for the purpose of establishing "a seminary of learning," the university opened its doors in April 1831, registering thirty-five male students to be taught by a faculty of four, which included the school's first president, a man named Alva Woods. Woods was apparently a pretty strict fellow, too strict for some of his students, who weren't shy about responding to his discipline.

A fellow named Clement Clay, who later became a U. S. Senator, wrote a letter to his father in 1834, describing "an open and audacious rebellion" in which a group of students chased Woods across campus one night, throwing stones and firing pistols at him. Woods got away by jumping through an open dormitory window and hiding till the posse had passed.

These student "riots" continued, off and on, for the next two years. Finally things came to a head. When forty-six students snuck off to see a circus in 1836, Woods suspended the whole lot, touching off a row that culminated in a group of the undergraduates invading the president's office with bullwhips in their hands. Figuring discretion was the better part of valor, Woods resigned soon thereafter.

Even then, the university had problems turning sons of pioneers into gentlemen and scholars. An item published in a New Orleans newspaper in the summer of 1837 described some pretty singular student-faculty relations on the Tuscaloosa campus:

> Some of the Professors of the Alabama University at Tuscaloosa, lately fired several pistols at some refractory students. The students returned the fire, and the Alma Mater of our sister State was suddenly converted into a scene of commotion and smoke.

Now *that's* what you call student unrest.

———

Tuscaloosa's boom years came to a halt when the state capital was moved to Montgomery in 1846. Nineteen years later the city was sacked by federal troops under the leadership of Union General John T. Croxton. "Croxton's Raiders," as they were called, were slightly delayed at the edge of town by Confederate cadets from the university. When they finally reached the campus, the Union troops burned all but four of the college's buildings, despite pleas from some of the city's leading citizens to spare them. One account described the burning as it looked to the retreating cadets: "The morning skies were darkened with billows of black smoke and by noon of that day, April 4, 1865, the University of Alabama lay in ashes." It's memories like that that make resentment die hard.

In the years following Reconstruction, Tuscaloosa built itself back to respectability, although many of its biggest plantations were broken up and its manor houses sold at auction. The turn-of-the-century cotton trade, as well as the river and rail traffic that passed through the city, helped get Tuscaloosa back on its feet.

So this was the town in which Oscar Nix and I arrived on the afternoon of September 8, 1930.

J. W. Rogers had seen us walking out of Vina that morning, our belongings under our arms, and he told us there was no way he'd let us hike those hundred miles to the university. That was no way to start our college careers, he told us. So he hailed the Rev. H. T. Vaughan, a Baptist preacher who lived two doors up the street from his store, and he told Brother Vaughan to fill up his car with gasoline and drive us to Tuscaloosa. That's how we wound up making the trip that day, in Brother Vaughan's 1927 two-seater Ford.

We didn't have any specific plans. No one at the university knew we were coming. There were no application or admission forms to fill out. This was a year into the Depression, and the college was accepting nearly anyone who could pay the bill. Now, paying the bill—that was something else I didn't have any specific plans about. But I figured we'd cross that bridge when we came to it.

We came to it that afternoon, when Spud—that's what everyone called Oscar—and I found our way to the office of George H.

Denny, president of the University of Alabama. This was the hardest of times for colleges around the country, many of which had been forced to close their doors. But the University of Alabama's doors had stayed open, thanks almost entirely to the financial wizardry and political savvy of George Denny. He was a no-nonsense fellow, a bottom-line autocrat who had ruled his campus kingdom with steel will and an iron fist ever since assuming its presidency in 1912, the year before I was born. Whether you were an employee or one of the three thousand students attending the university at the time I arrived, you jumped when George Denny said jump, because there would be hell to pay if you didn't. Everybody was afraid of George Denny.

Everyone, that is, except this sixteen-year-old from Gober Ridge. First of all, I didn't know enough to be afraid. I'd never met George Denny, or any man like him, in my life. Second, I had my father's training behind me, that fearlessness he'd taught me to have. And third, there was the fact that I didn't own a thing on this earth, and when you've got nothing to hold on to, nothing to lose, well, what the hell is there to be afraid of?

Spud and I walked into Denny's office, and there he was, behind a desk big enough to make a bed on. He looked up at us as if we had come from some other planet, two kids there to waste his time.

"What do you want?" he asked.

I started to tell him our situation, that we were there to go to school, that we had no money but we were planning to find work, and we were hoping to get our fees deferred until we could get ourselves set up.

"Now hold it right there," he said. "Do you mean to tell me that you came here to this university without a penny, and with no way to *get* any money, with parents that have none, with no brothers old enough to work and help you out? Do you think you can just walk into a university like this, just like that?"

"Well," I said, "I came to try. You have the power to keep me out, I guess."

"You kept your*self* out!" he said. "You've come here with nothing. You haven't tried hard enough."

"Wait a minute," I said. "What do you know about how hard I've tried? I've had to work most of my life to help my parents keep things together. My mama's been sick all this past summer, laid up in bed. She has nine children. We've had a bad drought this season. I've been dealing with all this, with human need here, bedrock stuff. I haven't had much time for high finance, but I do aim to get in this university."

Dr. Denny was not impressed.

"Go home," he said. "Get out of here and go on. I don't have time for your troubles."

He drove us out of the temple is what he did. We got back outside his office and Brother Vaughan was sitting there, real steamed. He'd heard the whole conversation, and he was about as close to physical violence as a man of the cloth could get. He was all for packing ourselves back in the car and taking us home. But I told him no, this was just the opening round.

Spud looked at me like I was crazy, but there was no way I was giving up. We thanked Brother Vaughan for the ride, sent him on back to Vina and went about finding some way to get ourselves into this college.

I'll never forget the first night we spent in Tuscaloosa. It was under a truck, parked out front of the home of the university's superintendent of buildings and grounds, a former Tuscaloosa County sheriff named Perry B. Hughes. We'd gone by his home late in the day, looking for work, and when he answered the door, he called out to his wife.

"Come on out here and take a look at this," he said. "This is the damnedest thing I ever saw. Here's two fellows that've got enough gall to think they're gonna enter the university without a dime."

Hughes had nothing for us, but as we were leaving, I saw a truck parked out front. It was getting dark and starting to drizzle, and we had nowhere to sleep. So I asked if he'd mind if we spent the night under that truck. I know he thought I was crazy. So did Spud. But that's where we slept that night, if you want to call it sleeping. It was hard, and it was cold, and when I got up in the morning, my body was so sore I said to Spud, "Now I know what it feels like to be old."

Spud's spirits weren't quite so high.

"Carl, I've thought about this all night," he said, struggling to sit up. "I hate to leave you but, by God, I'm going home."

"The hell you are," I said. "You aren't going to leave me because I'm not going to *let* you. We're going to stay here and see this through, fight a good fight."

This was a Saturday morning. We spent all day finding a small apartment, where we talked the landlady into deferring the rent. We went looking for work in town, but there was none. Monday morning we showed up at registration with our shoes shined, wearing our best clothes, and praying we didn't run into Dr. Denny.

We were lucky. The man we wound up dealing with was Dr. Denny's secretary, Ralph E. Adams. I told him we had been to see the president, and that was the truth. Of course I left out the details of our meeting. I also gave Adams my twenty-five-dollar check as an advance against the twenty dollars tuition each that it would cost Spud and me for a semester of classes. Adams went looking for Denny to okay this deal, and I thought we were sunk. But he couldn't find the president, so we were in—at least until the bill came due in three months.

Things seemed to fall in line after that. Perry Hughes hired both Spud and me to work on the buildings and grounds crew, trimming bushes and such. It wasn't long before I'd found two other jobs as well: firing the boilers in the college's power plant in the mornings and picking up and delivering campus laundry and dry cleaning in the afternoons. Hell, I could have carried two more jobs. If there was one thing I'd learned in my years on the farm, it was how to work.

I took the maximum eighteen hours of classes as well, figuring that was what I had come for, the schoolwork. I wish studying had been all there was to being a student, but I found out pretty quickly that there were sides to this university life that I hadn't imagined.

The vast majority of University of Alabama students were well-heeled sons and daughters of the Black Belt and Birmingham. The fraternity and sorority system that was so much a part of the university's social life meant a lot to most of them. I was never real comfortable with the whole idea of fraternities. There was something a little too exclusive about it all. Most of it struck me as downright silly. But I never really had to make a choice one way or the other that first year—there weren't too many students like Spud and me at the university, and what few there were did not draw much interest from the Greeks. As social circles went, hillbillies were rated pretty low.

But the freshman caps were something I couldn't avoid, these little beanies all first-year students were required to wear, identifying them as freshmen.

I had a real hard time with that cap. First, they made you pay a dollar to buy one, which was a lot of money to boys like Spud and me. And you had no choice, you had to buy a hat. That bothered me, too, but that was part of starting college, they said. And with that hat on your head, you were a target. The upperclassmen would come around and just basically beat the hell out of you, then go on. There was nothing you could do about it, no appeal to take. Where I was raised, when a fellow attacked you like that, you fought back. But here you were supposed to take it, even enjoy it. To me, it was just another example of social stratification, like the fraternities. It was just about the most demeaning thing I ever had to go through. And it gave me my first introduction to Big Bill Lee.

That was during my first day at the university. I was hustling around getting Spud and myself registered when this huge fellow shoved me from behind. He was as big as a house, and awful mean-looking. He asked me where my cap was. I told him I hadn't gotten around to buying it yet, and he told me I'd better get my ass down there and do it. It was all I could do to hold back from laying into this bully. He might have killed me, but so be it. The idea of a damn fool like that being allowed to push people around was too much for me to bear. It was only the fact that Spud and I were doing all we could to get into school that held me back. And it was only later that I found out this bully was a freshman *himself*—Big Bill Lee, a football star. I'd meet up with Big Bill more than once later in my life.

But Spud and I had more important things to do that first

semester than worry about all this silly social nonsense—things like finding a place to live.

It wasn't long before our landlady found a rent-paying tenant and Spud and I found ourselves out in the street. The pay from our jobs was going toward tuition and books. We had a dollar each to eat on for a week. Rent was something we could not afford, so we went hunting for someplace to stay. And we found it, behind fraternity row, in the old campus observatory.

This was one of the four buildings Croxton's Raiders had spared in the Civil War. It was abandoned now. You could hardly see it for the vines growing up its walls. The rooms were empty, some without floors. But when I looked closer and actually went inside, I found two students staying there, squatters, so to speak. One of them, a fellow named Virgil Lee Bedsole, went on to head the department of archives and history at Louisiana State University. The other, James Coley Etheridge, went on to become an attorney in Washington.

But back then they were just two boys in the same boat as Spud and I, looking for a cheap place to live and finding it in this old abandoned building. Virgil's chief concern was that we might blow his cover. Once I convinced him we would not, Spud and I moved in.

We got things set up there pretty good. Spud and I slept in one room, and we built fires and cooked in another. We had no trouble finding fuel for our fires. They were throwing away more good wood around campus than anybody would need, so we made a habit of picking that up. Things went fine until a couple of those damn fraternity fellows walked by one day and saw the smoke. They couldn't stand the idea that a couple of country fellows like us were getting by in this way, so they reported us.

Fortunately the man who got the call was a fellow I'd seen working around campus, and he'd seen me. He was a sergeant at arms of sorts, a university employee, dressed in overalls, kind of dirty and grimed up. He took a liking to us—I think he felt closer to me and Spud than he did to the students who had made the complaint. In fact, he wound up showing us how to tie into the building's electrical wires, so we could start cooking on a hot plate.

We even found a couple of old beds—no mattresses, just beds. That's how I pressed my pants—by sleeping on them. I'd lay them out with the crease just right, then spread newspaper over the top and sleep on top of that. I'd wake up in the morning with a crisply creased pair of pants ready to go.

There were a few inconveniences—like the rats. God, they were terrible, just horrible. I never saw so many rats as there were in that old building. They were everywhere, but we couldn't do much about them without revealing our hand. Some poison eventually got that problem under control, but another pest appeared one night, after I'd finished my standard 10-to-2-A.M. study session. I'd just fallen asleep when lo and behold, out of hell came these chinches, what some people call bedbugs. I could feel them crawling across me there in the darkness.

I turned to Spud and said, "Spud, are you being eaten by chinches?"

He muttered something, hardly awake. So I got up, turned on the light, pulled back the cover and there they were, hundreds of them. *Thousands* of them.

That was it for Spud.

"No more," he said, leaping out of bed, jumping around and brushing the bugs off him. "I can't take any more of this, Carl. I'm going home."

"No, hell," I said. "You're not going *anywhere* until we get rid of these chinches."

So we took a pile of newspapers—this was on a Sunday night—and I said, "Come on, we'll burn these sons of bitches to death."

And we did. Smoke once again rose from the observatory, once again the fraternity boys made an emergency call, and once again a college official showed up. This time it was a professor of English history named Clanton Ware Williams.

Professor Williams helped us put out the fire, then he took a close look at what we had been doing there. As we were getting everything squared away, he said to me, "You know, I could use a fellow with your apparent imagination, with your apparent willing-

ness to work hard, with your apparent ability to get things done and
to deal with some of the harsher realities of life without growing too
harsh yourself."

I said, "Oh, yeah, that would suit me fine. I could use another
job. What do you have in mind?"

He said, "There's a hell of a lot of people taking English history
this semester, and I'm the only one here who teaches it. That means
I've got a hell of a lot of papers to grade. I'm a multiple-choice sort
of tester, and I could use someone to be my paper grader."

"Well," I said, "I'm a multiple-choice sort of fellow."

So, by the end of my first year in college, I was working five
jobs, making enough money to mail a little home every week, and I
was pulling down eighteen hours a semester with an A average.

Not bad for a hillbilly.

By the time I began my second year of college, the goose was hanging pretty high, as folks back home would put it. Spud and I were
still camping in the observatory, but I had made a mark on campus,
both in classes and with my jobs. By then it was hard to avoid Dr.
Denny's eye—I think he knew about these students who were holed
up in that old building, but I think he just looked the other way. I'm
not sure exactly why, but when I finally came face to face with him
at the start of my sophomore year, rather than throw me off campus
as a renegade who had defied his orders, he gave me yet another job
—as his houseboy.

The president's mansion at the University of Alabama is a stun-
ning sight, especially to a boy born in a log cabin and raised in hills
where the biggest building around is the local feed store. The mansion was another of the four structures spared by Croxton's men in
1865. Built in 1840, it's a classic of colonial design, with six columns
out front, a pair of winding stairs leading to the front entrance and
an overhanging iron balcony above the front door.

A staff of servants took care of the three-story house and the
needs of the three Denny children. I did some floor waxing and
furniture dusting, but basically my job was to help Mrs. Denny with
whatever she needed. Mostly she needed help with her flower beds.

Occasionally Dr. Denny might ask me to tend to an odd job—like the time he sent me shinnying up a tree to saw off a dead limb and I wound up landing the huge limb on the front sidewalk, smashing the cement to pieces. But my main duty was keeping Mrs. Denny out of the boss's hair. If I could do that, as far as he was concerned, I was doing my job.

Dr. Denny ran as tight a ship inside his home as he did outside. Every week Mrs. Denny would write up a grocery list and hand it to me to carry to Dr. Denny who was already at his office, which was located about a block and a half away. He'd check it over and change just about every item. If she had written down, say, three dozen eggs, he'd shake his head, grunt, and mark out "three" and write "two." If she had ten pounds of potatoes, he'd grunt, strike out "ten" and write "five." He'd go over the entire list like that, raking it with a fine-tooth comb. When he was finished I took the list back to Mrs. Denny and she would take it to the store.

Weekends I was on my own, as far as the Dennys were concerned. Football at the University of Alabama is, of course, close to a religion, and it was no different back then. Even in the 1930s, the Crimson Tide was among the top teams in the nation. During my six years at the university, 'Bama football teams won a total of fifty games and lost only six. They went to the Rose Bowl twice, winning both games. The first of those two wins, in 1931, was described in the university's student newspaper in geographically breathless terms:

> Alabama, under the unfailing leadership of William Wallace Wade, gains the justly-earned title of Champions of the known Universe. . . . From England's foggy Thames to Mother India's sacred Ganges, from Brazil's copper Amazon to Nippon's snow-capped Fujiwara. The Crimson Tide rolls on.

Saturday afternoons it seemed the entire city of Tuscaloosa was jammed into Denny Stadium to see the game. I was there, too, but I didn't care much about what was happening down on the field. I had my own game to play in the grandstands.

People get their recreation in so many ways. I always got mine by reading, and in college I got it as well from finding and finishing jobs. That was a real challenge to me, waking up every day and saying, Now here are all the things I've got to do today—the jobs I've got to work, the classes I've got to attend, the studying I've got to do. It was a game, getting all that done—making my grades, paying my bills, sending my folks a little money. That was *my* football game.

So Saturday afternoons, while the players were pitching pigskins, I was pitching sodas and peanuts. I missed the excitement on the field, but I had my own excitement, selling those Coca-Colas coming and going. A dime apiece, and I kept a penny for each one. Some Saturdays I'd make as much as eighteen dollars, if it was hot enough. And I needed all I could make, especially after a letter arrived during that second year at school.

It was from my mother, telling me times had gotten even harder than ever back home. She said they'd had to sell their cotton that year for four and three quarter cents a pound, the lowest price it had ever gone for. It had been another dry year, and they didn't make any corn to speak of. She said she hated worse than anything in the world to write me this letter, because she knew I was having a pretty tight squeeze myself, but she said they had to have some help, and they didn't know where it was going to come from.

Well, I had a small postal savings account I had built up, with about one hundred and twenty dollars in it, and I went down and checked it out and mailed it to Mama, every cent of it. From that day forward, until she died in 1963—four months before my daddy passed away—I sent her money each and every week.

I did that, and I found more work—in the men's dining room, where I waited tables in exchange for meals. Every little bit counted, as far as money was concerned, and that waiter's job brought me right into the middle of campus life as well. The table I was assigned belonged to the football team. I was eventually hired as a tutor for the team as well, so I got a pretty good look at both the best and the worst of what the Alabama football program produced during those years.

The worst was my old antagonist, Big Bill Lee. The last I'd seen him was at the receiving end of one of his shoves. Now he was a

near three-hundred-pound All-American football player and wres-
tler, ordering the waiters around as if he were royalty. Thirty years
later, when I was making my final campaign for Congress in 1964, I
ran into Lee down in Greene County, where he had earned himself
quite a reputation as county sheriff. He was as big as he'd been in
college, bigger even. We got to joking about the old days, about
how he'd thrashed me around and how I was back now to give him
the whipping he deserved. He thought that was awful funny.

Somebody came in to have a warrant signed and Lee stepped
off into an office. I turned to the fellow next to me and said, "What
kind of sheriff is old Bill making here?"

The fellow said, "Oh, he's a fine sheriff. He's *our* answer to
civil rights, our answer to the integration problem."

Greene County was about eighty percent black at that time.

I asked Lee about that when he came back out. I said, "Bill,
you have the reputation of being pretty rough with these people
down here."

He said, "Aw, I don't go to court and fool with all that." He
said, "I know the judge pretty well, and we get along good. He
leaves it to me to do whatever needs to be done around here."

I said, "Well now, Big Bill, if you don't take 'em to court, what
the hell *do* you do with these people you arrest out here?"

He said, "I just whup the hell out of 'em and go on."

I asked him if that ever got him into any trouble.

"Hell, no," he said. "There's a few of these damn fool niggers
around here that don't like it and don't like me on that account. But
once I give one a whupping, they don't complain much after that."

I'll say this for Big Bill. He was consistent. He never changed a
bit from the first day I met him. But Greene County changed, after
the Voting Rights Act of 1965. The passage of that law sparked
protests and violence throughout the state, as thousands of blacks
registered to vote. Some of that violence occurred in Greene
County, where, in 1966, Bill Lee waded into a crowd of blacks
gathered in front of the Greene County courthouse, whacked the
leader, a man named Thomas Gilmore, in the head and arrested
him.

Four years later Bill Lee lost his job when the voters of Greene

County elected a black man to replace him. That man became only the second black ever elected sheriff in Alabama. He was a Baptist preacher, a disciple of Martin Luther King, and as sheriff he refused to wear either a uniform, a badge or a gun.

His name was Thomas Gilmore.

There was another fellow piling on the biscuits at that University of Alabama football table who never changed. He was one of the players I tutored, a fellow named Paul Bryant, better known, I guess, as Bear. It was clear back then that he was different from most of the other fellows on that team.

First of all, he was just plain smarter than the average football player. I noticed right off in the tutoring sessions how serious he was about doing what he was there to do. He was actually interested in learning. He asked questions, which, believe me, set him apart right off the bat.

Bear was an extraordinarily good football player, but we became friends aside from that. We kept in touch over the years, as I went off to Washington and he became one of the most fabled coaches in sports. When I ran into him down in Birmingham one afternoon in 1982, I was no longer a Congressman. I was back to practicing law, and Bear had just had a heart attack. But he showed no signs of slacking off.

I said, "Now, Bear, you've had your warning. Heart attacks don't quit after one," I said. "They keep coming at you, one after the other, unless you slow down."

"Yeah, I hear you," he said.

"You're at the top of the heap now," I said. "You're the All-American coach, a legend. And you're still alive. So, for God's sake, throw that damn stuff away now and get you something to do that you can enjoy, something that will not be a huge physical strain on you."

Well, that made him mad. He said, "Hell, yeah, everyone's looking to give me advice now."

That's exactly what I was doing, giving him advice. I'd heard from the doctors and people around him that he'd had one hell of a heart attack. All I was trying to do was tell him that, damnit, I was afraid he was going to die.

That was the last time I saw Bear Bryant. A year later he was dead.

From the beginning I was ideologically as well as socially set apart from most of the other students at the university. There was no way they could fathom the world I had been raised in. To a lot of them I was the oddball in the observatory, the mountain boy. Even when Spud and I moved into a dormitory midway through our sophomore year, we were still looked on as outsiders. But in the classroom, where my grades were routinely at the top of the charts, I was pretty well accepted by my classmates. Some of them even made me their friend. One, a boy named John Bates, challenged me to see who would make a better grade in our European history class. Twenty-five years later I ran into Bates in the political arena.

I'd been in Congress ten years by then, well established as a liberal, and Bates had become very conservative, working with a big anti-labor outfit that had a factory of some sort in Decatur. He came to talk to me about the horrible things organized labor was doing to everybody, and he was so damn smart he knew just exactly how to make it sound convincing, very impressive.

But when he got through, I said, "Now listen, Bates. Damnit, I represent a constituency that has a base of about ten thousand workers, industrial workers—coal miners, coal haulers, coal washers and every other job that goes with coal. And I think the outfit you work for is just about the most anti-union group I've ever known of.

"So you can just stop right now," I told him. "Don't say anything more, because personally I like you. I remember the days back in school when we competed for grades."

Then I kind of smiled, and said, "I also remember that I *beat* you, Bates."

I was always a pretty competitive person. I think most of my teachers appreciated that, although most of them were as befuddled as my classmates by my background, the way I lived and my perspective on things. That all adds up to a fellow's politics, and there was a particular professor named Charles G. Summersell who, although he gave me one of only two A's earned in his freshman political science class, could never understand my liberal leanings. At the end of that semester he made me stand up and he told these folks that I'd made the grade under harder conditions than any student he'd ever had. Years later, after I'd gotten my career in Congress going and it was clear I was about the most liberal thing coming out of these parts, Summersell would shake his head and say I'd made the grade but I must have missed the *point.*

This was, after all, the heart of Dixie. And I was clearly something more radical than they were used to on the staid grounds of the university. It might have been refreshing to see someone who went his own way and thought for himself, but it was threatening as well. I'm sure it was a mixture of those feelings that explained the blend of affection and alarm I felt from the faculty and administration, especially when I became president of the student body.

That was in 1935. I had gotten my undergraduate degree in 1933, gaining a year by taking extra classes each summer and graduating with honors. I took off from work the day of graduation, found a suit for five dollars, bought it and brought it back to wear at that night's ceremonies. I then immediately entered the university's law school, where I spent my first year taking a full load of law courses and teaching three undergraduate history classes on the side. It was then that I decided to run for student body president, who at that time could be elected from either graduate or undergraduate students.

This was no idle decision. The list of former University of Alabama student body presidents included Lister Hill and John Sparkman, both of whom would become U. S. Senators and whom I eventually joined as part of one of the strongest liberal contingents to serve in Congress from any single state in the country's history. In Alabama, the university had long been known as a breeding ground for future politicians. Campus politics was a deadly serious business. For me, it was a first step toward the U. S. House of Representatives.

The idea of this hillbilly running for Alabama student body president might have seemed ludicrous to those of my classmates who ridiculed me in my undergraduate years, who actually moved away from me when I sat near them in class. But it wasn't their votes I went after. I studied the college's registration rolls, found that nearly half the students were from out of state, and that's who I went after. I also went after the non-Greeks, my fellow social outcasts who were not part of the fraternity and sorority systems.

By the time I finished my undergraduate studies I had been invited to join three different fraternities, but I just laughed at those folks. Me, belong to a damn outfit like that? I never did regard myself as a joiner.

So it was pretty much an independent campaign I ran, not too different in a lot of ways from the approach I took when I went after a seat in Congress. I kept my hands on all the reins I could, I went after the votes of people who were relatively dispossessed, and I went after the *female* vote, involving coeds in my campaign as well as courting their ballots.

I always paid a lot of attention to organizing women, then and in the years to come. I don't know why, but women generally seem to be better campaign workers than men. Maybe God made them that way, but I think there's more to it than that. I think it has something to do with power and with what power does to men. Power can seduce a man, and pretty soon, instead of helping you, he gets to wanting to taste some of it for himself. I know there's nothing very scientific about this, but I've found that women tend to be more diligent and stay more loyal. If they're with you, by God, they're with you all the way, and they give it all they've got.

I made sure they were with me in that spring of 1935 by throwing a dance that pretty much flew in the face of the school's Greek outfits. A girl named John Effie Gilmore helped me put it together. We invited all the independent girls, the ones who weren't in a sorority. About eight hundred and fifty showed up, most of them girls that had never been invited to a dance in their lives. And those old gals had the biggest time I've ever seen, just cutting up and dancing those old country dances. Yes sir, it was a real night for the have-nots.

When the returns came in for that election—the first in my life —I was the winner by a two-to-one margin, the largest in the

school's history. That night's celebration party was one neither I nor
Dr. Denny soon forgot.

Some of the boys who had supported me went on over to
Greene County, came back with two barrels of whiskey in the back
of a pickup truck and set them up in front of the student union
building. It happened that every evening, like clockwork, Dr. Denny
would stop by the post office, the last thing he did at night before
going home. The post office, of course, was in the back of the
student union building. He'd go in the back and come out the front.

Well, he came out that night, saw those barrels of liquor sitting
there and a bunch of drunks hanging around it, and he just snorted.

"Pigs. *Pigs!*" he said. "The modern student has grown to be
nothing but a pig."

And he went on home.

Looking back on it, it's pretty clear that the way I approached my
job as president of the student body at the University of Alabama
was pretty much the way I approached my job later on in life as a
U. S. Congressman. It was basically the less privileged students who
put me in office, and they were my top priority once I got there. I
always believed in giving people something tangible instead of a lot
of lip service and hot air. In the case of my student body presidency,
I started with building courting benches.

When I first got to the university, I'd never done much courting really. And I didn't have too much time for that once I was
there. But I did get out once or twice. And I remember the first time
I did. I met a gal of like mind, and we took off one Sunday afternoon, went on up to the hill behind the engineering building. We
carried a sandwich up there, sat on a log where we had a good view
of the mountainside and the little stream that went through the
bottom. Then I looked down and I said, "My *God,* what is this?"

The whole hillside was covered with boys and girls like us, who
didn't have access to the courting rooms over at the sorority houses.
They were lying on blankets all over that hillside, doing things I'd
never seen before.

Not that my mission was to pull them off those blankets, but I thought those students should have as proper a place to court as their wealthier classmates. So I let Dr. Denny know I was writing a check off student funds to buy fifty courting benches. They went up, they got heavy use, and I think some of them are still there.

Dr. Denny balked a little at spending that money, but the benches were a minor issue. When I confronted him about the college bookstore, however, that launched a major battle. We'd been developing the idea for some time that the students ought to own the bookstore. What we didn't know was that Dr. Denny himself owned a large interest in the supply company that owned and operated the store. We had a long fight about that one. The college ended up hanging on to its ownership, but we got them to slice the markup on the books they were selling to students.

Ralph Adams, the president's secretary, still remembered that fight years later, long after I'd been in Congress. He said, "You know, the funny thing is instead of you being afraid of the establishment at the university, the way most students would be, they were all so damn afraid of you that they didn't know which way they were going.

"We used to hate to see you coming," he said. "God, we didn't know what you were going to come up with next."

I hate to sound like a do-gooder or some holier-than-thou sort of person, but I've just always believed there are times when some things just look like they're pretty clearly right or wrong. That's why I went about putting the university's student honor code back into operation. It had been dropped a while back, and there were so damn many people cheating in their classes that it was obvious to anyone who had any sense of moral rectitude at all that something had to be done. Of course it was no time at all before this ran me up against Dr. Denny again.

There was this one girl from Mobile who came from pretty rich and powerful parents. The honor council had such a blatant cheating case against her that we had no choice but to give her the works. Dr. Denny stepped in and tried to get me to reverse all that and let her continue in school. He said, "Don't you know I have a university to run here, that you have to run an institution so as to accomplish its broader and greater aims?"

I said, "Yeah, but hell, what's it all mean if you're going to let people get through by cheating?"

We expelled the girl.

Racism wasn't something I saw a lot of at the university, although it was definitely there. Tuscaloosa was a city full of black people, but you rarely saw one on the Alabama campus, which is where I spent almost all my time. It was a completely insulated situation. The only blacks you saw were the one or two who worked in the kitchens.

One of those blacks was a man named Jim Collins, a cook in the dining hall where I was headwaiter. The students called him Uncle Jim. No one knew much about him, but he and I got to be closely acquainted, working with the food and all. And it wasn't long before I discovered there was a lot more to Jim Collins than met the eye.

He didn't usually talk about personal things, but one day he began telling me about his home life, and lo and behold I found out he had five children and every one of them was a graduate of a big university in the North or the West, two or three of them with master's degrees. Here was a man situated with almost no real opportunity for himself, with no chance to do much more for himself than to be a cook, which he had been all his life, and he had put five kids through college. I didn't know that happened in the South. And I never forgot it.

Neither did I ever forget the student I met at the 1935 National Student Federation convention in Kansas City. He was a black man, president of the student body at Morehouse College in Atlanta, an extremely bright fellow. We were riding back together on the train from Kansas City. In those days, when you crossed the Mason-Dixon line headed south, the trains became segregated.

We were north of Memphis when here came the conductor, telling us we had to move apart. I said, "Oh, let this go. We have some things to talk about."

He said, "Mister, I don't make these laws, but I sure do have to enforce them." This was a black conductor.

What he did was draw a curtain between the black fellow and

me. So as soon as he left I just stepped around that curtain and we went on talking, and we went on like that clear on through to Birmingham. We discussed a lot of things, but what we talked about most was racism. What I got from this fellow was that there were two or three basic things that the black man really resented. He resented going to your home and having to take off his hat and go to the back to come in. He resented having any business's doors closed to him simply because he was black. And he resented the fact that his children would have school doors closed to them.

I never forgot that ride or that talk. Of course back on the Alabama campus, such talk was unheard of. That same year, 1935, one of the university's English professors, a man named Clarence Cason, published a book called *90 Degrees in the Shade.* I had been one of Cason's students as an undergraduate—one of his favorite students, as a matter of fact—and I read the book with a lot of interest. It just barely touched on this matter of race, but it made the point that at some time or other we would have to solve this problem.

That was enough to bring on the wrath of editorial writers throughout the South, Alabamians in particular. Most of Cason's colleagues on the university faculty were flag-waving Confederates, and they roundly condemned him.

The criticism apparently took its toll. Clarence Cason went down to his office late one night that year, and when he didn't return home by the next morning, his wife notified the police. They unlocked the door to his office in Morgan Hall, and there he laid, across his desk. He'd put the barrel of a pistol in his mouth and pulled the trigger.

That was in the thirties, but sentiments in the South had hardly changed by the sixties. This Confederacy is an absorbing thing. It's had such an enormous effect on Alabama boys and girls through the decades, it's almost unimaginable. When I got to Congress, there sat one hundred representatives from the Old South. You had to have at least some of their votes to pass your bills, and you damn sure had to have them to pass the test with your own voters if you were from the South yourself. If word got out that you varied from the Confederate line in the slightest, you were in trouble.

The day I was elected to the House of Representatives Rules Committee, Harry Byrd, the archetypal arch-conservative Senator from Virginia, was speaking to the Cotton Council in Memphis. Somebody gave him the word, and he stopped his speech.

"Gentlemen," he announced, "a terrible thing has just happened this morning in the Congress of the United States."

Everybody was on edge to hear what horrible news he had to deliver.

"This morning at nine-thirty," he said, "Carl Elliott of Alabama was elected to the House Rules Committee.

"This," he said, "might be the darkest day of this republic."

Now *that's* the kind of nonsense you had to put up with.

But that was still far in the future as I entered my last semester of law school. I had worked in 1932 as a local manager for Franklin Roosevelt's presidential election campaign and ended up going to Washington in the spring of 1936 in my capacity as the university's student body president to testify for a Works Progress Administration bill for federal scholarships to needy college students, something called the American Youth Act. I never forgot how hard it had been to get my education and how much it meant to me. If there was one issue that became a crusade in my life, the opportunity for education for the poor was it.

When I got to Washington that spring, Hugo Black, who was in the Senate and would within a year be on the U. S. Supreme Court, arranged a visit for me to the White House. He wrote me out a pass, and that piece of paper took me right to the door of the Oval Office. When I was shown in, there was the President, seated at a small desk in the corner. Just him and me.

I had read everything that had been written about Roosevelt. I knew he'd be in a wheelchair, I knew he had a sense of humor, and I knew he was very, very smart, as agile a thinker as ever there was, at least in that office.

He asked me a little about my background and I told him. We talked some about the bill, about how we both felt it was a tragic waste to see young people with ability and potential miss the chance for an education simply because they had no money. Somehow he began talking about how much time he spent with his files, and how disorganized they got because he was so busy. He told me how he was on the go from the time he rose at six in the morning until he wound down about midnight.

I said, "It sounds to me like you don't get enough sleep."

He chuckled at that. He wound up giving me about a half an hour of his time. I didn't really consider how special that was at the time. I approached our conversation as a person-to-person thing, and so did he. It's only in retrospect, after seeing how completely burdened and understandably unavailable the man holding that office can be, that I truly appreciate the small piece of his morning Franklin Roosevelt shared with this farm boy.

He shared something else, too. It arrived in the mail after I got back to Tuscaloosa, a photograph of the President, signed, "To a New Voice in Education."

I spent the rest of that spring winding up my law school work and was given a nice send-off from my fellow students and the faculty by being selected the university's outstanding student of the year. But that honor did little to change President Denny's opinion of this rural rabble-rouser who had been such a thorn in his side for six years.

The day I graduated from law school was, I'm sure, one of the happier days in George Denny's life.

Time after time we go hungry. Sometimes our friends give us food. . . .
I have tried every way to look on the sunny side of life and yet how can
I? I don't want to be a beggar. I want work. I don't want things for
nothing. Can you point me to a job?
                    Vassie Burney of Cullman County, in a letter
                        to Franklin D. Roosevelt, January 19, 1936

FOUR

ॐ

MELONS AND MUD ROADS

When I arrived in the town of Russellville, Alabama, in July
1936, it was with nothing but a law degree, a suitcase and
the dream of going to Congress that I'd had since I was eight years
old. No money. No car. No place to live when I first got there.

Russellville is the seat of Franklin County, tucked up in the
northwest corner of the state, thirty miles from Gober Ridge. It was
at that time a town of about six thousand, in the midst of the Tennessee Valley Authority development, the massive dam-building
project that was a cornerstone of Franklin Roosevelt's New Deal
program, which had kicked into gear while I was in college.

Most of the people around Russellville worked at the dozen or
so dams in the surrounding Tennessee Valley, but any other work in
those parts was hard to come by in the lean Depression years. A
young lawyer hanging out his first shingle did whatever it took to
make ends meet. In my case that meant renting an office for five
dollars a month, firing the building's stove and doing janitorial work

to keep expenses down. I found a place to stay with my cousin W. A. Rea, who gave me a room and fed me for a total price of a dollar a day. Once those matters were settled, I turned to the courtroom, which was a pretty crowded place in those days.

People were looking for recreation as always and, with times so tight, they figured out the courtroom was a pretty good place to watch a show. They'd go on up to the courthouse and sit there and listen to the lawyers try those murder cases and every other kind of case, building up their own opinions on which lawyer was doing a pretty good job and which arguments he should or shouldn't be making. Court buffs was what they were. There were a lot of court buffs in Russellville, and I gave them plenty to talk about right off the bat.

These were awfully hard times, with a lot of down-and-out men who literally had no place to lay their heads. In Russellville, the town fathers had opened up an old vacant building for people who were down on their luck, a place for them to sleep, with coal-burning stoves for heat. It was a flophouse, I guess you'd call it.

Well, one night this old boy came in there looking to spend the night, and the floor was pretty crowded. He was a big fellow, and no sooner did he find him a spot than one of his buddies came in looking for the same thing. Now this second fellow had been drinking some, and he didn't think it was right that this big man was taking up so much room. So he picked up a coffeepot off the stove, walked over to this big fellow, who was sound asleep on his side, and poured that boiling-hot coffee into the big man's left ear.

That created quite a hullabaloo. The grand jury met and indicted this boy, charged him with assault with intent to murder, and I was employed to defend him. The first case of my career, and it attracted a good deal of attention.

We had a young prosecutor up there, and he was one of these fellows that really bore down hard. He made a very strong case. When the jury brought in a verdict of innocent, that prosecutor just had a fit. He had the jury polled. He complained to the judge. And the judge, he was concerned about it too. He said it seemed unusual that a man could pour a cup of hot coffee in another man's ear and get off scot-free. He asked the jury foreman if he could explain the decision.

"I'll just tell you the truth, your honor," said the foreman, a fellow from over in Red Bay named David Morrow.

"This is Carl Elliott's first case," he said. "And we think it's more important to the welfare of this county that he win his first case than it is for some fellow to get convicted for a little flare-up that don't amount to much."

I couldn't believe my ears. And the judge, he was absolutely floored.

There were about a dozen attorneys in Russellville, and I took whatever work was available. Anybody who wanted to hire a lawyer could certainly get me if he couldn't get anyone else. I went to court every day, whether I had a case or not. And I began to get cases, many of them involving the TVA, most representing small farmers and landowners who stood to lose much or all of their land to the rerouted streams and lakes being formed by the dams that had gone up. In lower courts and circuit courts, in places like Decatur and Tuscumbia, I found myself going up against the well-trained and well-funded lawyers working for the TVA. I won my share of cases, and I lost my share too. But more importantly, I began to get the reputation of a fellow who stuck up for the little man, who believed everybody ought to get a fair shake.

Of course when you take on clients like that, not many of them can pay an attorney's fee. Most of these men had no money to speak of, but they insisted on paying me something. They'd offer a dog or a mule, or maybe some watermelons if it was that time of year. The animals were more trouble than they were worth—a mule eats a lot of feed. But I have to say I never turned down a watermelon in my life.

After six months in Russellville, I moved south to Jasper, a town closer to the center of Alabama's nine-county Seventh Congressional District and a place better suited to a young fellow with long-range political plans.

Jasper was—and is—a Walker County town built on the fortunes of coal. And coal runs pretty rich beneath the red clay and thin topsoil in these parts. It was coking coal combined with Alabama iron ore that turned Birmingham's furnaces into one of the world's leading producers of pig iron in the late nineteenth century, making it the industrial capital of the post-Civil War South.

But digging coal was a primitive and dangerous business. The men inside the mines risked their lives every time they went down, and by the turn of the century they were pushing for a fairer shake from the coal companies. Union organizers started showing up in the fields. In the winter of 1920–21, Alabama miners staged what was the largest mine workers' strike in the nation up to that time, protesting low wages and inhuman working conditions. The fires were fanned by the attitudes of Alabamians outraged at the United Mine Workers of America's policy of organizing local unions on a nonsegregated basis. When nearly twelve thousand Alabama mine workers responded to the strike call on September 7, 1920, the coal companies quickly struck back—with evictions, gunmen, scabs, racial attacks, false charges, arrests and numerous assaults against miners. The miners held firm until February, when Governor Thomas E. Kilby finally stopped the strike by ruling in favor of the workers.

That Alabama strike was a foreshadowing of the bloody coalfield battles that would take place in the 1920s in places like Harlan County, Kentucky, and Mingo County, West Virginia. John L. Lewis, the fabled UMW president, described the Alabama conflict as "the baby figure of the giant mass of things to come." Lewis told me years later, when I was in Congress, that, of the thousands of small coal communities in which the UMW had organized unions across the country over the years, there were no better union strongholds than the towns that had pulled together up in these hills in 1920, places like Carbon Hill, Cordova, Dora, Sipsey, Brilliant and a hundred more like them.

Coal miners were mostly the people I represented when I set up my practice in Jasper in 1936. There was a lot of legal work around this town then, maybe thirty lawyers. Half of them represented the interests of the coal companies, and the rest, well, coal mines were falling in on people right and left, so there were a pretty good number of lawsuits, for liability, negligence, workmen's compensation and such. I defended quite a few criminal cases during my career in Jasper, but the bulk of my early work was in damage suits.

No one had heard of black lung at that time. But forty years later, after my Congressional career was through, I came back to Jasper and wound up picking up where I left off, in a manner of speaking, representing black lung victims. This was in the 1970s, when it had finally been established that many of the men who had spent their lives in those mines had had their lungs ruined and that they were due some sort of compensation for their suffering. Of course the coal companies didn't make it easy for these men. We had to fight hard to win each and every judgment, but we did pretty well. I took cases from all across the southeastern United States during that decade, winning more than four million dollars in black lung compensations before the Reagan administration rolled back the laws and the payments to these people. You'll still see more than a few men walking through these towns today, breathing through two clear tubes running out of their nostrils—the badge of a black lung victim.

The miners I represented in the 1930s and '40s in Jasper were hardly more able to pay their bills than the small farmers I had represented in Russellville. The average annual income of people living in Walker County at that time was about six hundred dollars, which is exactly what I earned my first year practicing law in Jasper. And that was fine with me. I was developing something more valuable than a bank account. I was working to build what I've always believed is the foundation of any political base—a good reputation. I never considered any case a loss, and I never considered any action too rash if it seemed like the right thing to do.

That's why, in the winter of 1937, I decided to stop a train.

Things had gotten pretty harsh around here. Snow was twelve to fifteen inches deep, with more on the way. On this particular morning, I ran into the sheriff. I mean, I *ran* into the sheriff—my car slid on a patch of snow and smashed right into his. He wasn't too upset about that, and neither was I. What we, and just about everybody else around town, were most concerned about was how bad the weather was and how more people in town were without heat than with it. The same with food.

Well, I went down to my office that morning and looked up an old Alabama code I'd come across at some time or other, a section or two of old Alabama law that dealt with that very thing, with people going through times of severe hardship. The code specifically said that, under those conditions, people who had no other recourse could take food and any other necessary provisions off a train, if a train carrying such provisions were within reach.

It didn't take a lot of looking to learn a train was leaving Birmingham that morning, loaded with coal and other freight, headed toward Chicago. I went down to the Jasper station about the time that train would be passing through, stepped onto the tracks and flagged it down when it came within sight. A crowd of about a couple of dozen folks had gathered up on the platform by then, to see what the hell was going to happen here.

When the train came to a stop, I told the engineer I had to take the coal and whatever food he might have off his train.

He said, "You *what?*"

I told him again. The crowd was getting pretty good-sized by that time. The engineer looked over at them, then back at me and told me he had no orders to let coal or anything else off that train.

I told him he didn't need any orders. I said these people standing here without heat in their homes or food in their mouths were all the orders he needed.

He said, "But you can't just flag down a train and start *unloading* it!"

I said, "You can *this* one."

And that's what we did, emptied a couple of cars of coal and Irish potatoes and piled them up in back of the depot. Then I sent out word that we had coal and potatoes for those that needed them.

Every now and then someone still reminds me of that day. I was in Birmingham not long ago, and a fellow stopped me on the street, shook his head and smiled.

"Well, well, well," he said. "If it ain't old 'Coal and Potatoes.' "

I was learning as much as I could about the law in those days, but I was also learning as much as I could about the people in these parts, what made them tick, what their needs were, what they were missing in their lives and how somebody might be able to help them get it. You might call it taking the pulse of the people.

That's what I thought Franklin Roosevelt was able to do. All you had to do at that time was turn on the radio and nearly every night you'd hear him and one of his "fireside chats." I listened to those religiously while I was a student at the university, and he captivated me the same way he did just about the entire country. When he discussed the starvation of the people in America and would pronounce, "I tell you, it's time for a *new deal!*"—well, every man who ever played cards knew what a deal was. And here's this man telling them it was time for a new one. Toss in your hands and let's start fresh, he was saying. And there were plenty eager to listen.

America's twelve million unemployed wage earners—one out of every four breadwinners in the nation—were listening. The people whose life savings were lost when more than five thousand banks failed were listening. The 273,000 families who were evicted from their homes in 1932 alone were listening.

Basic justice and a level playing field is what that new deal was about, giving everyone a fair shake and offering a helping hand to those who needed and deserved it. These were principles I'd always believed in, and I knew from the beginning that politics was the best place to do something about it.

The hard times of the Depression, Franklin Roosevelt's promise of a new deal and my own first steps in politics had all converged while I was still a law student at the university, in the fall of 1933.

There was a big fuss that fall in the community of Tuscaloosa about several large chain stores coming in and pushing aside the small mom and pop operations that abounded throughout the smaller towns. The buying power of these chains was so superior that the small shops just couldn't compete. Not much has changed in the half century since then. Everywhere you turn today, from restaurants and grocery stores to hotels and hospitals, small independently owned businesses are facing extinction at the hands of these juggernauts with their economies of size.

Well, the small shops in Tuscaloosa decided to do something about it. It was crude, but they formed a coalition and went out to

Margaret Bonds Massey, my great-grandmother, with her granddaughter Claudia in 1905.

Andrew Jackson Massey, the boy whipped by Confederate "rangers" while his father was away fighting in the Civil War, and his seven children in 1906. My mother, Nora, age eighteen, stands at right.

G. W. (Will) Elliott and his new wife Nora in January 1913. (Carl Elliott, Sr., collection)

Senator J. Thomas
"Cotton Tom" Heflin.

Senator Hugo Black in 1937, the
year he was appointed a Supreme
Court justice.

In 1932 I was working as a member of the University of Alabama's building and grounds crew, among other jobs.

George H. Denny, President of the University of Alabama during my six years there.

Greene County Sheriff W. E. (Big Bill) Lee, 1966.

Student Body President Carl
Elliott, May 5, 1936.

Candidate Carl Elliott in 1948.

Campaign literature from my 1948 run for Congress.

The newly elected Congressman with my parents and siblings. Seated, left to right: Jewel, Martha Jean, G. W. Elliott, Mrs. G. W. Elliott, Willie Mae and Mable. Standing: me, Gober, Hoyt, Ernest and Ernie.

As a young Congressman at home with my constituents in December 1951.

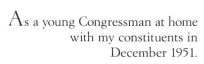

Two coal miners at the mouth of a "wagon mine" near Cardiff, Alabama, 1930.

"Kissin'" Jim Folsom visits New York City, March 1948.

Senator Lister Hill, October 1944.

With my wife, Jane, and our children (from left: Martha, John, Lenora, and Carl Jr.) in Washington, June 1957.

The Dixiecrat leaders arrive in Birmingham in July 1948 for their convention. From left: former Alabama governor Frank Dixon, presidential elector Horace Wilkinson, Sidney Smyer of Birmingham, and Fielding Wright of Jackson, Mississippi.

A bookmobile in rural Cullman County, 1957 (note the wheelbarrow used to return the books).

hire someone to make speeches on street corners in front of their stores, to stir up some crowds and get them thinking about what was going on. The man they wound up hiring was me. I went around on Saturdays, climbing up on a box or sometimes simply standing on the hood of a car, making speeches to whatever kind of crowd collected. I made as many as fifteen a day, a dollar a speech. There were some hecklers, but there were plenty of sympathetic listeners as well. I saw it all as good training, and when I looked down at these people I was speaking to, so many of them unshaven, poorly dressed and practically unshod, I knew just why Franklin Roosevelt was such a popular man. He was aware of these people and he felt for them, and they knew it. I was a New Deal man long before there was a New Deal, and I was definitely one thereafter.

Of course the suffering of the Depression made liberals out of a lot of folks. The way most of us saw it, we were all in this thing together. When it came to politics, there were several Alabamians who began making a pretty good name for themselves as liberals at that time. One of the first I met was Lister Hill.

Hill was at the head of a wave of progressive Southern Democrats whose careers blossomed with the New Deal. He was instrumental in the creation of the Tennessee Valley Authority, and in 1940 he stepped into the national spotlight when he was selected to place Franklin Roosevelt's name before the Democratic national convention as a candidate for an unprecedented third presidential term, a rare opportunity for a first-term Senator. The speech itself was a disaster, with Lister's drawn-out oratorical style disappointing the rowdy conventioneers in Chicago, who were hoping to be whipped into a frenzy. Still, Hill's career flourished. There was a strong feeling among some that if Roosevelt hadn't died in office during his fourth term, leaving the presidency to Harry Truman, Lister Hill would have been the Democratic presidential candidate in 1948.

But in the fall of 1937, Hill was an eighth-term Congressman considering making a move for the Senate but not sure when that move should be made. In August of that year, President Roosevelt made the move for him, by appointing Alabama Senator Hugo Black to the U. S. Supreme Court and creating a vacancy to be filled in a January primary. When Hill ran for that Senate seat, I was his Walker County campaign manager, working to get him as many of the county's votes as I could.

What I liked about Lister was that although he came from a rich and powerful background, his heart still beat to the tune of the common man. His father was a surgeon in Montgomery, the first doctor to perform a suture on a human heart—that heart, by the way, belonged to a black man.

Lister was a Beau Brummell kind of fellow, as conservative in his personal behavior as he was liberal in his politics. And he knew the art of politics. He had a real feel for the direction in which the people were going. You could follow him, and he wouldn't get you lost out in the mire somewhere. When I eventually came to Congress, it was with Lister that I ultimately hammered out what I consider the crowning achievement of my career, the National Defense Education Act.

But in the late 1930s and '40s I was out to learn the art of politics for myself, and there was no rushing that process. Not much sense that politics makes was ever put into a book. It's something you learn by doing. I eventually made twenty-one campaigns in my own career, and I feel that I gathered something from every one of them. A lot of other folks gathered a lot about me from them as well. Politics, you see, prior to this age of what they call mass media, was largely based on word of mouth.

By 1940, I figured the word on Carl Elliott was good enough to give it a go myself, so I made my first foray into the political ring. I didn't feel I was ready to run for Congress yet, but I felt ready to run for *something.* I wound up running for Judge of the Walker County Court against a fellow named J. B. Powell. Everyone called him Jim Bird, and he was a wise old political owl. Sixty-one years old, to be exact, and he didn't let anyone forget that I was only twenty-six.

"Carl Elliott is a fine boy," he'd say. "He's got the best education you ever saw. He's smarter than any of us. He'll make a fine politician someday, but he's not right for this job.

"He came in here with nothing but a traveling bag, and that's what he's been up till now—a suitcase lawyer. He'll be disappointed when he loses this race, I'm sure he will. He'll get that traveling bag and he'll throw his shirts in it and he'll go on down the road. You'll never see him again.

"But old Jim, I'll still be here, with my nine children and my grandchildren. I'll be standing at the window, watching down the road to see the light turn the curve, bringing home my children, who will be out with your children, long after you've forgotten Carl Elliott's name."

Jim Bird had a way with more than words. Jasper was a small town then, but not too small to have a few ladies of the night among the population. Everyone knew who they were, which is what Jim Bird and his supporters counted on when these painted women began showing up in the nicer parts of town, knocking on doors and announcing, "Hi! We're friends of Carl, and we're here to ask you to vote for him for county judge!"

A variation on that same theme were several of the county's more successful bootleggers, who came down from the hills during that campaign to cruise around town in cars with "Vote for Carl" signs mounted on the tops.

I made sixty-two speeches during that campaign, but I couldn't match the judge. He beat me by three hundred votes.

I went three thousand six hundred dollars in debt on that campaign. In fact, I don't think I've ever finished a political race that paid for itself. It's awful hard to do. But still I can't see any other way around it. This business of Senators and Congressmen massing contributions and building up campaign war chests has predictably gotten to the point where people are asking hard questions about who our representatives are actually representing. And something's really out of kilter when these fellows are free to *take* that money with them and put it in their own pockets when they decide to leave office.

I've just always figured a fellow should pay his own freight as he goes. The day after that 1940 election, I went back to my law office, licked my wounds a little bit, then got to work, to start paying back my debts from that campaign. And a month after that, in June

1940, I married Jane Hamilton, the woman who stayed my wife to the day she died in 1985.

She was the girl, the only girl I'd ever met that I wanted to marry. She was a clerk in a federal office in Jasper when I first saw her, not even out of high school. It wasn't until a year later that I actually asked her out. For our first date I took her to a wrestling match, and I don't think she ever let me forget that. She was twenty years old when I married her. She had a fairly good education from Christian College in Missouri. She was very loyal. We made a good team.

By the time our first child, Carl, Jr., was born in 1941, I'd paid off the debts from my first campaign and was making regular trips down to Tuscaloosa, for this or that political function, most of them at the university, which, with its long list of politically active alumni, was a crossroads for the state's past, present and future leaders. It was at a banquet there that spring that I met an eager young man, an undergraduate student seemingly of the sort I had been—clearly ambitious, and not one bit intimidated by this scene of Alabama statesmen all around him. He stopped me as the dinner was breaking up and Jane and I were making our way out the door to our car.

He was a very intense young fellow, clearly on the make, really on the rise. I didn't know who he was, but he told me he knew all about me, told me how much he thought of me, of the career I'd had at the university and of the work I'd done since. I listened to him while he talked about all the books he'd read on politics, and all the plans he had for himself. I listened for about half an hour. He had me cornered. Finally, Jane pulled me into the car, and this boy was still talking as we pulled away, telling me I was the greatest man that's ever been and maybe we'd cross paths again.

When we got going toward home, Jane asked, "Who *was* that?"

"Don't know him," I told her. "I think he said his name's George Wallace."

There were plenty of men I worked with and for on the Alabama political scene during the 1940s, but none had the impact of Jim

Folsom. Big Jim, they called him, for obvious reasons. A bear of a man, he towered six feet eight inches tall and tipped the scales at more than two hundred fifty pounds, with a big shock of thick black hair sprouting from his head. He wore a size sixteen shoe. A lot of folks compared him to the comic-strip character Lil Abner, not just because of his physical appearance but because of his hillbilly background.

Folsom came out of what they call "wire-grass country," the southeast corner of the state, where the flatland soil was just as sandy and the people just as poor as up in the northern hills. By the time he stepped on the political scene, running for governor in 1942, Folsom had moved up to my territory, living and selling insurance in Cullman, some forty miles east of Jasper.

There were plenty of people who ridiculed Jim Folsom for his down-home demeanor and his corn-pone antics, but they underestimated the big man's appeal. When he took to stumping the state in 1942, Alabamians were in for a show the likes of which they'd never seen before. Attacking the "Big Mules" of industry and agriculture, Folsom courted the votes of the little men, the people who lived around the "branch heads" of isolated mountain streams tucked up in the hills and hollows, people who took their crops to markets on dirt roads that turned to quagmires when it rained. Folsom lured those people out of their branch heads with his trademark invitation "Y'all come!" He warmed them up at each speaking stop with some musical entertainment from a string band called the Strawberry Pickers. Then he'd climb on stage waving a corn-shuck mop and vow to sweep the statehouse clean of corrupt politicians. He promised to pave those roads they'd ridden in on. He pointed out how thinly represented in the state legislature they were compared to their wealthier fellow Alabamians to the south, and he promised to reapportion that legislature.

Jim Folsom was Populism incarnate, an Andrew Jackson man of the first order. In fact, his platform was called the "People's Program." It was a grass-roots approach from the bottom up. When he closed his speeches by passing copper "suds buckets" through the crowd, asking them to ante up whatever nickels and dimes they could spare, the buckets came back full and the people went home fired up.

To me, at least early in his career, Jim Folsom represented everything I believed in, the eternity of the hopes of mankind. He knew how to speak the people's language better than just about anybody I'd ever heard. To him, everyone was just "fokes." But he wasn't as simple as his critics made him out to be. He was a showman all right. Every move was a show to the big man. But every show had a purpose. He was, as they say, dumb as a fox.

I liked what I saw in Jim Folsom, and I was happy to be his Walker County campaign manager in 1942, along with my friend Lecil Gray. As it turned out, Walker was the only county Folsom carried in that race, but when he ran again in 1946 he stunned the state and stepped onto the national scene by becoming Alabama's most visible governor of the century. George Wallace would later take that title, but back when Big Jim was riding high, Wallace was, like me, just another face in the Folsom crowd. In 1954, Wallace was Folsom's southern Alabama campaign manager, writing the bulk of Big Jim's speeches before better possibilities elsewhere and the lure of racism pulled him away from the Folsom fold. Loyalty was never one of George Wallace's strong suits.

There was a lot about Jim Folsom that was embarrassing to more staid Alabamians, even those among Folsom's allies—people like Lister Hill, whose approach to his constituency was always more paternalistic and refined. Big Jim's backslapping antics made more polished men like Lister Hill uncomfortable, but everyone came to recognize the big man's power and so they put up with his excesses —at least in the beginning. And Big Jim really had some power for a while, although, as it turned out, not as much as he believed.

He wasn't in office but two years when he announced his candidacy for the United States presidency in January 1948. But that dream was short-lived. In March of that year, it came out that Folsom had fathered an illegitimate son during the 1946 gubernatorial campaign. His critics had a field day with that one, latching onto his longtime nickname of "Kissin' Jim"—given for his practice of kissing all the women in his crowds. The presidency was out, and so was Folsom as governor in 1950.

Big Jim came back in 1954 and took the governorship again. But by then his drinking and rowdy public behavior were no longer as amusing or endearing as they had once been. He had risen to power as everyone's overgrown boy, full of mischief but easy to forgive. Now, however, his act had begun to wear thin. When it came to matters of race, Folsom was color-blind. This is the one thing that set him apart from even some of his most otherwise faithful followers, and it eventually proved his ultimate undoing.

In 1955, Jim made the mistake of inviting black New York Congressman Adam Clayton Powell, Jr., to share a Scotch and soda with him in the governor's mansion in Montgomery. This was an unheard-of sin, even to most otherwise progressive white Alabamians, and Folsom's career never recovered from it. From then on, he was branded as "host of the whiskey-drinking Negro Congressman from Harlem."

It was during Folsom's second administration that the national Young Democrats met in Oklahoma City. One of the leading candidates for the group's presidency was an Alabamian, so Big Jim rounded up as many of the state's legislators as he could get to go up there and see what we could do to help this young man out. I was one of those who went.

When a group of us wound up on a local television program for a panel discussion, Big Jim took center stage with a tumbler of bourbon in hand. The state of Oklahoma was, at the time, bone dry, so when the camera swung to Folsom, he raised his glass and announced to the viewing audience that this might look like whiskey he was drinking but it was actually "good ol' Oklahoma branch water." He laughed and began whacking the back of the fellow seated to his right, Pete Matthews, a state senator from down in Coosa County.

It was apparent that Jim was pretty liquored up, and as he went on rambling, he didn't get any soberer. People began to look at each other, and the newspaper people in the room started rushing up front like bees to honey, flashing their lights, writing in their notebooks.

I was seated to Folsom's left, but by the time the television cameras swung toward me, my seat was empty. People have sworn for years that I crawled out of that studio on my hands and knees. That's not true. But I was definitely bent real low as I made a quiet —and quick—exit.

By the end of that second term, Folsom's own whiskey drinking had gotten entirely out of hand. He had become a pretty pathetic figure, especially to people outside the state. It was late in Folsom's final term as governor that I ran into a former governor of Virginia named Bill Tuck one day in Congress. He stopped me in the hall and said, "What's with this goddamned fool Folsom?"

I was being asked that question more and more those days.

What Bill Tuck had wanted to tell me that day in Congress was his tale of a recent visit Folsom had made to Virginia. It seems Jim had stopped through the state searching for some graves of his ancestors. It happened that the Navy was launching a new cruiser out of Norfolk, so they invited Folsom to attend "to see 'em bust a bottle of champagne," is how Tuck put it.

Well, Big Jim could think of better things to do with a bottle than bust it. Bill Tuck saw that was true when the governor of Alabama came wobbling in late to that christening. When they took this new ship out into the Chesapeake Bay to show what it could do and to demonstrate a new airplane as well, Big Jim went along for the ride, hanging on the rail, doing his best to keep his lunch down. He was hardly watching the goings on when something went wrong with the plane. It turned upside down and crashed into the bay, right there in front of everyone.

"Well," said Big Jim, watching the parachutes of the two pilots float down toward the water, "if that ain't a show, I'll kiss your ass."

That's the way Bill Tuck told it, and that was Jim Folsom all over. It was sad to watch the twilight of Jim's career, to see him run again for governor in 1962, bringing his family with him as he made a statewide television appearance the night before that vote, and forgetting the names of his own children as he tried to introduce them. George Wallace won that election, leaving Folsom one more futile try for the governorship, in 1966, in the same race that marked the climax of my own career.

Jim Folsom was larger than life, for better *and* for worse. I prefer to think of the better. The big man's weaknesses were as huge as his appetite, but so were his heart and his vision—and his courage. He was ahead of his time on race relations and wasn't afraid to share his views.

"I could never get excited about my colored brothers," he said once. "They've been here three hundred years and I estimate they'll be here another three hundred years or more. I'm not going to get my ulcers in an uproar. I find them to be good citizens. If they had been making a living for me like they have for the Black Belt, I'd be proud of them instead of kicking them and cussing them all the time."

In his Christmas message to Alabama in 1949, he declared:

"As long as the Negroes are held down by deprivation and lack of opportunity, all the other people will be held down alongside them. Let's start talking fellowship and brotherly love, and doing unto others. And let's do more than talk about it; let's start living it."

One thing you can say about Big Jim Folsom is he lived it.

My own political career was temporarily put aside when America entered World War II in December 1941. My brother Gober entered the Army Air Corps that year, eventually flying with a Pacific bombardment group based in New Guinea. My brother Hoyt left the University of Alabama two years later to join the Army Quartermaster Corps. I also volunteered for the Army and on June 4, 1942, I became Private Carl A. Elliott, U. S. Infantry.

After going through basic training at Camp Wheeler, Georgia, infantry school at Fort Benning and more training at Camp Blanding, Florida, I was commissioned a first lieutenant in April 1944 and wound up at Camp Forest, near Manchester, Tennessee, training with Company A, First Battalion, 313th Infantry Regiment of the 79th Infantry Division, getting ready to go overseas.

They had us maneuvering through those Tennessee hills, getting ready for mountain combat. We were all eager to be shipped out, but meanwhile we trained, and we waited. Of course, when you get a bunch of soldiers sitting around with time on their hands, it isn't long before the cards come out, and my platoon learned pretty quickly that the Tennessee hills are not the safest place to find a game of poker.

We had pulled into a horse farm up there in those hills and set up for the evening when the owner of this farm, who had been friendly enough to let us camp on his land, came strolling down to see how we were doing. A group of us were playing cards, including this fellow named Henderson, who was not what you'd call shy. Henderson began taunting this fellow, daring him to come gamble with us.

"Now you boys oughtta be careful about that loose talk," the farmer said. "I own this beautiful farm, and I run these horses here, but the way I actually make my living is I play poker."

It sounded to me like this fellow was giving us fair warning. To Henderson, it sounded like bunk. He kept teasing this fellow, telling him his horses would belong to us when we were done with him.

Well, this fellow just smiled, sat down, and said one word: "Deal." It didn't take too many hands to see a shift in the money, like a sudden change in the weather. We'd all been paid that day, and by the end of that evening, around about midnight, I think this fellow had pocketed every dollar on that table. I know he had every dollar of mine. And I knew that better be the end of my poker-playing career, especially after I broke the news to Jane, who had been planning to bring her mother and baby Carl up to visit me for the weekend. Needless to say, that visit never happened. It took a couple of weeks, but Jane eventually cooled off. I never did get to hear what my mother-in-law thought of it all, and that's just as well.

By the middle of 1943 we were still in Tennessee, training around a place called Spencer Mountain, and I had been appointed the regiment's trial judge advocate, which meant I was the first one called when any of these soldiers got himself into a legal scrape. My first case gave me a good refresher course in mountain justice.

It seems one of our men had gotten involved with the daughter of a local farmer. The old fellow had absolutely no doubt that his daughter had been impregnated by our man, and he sent word that he was not going to wait too long to hear what we planned to do about it. I figured the first thing I'd better do was go down in those woods to see the father.

When I got there, he was sitting in the corner of his cabin, making a big show—clearly for my benefit—of polishing his rifle. This was not a military-issue rifle. It was a good old-fashioned mountain rifle. Basically, I was there to ask him if he was certain it was our man who had done this. He told me he had absolutely no doubt, and he added that he was not going to wait long for our verdict.

"That's the man," he said, rubbing his rifle, "and, by God, if the Army can't settle it, I can."

I got back to camp, gave the battalion commander all the details, then went back to my tent for the night. The next morning I pulled back the flap and there was the old fellow himself, rifle in hand, come to let me know there were no slow wheels of justice where he came from, and if he couldn't find this soldier, he could sure as hell find me. When he left, he promised we'd meet again, "real soon."

Sometimes fate steps into situations in strange ways. In this case, it did it by sending me off the side of a cliff.

The afternoon of the mountain man's visit, our platoon went up on a hillside for some maneuvers. We were climbing over a cliffside fence when the thing gave way as I was swinging across. By the time I was done rolling down that mountain, my head was banged up pretty good and I'd badly broken two bones in my right forearm. They carried me back to the hospital at Camp Forest, then moved me to a hospital in Atlanta, where I stayed for five months and two surgical operations. Meanwhile, our regiment shipped out without me.

On September 28, 1944, I was honorably discharged from the Army for the disabilities caused by my injuries. I never found out what became of the mountain man and his daughter, but the rest of my life I made a point to steer clear of Spencer Mountain.

Three days after I left the Army, I was back in my law office at Jasper, picking up where I had left off more than two years earlier. A month after that, our second child, Martha, was born.

A year later, in 1945, I was appointed a city judge in Jasper, taking a choice seat to watch the steady stream of humanity coming in and out of that courtroom. Depression or not, war or no war, times continued to be tough for these people, awfully tough. A fellow couldn't help but feel that, and I was feeling it mighty strongly by then. I was chomping at the bit to get the chance to start doing something about this politically. Meanwhile I tried to mete out justice in my own small way as best I could. More than a few times, I made that justice personal.

I remember one particular night when things got to me. It wasn't much different from any other. I looked out among all those tired faces, those poor fathers and sons, mothers and daughters who I realized didn't have a thing in the world. Most of them had been arrested for something connected with drinking, a lot of it out of pure desperation or simple surrender. I sat there looking at them, then I just stood up and announced that every case on that day's docket was hereby dismissed. Of course that didn't sit well with the people in there who had cases against someone—the storekeeper who had caught someone stealing a loaf of bread, for instance. But I just had to do it, to illustrate that these boys and girls had just about all they could carry.

It was about that time that I met up with a man who would be by my side throughout the rest of my life. He came from out of those coal mines, his heart beat to the tune of the common man, and despite the success he'd made of his life, he never forgot the hardships he and his family had endured in the life he'd been lucky enough to leave behind.

His name was Garve Ivey. He was five years younger than me, born and raised in a wilderness mining camp called Gamble Mines, near Jasper. There were dozens of camps just like that one scattered throughout these hills, clusters of company-built shacks gathered into villages with names like Slick Lizard, Dog Town, Nauvoo, Calumet, Good Springs. These homes, assigned by the coal companies to miners depending on the size of a man's family, with rent deducted from his monthly pay, were little more than lumber nailed together with tin on top. There was no heat other than the home's single fireplace. No yard, no electricity, no plumbing. Six or seven homes would share a single dug well, from which they'd carry their water. And the outhouses were emptied once a week, which made flies a constant presence in homes that didn't have the luxury of screens. One of Garve's most vivid memories was when the preacher would visit a miner's home for Sunday dinner, and the young boys would be given the job of standing by the table throughout the meal, waving away the flies with tree branches.

These homes were built on steep hillsides, with one step up to the back porch and as many as a dozen down from the front. Dogs playing in the dirt beneath the houses could be seen through the cracks between the boards of the wooden floors.

There were no roads in or out of most of these camps. The rail lines built to carry in equipment and carry out coal were the only means of transportation. So the families spent nearly their entire lives within the village, doing all their shopping at the company store, buying company-priced products with company scrip. That scrip was either paper money or tin coins the miners called "clacker," for the way they sounded when they were rubbed together. In Garve's village, clacker was worth one hundred cents on the dollar at the company store, but if a man wanted actual cash, his clacker would only get him fifty cents on the dollar.

It's easy to see the total control the companies had over the miners' lives. It's easy to see what Tennessee Ernie Ford was singing about in his song, "I Owe My Soul to the Company Store." And it's easy to see why Garve Ivey described his upbringing as "just that much short of slavery."

When Garve was twelve, a rock fell on his father's neck, breaking his back and rendering him totally disabled. The company settled by giving him a lump sum of seven hundred and fifty dollars and allowing him and his family to stay in their house as long as he lived. That was considered generous by company standards at the time. But three years later, when Garve's father was found dead from a fall off a railroad trestle, the company sent its condolences in the form of a notice telling Garve and his mother that they had thirty days to vacate the house. It was the county, not the coal company, that paid for the burial Garve's family couldn't afford.

That was in 1934, in the heart of the Depression. Garve was fifteen years old, grief-stricken from the sudden death of his father, and faced with the prospect of somehow caring for his mother and five younger brothers and sisters. Evicted from the camp, the family was able to set up on some land owned by Garve's brother-in-law, and Garve found a job repairing roads for the federal government's Works Progress Administration. That WPA job, as much as anything else, made a Democrat for life out of the grateful young Garve Ivey. His formal schooling had gone no further than the fifth grade when he was forced to quit and go to work to help his family. But Garve swore when he left that coal camp that neither he nor his family would ever have to come near that kind of hardship again, and he worked every day of the rest of his life to keep that vow.

By the time I met him in 1945, Garve had built a small business hauling cattle and produce. He'd taken a break to join the Army during the war, where he was one of the first men to hit the beach at Normandy. When he came home, he brought a Bronze Star, two oak leaf clusters, a Purple Heart and more than six thousand dollars in poker winnings. It was that money that helped him buy a café in Jasper, and it was at that café that Garve and I met and became fast friends. Pretty soon I became his attorney as well, handling the business deals Garve was always involved in, from running pool halls to starting up a chain of drive-in theaters.

Garve needed me for more than legal reasons. He had a hair-trigger temper that sometimes got him in trouble, and there weren't many people he trusted enough to get him out. The more he got to know me, the more he trusted me, not just as his lawyer but as his friend.

And I needed Garve. Any man who builds a political career needs someone he can totally count on, someone he can turn to for information and advice when the chips are down, someone beyond his circle of formal staff members. From the beginning of my political career, Garve Ivey was that man.

And the beginning of that political career was 1948.

Jane and I were the parents of three children by then, with my second son John born a year earlier. I was about as well known around the county as I was going to get, and I'd worked enough

campaigns for other Democrats to be pretty familiar with the entire
nine-county district. A fellow named Carter Manasco was up for
reelection to his fifth term as Congressman, having seven years earlier taken the place of none other than Will Bankhead, the man who
had planted the seed of my own dreams when I was eight. I took a
good look at Manasco, at my own situation, at my sense of the
connections I'd made with the people throughout this area—having
a sense was about as much science as there was to that—and I
decided the time had come. I could feel it. So, at the age of thirty-
four, I declared my candidacy for U. S. Congress.

I guess you could say I ran my campaign pretty much the way
I'd watched Jim Folsom run his. I did my footwork, making eighty-
five speeches in three months. Some Saturdays I made as many as
ten. I didn't let the people forget I was one of them, beginning with
my slogan: "From Farm Boy to Congress." Not the catchiest, most
imaginative phrase, but it did the job.

Like Big Jim, I walked the mud roads, promising to get them
paved. Like him, I passed the bucket, so to speak, taking whatever
folks wanted to contribute at the end of each speech. One meeting
with a crowd of one hundred yielded one hundred contributions of
a dollar apiece. Every one of those dollars helped, and more importantly, every one of those dollars was a vote.

Unlike Folsom, I focused real hard on education, telling those
miners and farmers that there was no reason on earth their children
shouldn't have schooling of the same quality as that of children who
live in large cities.

The similarities between the governor and me did not go unno-
ticed. One reporter covering that 1948 campaign wrote the following account:

> The tall fellow with the battered campaign hat wound up his
> speech and mopped his forehead.
> There was a pattering of handclaps, but applause seemed
> too formal for a crowd of fifteen. They stepped up to shake
> hands with the candidate.
> It was Saturday afternoon and he had provided the only

diversion around the country store where Alabama and Mississippi meet.

"Y'know," said a worn farmer, "you're the only political
candidate *has* ever come to this town in my memory."

An onlooker who had wandered up late asked curiously,
"Are you Jim Folsom?"

"No," said the candidate, "I'm Carl Elliott. Get it, Carl
Elliott."

Another of the county's small daily newspapers described the
mounting campaign in its own distinctive way:

> Congressman Manasco has been busy as a bee tending his po-
> litical fences since Congress adjourned in August. . . . He's
> gotta be re-elected again if he keeps his job, and his opposition
> will be nothing to sneeze at. Carl Elliott, popular and able
> young Jasper lawyer, has announced that he is going to run for
> the office. In fact, he's been running for quite a while now,
> getting around the nine-county Seventh District, shaking hands
> and passing out cards. Yessir, it ought to be a dilly of a cam-
> paign—clean of course but keen just the same.

It was a clean campaign. Manasco and I were joined by a third
candidate, a Haleyville lumberman named J. H. Kelly. Garve Ivey
worked Walker County for me, and my friend Lecil Gray used his
connections as probate judge to spread the word throughout the
district. It was Manasco I worried about most, of course, but he
wasn't too worried about me. He had come into Congress as part of
what was in essence the local Bankhead machine. Carter had
worked his way into the Bankhead political organization, and when
Will died in 1940, Manasco found himself in Congress. As soon as I
announced my candidacy and launched my campaign in '48, Carter
went to see Will's nephew, Walter Will Bankhead, as he often did
for political advice. In this case, Carter was wondering when he
should start his own campaign.

"It's too early," Walter Will told him.

A few weeks later, hearing how busy I'd been, Carter was back again.

"It's too early," Walter Will told him again.

Finally, not long after that, when it was apparent I'd picked up more momentum than either Manasco or the Bankheads could have imagined, Manasco was back with the same question.

"Carter," declared Walter Will, "it's too *late.*"

An incumbent is awfully hard to beat, but I guess you could say I snuck up on this one. When the final returns were in, Kelly had collected about two thousand votes. Manasco got thirteen thousand. And I had won by a landslide, with twenty-two thousand votes.

After twenty-six years of dreaming, I was finally on my way to Washington, D.C.

The House is composed of very good men, not shining, but honest and reasonably well-informed, and in time they will be found to improve. . . .

Fisher Ames, Representative from Massachusetts, writing to a constituent in May, 1789

FIVE

⧜

CAPITOL HILL AND COUPLING POLES

I was due in Washington January 3, 1949, for the convening of the Eighty-first Congress. But I had some things to take care of before then, one of which was to wrap up my law practice. I didn't expect to be getting back to that any time soon. Coming from a Democratic stronghold such as Alabama's Seventh Congressional District, where tradition generally holds that one good term deserves another, I figured I was going to be in Congress for a while. Ten years is about what I had in mind.

Of course I kept my home in Jasper, which I had bought in 1945 for five thousand dollars and on which I'd spent another seven thousand for repairs. House hunting in Washington would be more expensive, I knew, but when I went up in October with my first two staff members—my head secretary Hershell McNutt and my office secretary Cora Marlowe—I found what I was looking for the first day and bought it. I'm not much of a shopper, never have been. It's always seemed to me that you can waste enough time shopping to chew your whole life up. Get it done and get on with the important things—that's how I've always approached shopping.

I guess you'd call the house I bought a brick bungalow. I never have known exactly what a bungalow is, but that's what the ad in the newspaper called it, and when I saw it, it seemed to be just about what we'd need. Three bedrooms, in a nice, tree-shaded neighborhood called Alton Place, in the northwest section of the city. The price was $23,495—just about twice what our Jasper home had cost, which was fine with me. I wasn't in Washington to quibble about money. If money meant that much to me, I would have kept at my law business, which was earning me more than the $12,500 a freshman Congressman was paid in 1949. That salary was nothing I paid much attention to either. Hell, I would have paid *them* to come to Congress if I'd had to. The whole fabric of my life had been built around arriving there.

I wanted the people working for me to feel the same way. That's why I picked McNutt and Marlowe to join me. Cora had been my secretary in Jasper for years, as thorough, loyal and devoted as they come. My selection of Hershell was somewhat of a surprise to some people. He had nothing to do with politics—which is exactly why I picked him. He didn't come with any *barnacles* attached. I wanted a fellow fresh from the people, and Hershell was just that —a former teacher and high school principal. He was a man who didn't panic, and I liked that about him, liked that about any man. Those fellows that get beside themselves when the heat's on never did appeal to me. I might be wrong about that—some of the most successful people I know are gone to pieces most of the time—but personally that irks me.

I guess the dedication I expected in my staff was the same as what I demanded of myself. They almost never bothered me about anything personal. There wasn't any of this business of "I've got to take off early today to go watch my son play his first game of Pee-Wee football." It was the same for me. I knew going into this business that some things were going to have to be sacrificed to a certain extent. One of them was time with my family. I regretted it, but it was something I knew when I got into this.

We had grown to a family of six by the time we left for Washington three days after Christmas of 1948. Carl, Jr., was seven years old, Martha was four, John was one, and our infant daugher Lenora, born that October, was barely two months old. Jane brought Lenora up by train while the rest of us drove in my Ford. By the time Jane arrived, Lenora was awfully sick. We didn't know what exactly was wrong, but we knew we needed to find a doctor right away. When we wound up at the Washington, D.C., Children's Hospital, we weren't prepared for what the doctor there had to tell us.

"This child," he said, after looking Lenora over, "is going to die."

Our baby had spinal meningitis. Specifically, she had a form of the disease caused by an organism called *Neisseria meningitidis.* This is considered one of the worst types of meningitis there are, especially in infants. It can cause everything from brain abscesses to cerebral edema, which is swelling around the brain. The doctor told us he would do his best to break this thing up, but it was at an advanced stage, he said. When he told us late that night that Lenora had developed a second form of the disease as well—something called *influenza meningitis*—he was even more pessimistic about her chances.

It was an awful big load on all of us, a real hard way to ring in the new year. It threw a pretty big shadow over everything else, including the opening of Congress. I went, of course—there wasn't much else to do. But I went with a heavy heart, and it stayed that way for my first week in office, as I stopped in at the hospital each morning on my way to Capitol Hill, to see my daughter. Every morning I held my little finger down in front of her face, hoping she would reach up for it, as she had done when she was healthy. Words can't describe how I felt when, on the tenth day, Lenora's tiny hand came up and closed around my little finger.

She would stay in that hospital three more weeks, but I knew that day that my little girl was going to live.

"Do you solemnly swear that you will support and defend the Constitution of the United States against all enemies, foreign and domestic; that you will bear true faith and allegiance to the same; that you take

this obligation freely, without mental reservation or purpose of eva-
sion, and that you will well and faithfully discharge the duties of the
office on which you are about to enter, so help you God?"

This was the question put to more than one hundred new arriv-
als on the floor of the House of Representatives on January 3, 1949.
I was proud to be among them, eager to answer "I do," and fully
prepared to get on with the business of becoming a Congressman.

It's a business that takes time, and there's no rushing the process. Congress is an institution that has always valued, respected,
even worshiped the concept of time. It's a system based in large part
on seniority. Like children, newcomers are expected to be largely
seen and not heard. When they ask for something, they ask carefully
and with all due respect. And whatever they are given, they take it
without complaining. There is plenty of room to rise and to gain
respect of your own, but there are no shortcuts, at least not the way
I saw it. The way I looked at it, I was there to do everything I could
to learn all I could about my job, and I was ready to give it everything I had. There might be fellows who were smarter than me,
some more clever, some better connected, but there was nobody
who was ever going to be able to say he worked harder than I did.

Four hundred and thirty-five men answered the roll my first
day in the House chamber. The oldest of them was eighty-two-year-
old Adolph Sabath of Illinois, born in Czechoslovakia, who had first
been elected to Congress in 1907 and was now beginning his
twenty-second consecutive term as a Congressman from Chicago.
He had served forty-two years, longest in that House. Harry Truman was the eighth President under whom Sabath served.

Up on the rostrum was Speaker of the House Sam Rayburn of
Texas, who had come to Congress the year I was born and who had
no intention of ever leaving it. Short, stocky, bald, he had his hand
on the gavel and that was all he wanted. Rayburn had been briefly
married early in his life, but his real marriage was to this chamber.
Time and again, "Mr. Sam," as they called him, put his feelings in
unequivocal terms: "I love this House." Not the Senate. Not the
presidency. But the House.

I'd first met Rayburn when he came to Jasper in the fall of 1940
to help bury Will Bankhead. Bankhead's death was a turning point

in Rayburn's life, because that put Rayburn in the Speaker's seat where he remained for the rest of his life.

Rayburn took that seat immediately after Bankhead's state funeral on Monday, September 16, 1940. He made no acceptance speech but moved immediately on to the first order of business, which was appointing a committee of sixty-three House members to accompany Bankhead's body to Jasper for burial the next day. Also on that train to Jasper was President Franklin Roosevelt—the third time he had traveled to pay respects to a Speaker who died during his presidency (the previous two were Henry T. Rainey of Illinois in 1934 and Joseph W. Byrns of Tennessee in 1936).

In *Mr. Sam,* a biography of Rayburn written by a man named C. Dwight Dorough, Rayburn's memories of that journey to Jasper are described:

> . . . the dusty roads of Walker County, the hot Alabama sun, the Jasper First Methodist Church roped off with binder twine from a telephone pole to a soapbox, to a fireplug and to another telephone pole. The men in overalls and blue denim shirts . . . He sensed their grief. Fans and umbrellas gave the ladies some relief from the heat. When the prayer came over the loudspeaker, the men removed their sweat-stained hats. Because of the solemnity of the occasion, the people acknowledged Roosevelt's presence with only subdued applause and a nod of the head. A reporter heard a farmer remark, " 'Tain't no time for cheering."

That's about the way it was. I was Rayburn's personal escort that day and got to know him some as we sat and waited an hour at the station for the train to get ready to leave Jasper back toward Washington. Already he had the question on his mind of who'd be chosen as House majority leader, John McCormack of Massachusetts or Clifton Woodrum of Virginia. His clear preference was McCormack, and he was happy when that choice was made two days later. I kept up correspondence with Rayburn during the years that followed, so I was no stranger to Mr. Sam when I took my seat in the House.

Around me that first day were plenty of faces I'd come to know well in the years to come.

There was John Rankin of Mississippi, whose district bordered my own for a hundred miles, and who was the most irascible, adversarial, ornery individual I came across in all my years in the House. Anti-Negro, anti-Jew, Rankin was just about anti-everything. This would be his fifteenth term.

There was John McCormack, tall, lean, a man of precise routine. He always sat at the same corner table in the House dining room, always ordered the same lunch, never drank alcohol but couldn't say no to his only vice: ice cream. John McCormack was a key player among the inner circle of Sam Rayburn's men, the dozen or so Congressmen who were regularly invited at the end of the day to an office back behind the members' dining room for a gathering they called the "Board of Education." Actually, Rayburn himself never cared for that title. He just called it "downstairs." In any case, it was in this room full of black leather chairs and one black leather sofa that a small circle of men would share bourbon (usually Virginia Gentleman) and branch water and, in their words, "strike a blow for liberty." McCormack never partook of the liquor, but he could often be found later in the evening with his wife at the nearest Howard Johnson's. This would be John McCormack's twelfth term.

There were other names in that Eighty-first Congress who were well on their way to establishing themselves as memorable figures in our nation's history: Everett Dirksen of Illinois, in his ninth term; Albert Gore of Tennessee, starting his sixth; Brooks Hays of Arkansas and Mike Mansfield of Montana, both beginning their fourth terms; and Hale Boggs of Louisiana, returning for his third.

Notably absent was one of my neighbors in Alton Place, on whose wife I had spilled a pitcher of water while I was waiting tables at the University of Alabama when she and I were students there. Her name then was Claudia Alta Taylor. Her name now was Lady Bird Johnson, and her husband Lyndon had just been elected to the Senate after serving six terms in the House.

There were three second-termers on that floor who stood out even then and would make historical marks on the nation in the years to come. One of them was a small fellow from Oklahoma who was already being groomed by Sam Rayburn as an up-and-comer, already being invited to the Board of Education meetings. They called him the "Little Giant" back in his home state—Carl Albert, who would become Speaker of the House in the 1970s, overseeing Congress during the crisis of President Richard Nixon's resignation.

Richard Nixon himself was also beginning his second term, reelected from the Los Angeles district of California after spending his first term assigned to the Education and Labor Committee and to the Committee on Un-American Activities.

The last of that second-term threesome was John F. Kennedy of Massachusetts, already a standout because of the publicity surrounding his father, his wealthy family, his wartime heroics and his writing—his thesis at Harvard had become published as a history book titled *Why England Slept.* I'd read that book and was impressed. Any man who could write a book caught my attention, and Kennedy had written a good one.

Among the newcomers joining me on the floor that day were two men I would eventually join on the House Rules Committee— Homer Thornberry of Texas and Dick Bolling of Missouri. Dick would prove to be one of the brightest, ablest and most deeply respected members of the House, a man who understood its mechanics inside out and who understood *people* as well. Homer Thornberry was later appointed to the U. S. District Court in Texas.

Another Texan named Lloyd Bentsen was also a rookie that year. He eventually became Michael Dukakis' running mate in the 1988 presidential election, but the funny thing about Bentsen back then is he struck me from the beginning as a man who did not seem quite at ease in the House. That's just something you can *feel* from a fellow, and sure enough, Bentsen left Congress after only six years. I think money had a great value with him, and he later said his purpose for dropping out of the House was to make some money. He did that, and when he came back to Washington about a decade later, it was to the Senate, not the House.

There was plenty of ambition in that House chamber the day I first walked in in 1949—probably no more nor less than filled the room when the first Congress met in 1789 nor when the Hundred and Second convened in 1991. I saw men who had their eyes on specific positions from the beginning—some who aimed to become Speaker of the House, others who saw the House as a way to the Senate, and a few who had plans beyond that. They sought out allies and mentors, looked for the right man to take them under his wing, to groom them and prepare them for the next step up the ladder. I don't hold a thing against that approach. I respect and admire men with ambition, but I never had a lot of that, not personally. To some men a position of power can be an end in itself, but to me power is pointless if it's not a means to an end.

I had never lost sight of the ends at which I aimed. They were the same things I'd cared about from the time I was a boy: seeing that folks got what they deserved, good or bad; seeing that the less fortunate weren't denied at least the same opportunity to get an education, earn a decent income, have a home and raise a family as people who happened to be in better circumstances. I never forgot where I came from once I got to Congress, and I was never mesmerized by things like power and prestige.

But you need power and prestige to get things done in Congress. While, on the face of it, this body of men which meets each day at noon on the floor of the chamber of the House of Representatives in full view of the public works as a unit, creating, debating and ultimately passing the laws which govern our nation, the fact of the matter is that during the time I served there the actual decisions were not made out on the floor in front of the galleries of constituents (and today, in front of television cameras as well), but were hammered out behind closed doors, among key committees ruled by individuals who were able to obstruct legislation more often than create it, and who made behind-the-scenes deals with one another, trading favors—"paying back the meal," as some put it—too often without regard to the needs of the nation or even of their own constituency. The tactics of a select few autocratic individuals and overly influential—and largely unseen—power groups were a regrettable but unavoidable fact of life in the House of Representatives during the time I was a member.

An effective Congressman had to learn who those individuals

and groups were, whether he intended to join them or not. If he was sponsoring or supporting a bill, he had to learn how to approach these members, how to win their support or stem their opposition. There's no way around the fact that you've got to study your colleagues in Congress, learn what their strengths are as well as their weaknesses, understand where they come from, who their constituency is, what issues matter most to that constituency and therefore what issues might matter most to them.

There's an art to what they call counting votes, which is a simple matter of understanding what will impel a fellow to vote a certain way. In some cases it will be his union constituents, in some it will be his *non*union constituents. With some, there are large industries that have paid much of their campaign expenses, and they're beholden to those interests. I'm not saying they have to kowtow or kiss those interests' asses, but they must pay some attention to them.

When I came to Congress, an average campaign cost about a hundred thousand dollars. Mine was a lot lower than that; my first campaign cost about twelve thousand. That's because I had a constituency that was not as politically sophisticated as some, not as well educated as some (the average person in my district had about a sixth-grade education) and certainly not as affluent as most. There were hardly any places for me to get large political donations. Besides, nobody thought I would win that first time around. Nobody urged me to run, nobody bankrolled me. I just went out and *did* it.

So, when I came to Congress, I was freer than many of my colleagues to make my way on my own. The adage about being seen and not heard was not one I strictly observed, but I made damn sure that when I had something to say it was worth saying. "It's better to be silent and seem dumb," Sam Rayburn used to say, "than to speak and remove all doubt." There were times I wanted my voice to be heard, but I picked and chose them carefully.

Another often-quoted Rayburnism is one I heard the day I arrived in Congress. "To get along," I was told, "go along." Those were Rayburn's words all right, but people rarely point out that he added a qualifier to that quote. "To get along, go along," he said.

"But I've never asked a man to cast a vote that would violate his conscience or wreck him politically."

That is and always has been the Congressman's basic dilemma: balancing your allegiance to your constituents with your allegiance to your conscience and to your country. It's no simple trick to work to achieve goals of national purpose and at the same time convince your constituents that those purposes are in their best interests as well—especially, as I would ultimately find out, when the issue is one of race.

Congress is constantly criticized for the general inability of its members to rise above their parochial interests and look to the needs of the nation. It's a criticism with plenty of justification. For generations people have talked about ways to reform Congress, to make it more effective. They've talked about changing the seniority system. They've talked about limiting the number of terms a man can serve. They've talked about lengthening the two-year term so a man can have time to get something done before he has to worry about running for reelection again. Some of those reforms have happened.

But I never had any serious problems with the system as it was or as it is. There are ways to work with, through and around the roadblocks, and as far as I'm concerned, two years is plenty of time to get your job done and get it done effectively—*if* you are committed to making use of your time.

I guess I'm simply talking about dedication and effort here. There are plenty of distractions for a man who arrives in Washington with the title Congressman in front of his name. Every day there's someone or other inviting you to this function or that. Every night there's a party somewhere in the city, and a Congressman's name is on everyone's A list. On weekends there are plenty of ways to while away a day, from lunches to dinners to golf in between. A Congressman holds a seductive position in a very seductive city, and it's easy to see how some men lose sight of why they're there or of what their priorities are.

I never hit a golf ball in my life. I went to as few parties as possible, although those still kept me busy enough to wear out two tuxedos during the time I was in Washington. There were some invitations you just could not turn down, such as a presidential party. That's one RSVP for which a regret is never sent.

What did I do for fun? I studied bills, that's what. I worked on Saturdays, sharing lunch down in the House dining room with my fellow Alabama Congressman Albert Rains, who also came in on weekends. Maybe there are people who would say I was a workaholic. I know there are some who might say I was a stick-in-the-mud. But the way I saw it, I held a warrant from the three hundred thousand or so people of the Seventh District of Alabama to represent them in Congress, and on top of that I had a duty to the nation as a whole to tend to its needs as best I could. Everything else came second, as far as I was concerned.

I had a pretty regular routine right from the start. I'd get up about 6 A.M. and fetch the morning's Washington *Post* and the *Congressional Record* off the front doorstep. I'd read till I felt I had enough in my head to see me through the day. Then I'd drive to the Capitol. I wore out several Fords and two or three Plymouths during my years in Washington, mostly on trips home and especially on campaigns. One campaign could pretty much use up a car.

By about eight-fifteen I'd be at my office, on the first floor of the old House Office Building. My room had been vacated by a fellow named John Robsion, a thirteen-term Republican from Kentucky who had lost his seat in an election that saw the swing from the Republican-majority Eightieth Congress to our Democrat-controlled Eighty-first. That Eightieth Congress had been tagged the "Do-Nothing" Congress by a frustrated Harry Truman. The label wasn't entirely fair, but it was very effective.

There had been a recession during that 1947–48 term, and there was dissatisfaction throughout the land over the lingering restrictions left over from the war as well. When the Republicans of the Eightieth Congress pushed through the anti-labor Taft-Hartley Act, over President Truman's veto—an act which banned the closed shop, sympathy strikes and mass picketing, which made unions liable to lawsuits, which forced union officials to sign affidavits that they were not Communists and which gave the President authority to obtain injunctions to prevent strikes in interstate transportation, communications and public utilities—the American public said, "Enough!" Republican incumbents went down by the droves in the fall of 1948, as well as many Democrats who had sided with them on the Taft-Hartley Act. One such Democrat was the man I had defeated, Carter Manasco.

The room across the hall from mine had also been vacated that election by a two-term Congresswoman from California named Helen Gahagan Douglas. I only met her and her husband, the actor Melvyn Douglas, in passing that winter, but I saw Helen again two years later, after she had run for the Senate against Richard Nixon. Nixon chewed her up something awful in that race. Helen was a New Deal Democrat, a wealthy woman who had made housing for poor people her cause during the time she was in Congress. Nixon was really beginning to feel his oats on the Communism issue, and he laid into Douglas with everything he had, questioning her patriotism, saying she was "pink right down to her underwear."

It was in that 1950 campaign that Douglas came up with the nickname that stuck to Nixon throughout his career: "Tricky Dick." But to no avail. Nixon crushed her by nearly seven hundred thousand votes. When I saw her, she was still fussing and fuming about what all Nixon had done to her, how he had destroyed her. I don't know if Helen ever did quite get over that, but I do know she never did return to politics.

I spent most of my mornings reading and answering mail. Grandma Elliott's lessons about the importance of letters had stuck, and every day there were usually about a hundred letters in my mailbox from my constituents, most of them handwritten. Sam Rayburn had something to say about that matter, too, something I totally agreed with. "I have greater trust in people who send their Congressmen postal cards and handwritten letters on tablet paper," he said, "than those who send telegrams."

Midmorning was when my committee met, and it's true that a Congressman's entire career is steered by his committee assignments. Some men seek committees for just that purpose—to advance their careers. They might aim at one committee because of the prestige attached to it or its chairman, they may avoid another because of its controversial nature. Other men pick a committee because it's close to the interests of their own constituency. Still others choose a committee because of their own particular interest in particular issues.

It was the latter two reasons that guided me as I wrote the Democratic committee on committees soon after my election, listing my preferences for assignment. Each newcomer to Congress is allowed to list three choices, none of which he is guaranteed to receive. As with any wish list, you've got to be realistic. To write down the Rules Committee, or Ways and Means, or Appropriations would be wasting ink. Those are the three most prestigious committees in the House.

My first choice was Education and Labor. To get on that committee would be to just about completely fulfill my lifelong dream of being able to shape and steer this nation's educational system. That committee was closest to my heart from the beginning.

My second choice was Interstate and Foreign Commerce. I guess that goes back to the days I sat on the dirt bank at the edge of our farm, watching those Illinois Central trains roar past. It was also the committee on which Sam Rayburn had gotten his start. In later years, Sam urged me to find my way onto this committee, but by then I'd made my way into Education and had no interest.

My third choice was Veterans' Affairs. It was largely veterans' votes that had sent me to Congress, and I knew this committee would be closest to what mattered in their lives.

Veterans' Affairs is where I wound up for my freshman term, under the chairmanship of none other than John Rankin.

Rankin was a racist to the first degree, using that issue to solidify his position in his home state of Mississippi. He was contentious, outspoken and always spoiling for a fight, whether it was about race or anything else under the sky. You might think a man wouldn't last in Congress with those qualities, but John Rankin managed to stay for sixteen consecutive terms.

I had no taste for Rankin's virulent racism, but this was one case where Sam Rayburn's "go along, get along" philosophy applied. Besides, I'd learned early on in life that you can only afford to get offended about so many things, so you've got to pick and choose the spots to spend your steam on. Hopefully those spots are on something you can change. God knows there was no changing John Rankin.

Some people are disappointed when they first see the proceedings on the floor of the House chamber. The setting only fuels the hopes for high drama: rows of stuffed leather chairs, thick maroon carpeting, dark polished woodwork, brass spittoons along the back railings, pages dressed in navy blue and white clutching sheaves of papers as they dart up and down the aisles. The mind swims with visions of grand debates, stirring speeches, moments of conflict and courage, possibly even heroism. What transpires instead is a scene something on the order of my colleague Dick Bolling's description of a constituent's visit to the House chamber, in his book *House Out of Order*:

> An elderly man ascends the dais flanked by flags, and raps the gavel. His opening remark is the customary "The House will be in order." The chaplain of the House gives the customary opening prayer. Something called the "Journal" is ordered read and approved.
>
> The constituent, briefed beforehand by his Congressman, recognizes the man with the gavel as the Speaker of the House. To the Speaker's right is a silver-encrusted black staff called the Mace. Seated below the Speaker at a semicircular desk are employees of the House writing industriously in ledgers. Others, the tally clerk and bill clerk and their assistants, sit looking solemn and wise awaiting their work. Official reporters stand with their stenographic notebooks. Around the Chamber fresh-faced page boys move, carrying messages and running errands for the men and women Members of the House.
>
> The constituent leans forward in expectation of the first act of this day's legislative drama as several Members rise and seek recognition from the Speaker.

"The Gentleman from Tennessee," the Speaker intones. The recognized Member says a few inaudible sentences.

"Without objection, so ordered," the Speaker says.

Now one of the Members leaves his seat and walks to a chest-high lectern equipped with a microphone.

"Ah," says the citizen-constituent to himself.

The Member at the microphone coughs, rebuttons his suit coat, and, after glancing solemnly at the sparsely filled galleries, begins to address his colleagues on the topic of preservation of marine life along the Florida shores.

The constituent, after a few minutes' concentration, shifts inattentively in his upholstered seat. Perhaps the major discussion of the day comes later on, he thinks, as the Member talks on about the breeding and feeding of the infant shrimp. None of the Members seem to be listening either.

Aren't there supposed to be 435 Members of the House in attendance, he asks himself, instead of the 50 Members now present? And those 50 are reading newspapers, talking to one another, or moving, indeed, milling about seemingly with no apparent purpose. One Member, hands folded across his stomach, appears to be dozing.

The Member from Florida begins to gesture at the microphone and warns that the supply of bait shrimp will certainly diminish, with consequent disaster to the economy of his "Sunshine State." One, perhaps, two, Members in the back row, laugh. . . .

Another Member rises and, addressing the Speaker, "suggests" the "absence of a quorum." Another Member rises and says, "Mr. Speaker, I move a call of the House." The Speaker instructs the attendance clerk to call the roll of Members, which will take about twenty-five minutes. Three bells are sounded. These ring throughout the House wing of the Capitol, and in each Member's office located in one of two House Office Buildings a block away. . . .

The constituent's hopes are rallied. Upon completion of the roll, the clerk hands the Speaker a slip of paper. The

Speaker announces, "Three hundred and sixty-seven Members having answered to their names, a quorum is present."

Incredible. There are still only about fifty Members on the floor. The constituent now realizes he has been watching the most august kind of revolving-door game. Most members simply walked in, answered to their names, and walked out again.

Unfortunately, the picture Dick Bolling paints is an accurate one. But even within what can seem like a stilted, static situation there's a lot a man can learn—that he *must* learn—to have an effect in this place, to put a bill through and get a law passed, a law whose effects radiate far outside the walls of that chamber, a law that affects and changes lives. I came to Congress to make laws like that, and I knew, in order to do that, I was going to have to have the patience to sit through scenes like the one Dick Bolling describes— not just to sit through them, but to *learn* from them.

What, you ask, can a man possibly learn in a setting like that? The answer is the rules.

That was one secret to John Rankin's success—he was simply one of the best damn parliamentarians on the floor of the House. He knew the ins and outs of every procedural step, and he could play those thousands of legislative strings like a harp. Clarence Cannon of Missouri was another parliamentary giant when I joined Congress. In later years, Dick Bolling would establish himself as just about the best there was at knowing the rules.

The House of Representatives speaks a language all its own. Every movement made, every sentence uttered, is steered by an incredibly complex network of intricate rules, more than ten thousand rules, each one created with a specific, finely targeted purpose. To an outsider or a newcomer, the language on the floor of the House can sound numbing, the "readings," the "motions," the "objections," the "so ordereds." But there is a delicacy and a purpose to these minute procedures, a careful path of positioning much like a chess game.

I was never one for chess, but I took to learning those rules like a trout takes to a fly. I studied them every day, knowing that these were the weapons a man had to have to really make a mark in the

House. He had to know the rules, and he had to have patience, and he had to have perseverance.

Dick Bolling's fictional constituent displayed none of these, and I don't blame him. This wasn't that constituent's job. But it was mine. And I guarantee, on most any day during my time in Congress, I was a sure bet to be among the members that constituent saw on the floor.

There was no place else I'd rather be.

I always felt there was more to my job than simply making my constituents happy, although God knows I did all I could to take care of their needs. There are enough roads, hospitals, houses, schools, dams, armories and libraries throughout these hills to attest to that. Plenty of them still bear my name: the library here in Jasper, a lake up near Russellville, more than two dozen housing projects throughout this district. I'm pretty sure most people today have no idea who this Elliott fellow was—or is. That doesn't bother me any. I didn't get those things built so they'd have my name on them. I just wanted to get them built.

But I wanted more, and that's where some of my colleagues thought I was wasting my time, even hurting myself. I always had it in my head that it was as important to be a national Congressman— an *American* Congressman—as it was to be an Alabama Congressman. Maybe that comes straight from the civics books, maybe it's simplistic, but there it is. The way I saw it, somebody's got to mind the store, and if Congress doesn't do it, if every man's just looking out for himself and his friends, nobody's tending the store. I wanted to hear what *America's* problems were. I wanted to learn who was running this country, and I wanted to have a say in that, for the sake of the things I believed in, of the *country* I believed in.

There are plenty of Congressmen who go through their terms and don't ever create anything, don't sponsor anything of any significance. They tiptoe through their terms, dodging anything that might create a stir back home, playing to their constituents and holding on to their seats. You've got to stick your neck out sometimes to get something done, and I think it's sad to say not every person who goes to Congress is willing to do that.

I remember one fellow coming up to me, a Congressman from Mississippi named Arthur Winstead, not one of my favorite people in the House. We started talking about this very issue, and he told me he couldn't understand why a man would want to go around shaking trees, as he put it.

"These do-gooders like you," he said, "you all go all over the country and the countryside stirring up trouble for the rest of us and making nothing but trouble for yourself.

"I'll tell you what I do," he said. "I spend as much time as I can back home, sitting on the coupling poles of the wagons of my constituents. I know what they want and I get it for them. And every fall, when I go home, I can take it easy, look over my farm, cut my woodland over, relax.

"And you," he said, "you've got nothing but worries, nothing but problems, one right after the other, because all you're doing is going around shaking trees."

I knew more than a few coupling-pole Congressmen during my years in the House, and maybe they were right, maybe they knew more than I did. But I never doubted the way I approached things, and I don't doubt it today, even after all that's happened. Sooner or later a fellow's got to reckon with his own conscience, and if there's anything that bothers him about the way he did things, it can get awfully hard to sleep at night. And all the woodland in the world won't help you then.

Lord knows I could have reached out and grabbed some for myself back then. If I'd taken all that was offered me, both legitimately and otherwise, during my years in Congress, I'd be a rich man today. It amazes me to this day the way some people will approach a Congressman.

The issue of patronage doesn't have to be as sticky as some make it out to be. When a Congressman takes office, there are certain jobs back in his home district that it's his responsibility, his duty and in many cases his pleasure to fill. Some use those opportunities to pay back political favors, but I didn't have that many favors to repay. So I was able to approach that part of my job the way I believed it should be approached. I served the public—not my friends, not my family. There were many times friends and even relatives of mine asked me to help them get this job or that, and I wouldn't do it because I didn't think it was fair to all the other people interested. Many a time I watched a kinsman leave my office angry because I wouldn't give him a particular appointment.

There were some who didn't come to ask. They came to *buy* my help. Early on, one old boy walked into my Congressional office in downtown Jasper. He was interested in a post office job way up in Winston County. There were about a hundred rural post offices just like it all over my district. This fellow walked in and said, "So how much is it?"

I said, "How much is what?"

"That post office up there," he said.

I said, "There ain't no price *to* it, you sorry son of a bitch, and I'll throw you out this goddamn window unless you leave my office immediately.

"It's three floors down to that sidewalk there," I said, "and that's where your ass will be if you don't leave my sight right now."

I wasn't naive. I knew that sort of thing happened, but I bent over backward my whole career to be the other way about anything that even *looked* like a bribe. That made things real simple. When you start edging toward the line, pretty soon you're over it and you don't even know it.

The same thing happened on a larger scale in Washington during my last term in Congress. I was on the Rules Committee then, getting set to cast what would be the deciding vote on Medicare. A few days before the vote, one of the biggest—literally and figuratively—doctors in Alabama came to see me at my office in the House. He said, "I understand you're broke from your campaign."

This was in 1964, when I'd had to run a statewide race to keep my seat. I said, "That's right, I am. What about it?"

He said, "Well, you must need some money to clear up your bills. And I have money."

"Good," I said. "Glad you got it."

Then he said, "But *you've* got something *I* want."

"What's that?" I said.

"You're going to cast a vote tomorrow," he said, "on whether Medicare goes to the House floor for debate."

"Yep, that's right."

"Well, I got money, and you *need* money. So let's close the deal."

That did it.

"Now you listen," I said, "and you listen straight, you big bloated son of a bitch. It doesn't make any difference to me that you think you're somebody real important or that you were sent here by somebody real important like the AMA.

"The fact is," I said, "you belong to a segment of the people I don't belong to. I don't believe you ought to be able to buy something like this, something that belongs to the people. And I can't even imagine what the people would do to you if they knew what you came here for today. So you just get your fat ass out of here right now, or I'll put it on the pavement myself."

I went out the next week and cast my vote for Medicare. It went before the House, but before it got through, the Speaker, John McCormack, adjourned the House for the fall. This was an election year, and he wanted to wait on an issue like this until the new Congress. By then I was gone, but I still felt a part of Medicare when it passed.

And I still smile when I think of the look on that doctor's face as he backed out of my office.

It is a tale in which the echoes of past failures haunt a people's hopes for the future. The burden of its telling compels recounting the ancient and unsolved puzzles of democracy and of race.

William D. Barnard, Dixiecrats and Democrats

SIX

"TO BREAK OUR CHAINS"

There is no understanding the racial conflagration that engulfed Alabama and the South in the early 1960s and that swept aside so much of what I and many men like me had worked for and believed in without understanding the dynamics that created those curious political characters called the Dixiecrats.

They were formally born in 1948, the same year I was elected to Congress, but these renegade rebels and segregationists who rallied beneath the Alabama Democratic Party's banner of a white rooster and the slogan of "States' Rights" had been building their strength since Franklin Roosevelt's New Deal first descended on the land. Their slogan was a throwback to antebellum days, a Southern version of "Don't Tread on Me."

While poor people across the South welcomed the federal government programs and agencies Roosevelt created to pull them out of the misery of the Depression, the states' righters recoiled in alarm. All they cared about was the control they had over both the economies and people of their states. When they saw the federal government reaching into their own backyards with these social programs, they knew other programs couldn't be far behind—programs that would pull poor people up, white and black alike. Loss of economic control in any sense was alarming to these mostly conservative coalitions of Southerners; but loss of control over the Negro was more than alarming—it was absolutely unthinkable.

As long as the country was gripped in the crisis of the Depression, there was no way to resist the force of Franklin Roosevelt and his New Deal. But by the end of the 1930s, when the worst part of the Depression had passed, there was a swelling of anti-New Deal sentiment among conservatives in the South, on both racial and economic grounds. When the President tried to enlarge the Supreme Court in 1937, Southern conservatives saw it as a signal for more federal laws to interfere with their lives. When Roosevelt identified the South in 1938 as "the nation's number one economic problem," the conservative businessmen who controlled the Dixie economy were insulted. Mrs. Roosevelt's open efforts on behalf of blacks rubbed the states' righters' sores even rawer and drew the segregationists to their cause.

In December 1942 a fellow named Frank Dixon was just leaving the governorship of Alabama. I'd met Dixon when he was campaigning for governor in 1934 and I was a student at the University of Alabama. I was impressed with his seriousness and his dedication to his beliefs. He seemed like a real thorough man. But he was about as far away from me philosophically and politically as a man could get. I had a distaste for Dixon's programs practically all across the board. I believed in our federal government a lot more than he did, and I believed blacks should be treated like people, not like a disposable problem, a threat to be suppressed at any cost.

Dixon lost that 1934 race but was elected in 1938 and stayed in the statehouse for one term. On his way out in 1942, he made a speech before a group called the Southern Society of New York. Included in that speech was a prophecy:

"Suggestions are rife," Dixon said, "as to the formation of a Southern Democratic party, the election of unpledged representatives to the electoral college. Ways and means are being discussed

daily to break our chains. We will find some way and find it regardless of the effect on national elections. . . ."

At the time it didn't seem that the states' righters would have a
chance in hell of making Dixon's warning of a breakaway from the
national Democratic Party come true. Liberalism was still, on the
whole, riding high, even in the South. There were a few danger
signals, such as Lister Hill's close Senatorial win in 1944, after a
campaign in which his conservative opponent, a Birmingham lawyer
named James Simpson, raised the racial issue. Lister responded by
conceding to segregationism, stressing his commitment to "the existing social order" and thereby sidestepping, for the time being, the
same racial fork that eventually skewered me and more than a few
other liberals like me throughout the South.

The issue of race has been laced through the fabric of life in the
South since the creation of this nation. But as long as the system of
segregation remained institutionalized, as long as the black people
who lived in the South remained powerless and subservient, bound
by state laws they had no say in making, they posed no threat,
political or otherwise, to the white power structure. Few of even the
most liberal Southern politicians took a stand on the issue of race in
the first half of this century, because there was no issue on which to
stand.

But once a serious movement was made by the federal government to force integration on the largely unwilling South, a line was
drawn in the sand, a line based on nothing but the issue of racial
segregation, and every Southern politician eventually had to show
on which side of that line he stood.

George Wallace used that very image in his 1963 gubernatorial
inaugural speech: "I draw the line in the dust and throw the gauntlet
at the feet of tyranny and I say segregation now, segregation tomorrow, segregation forever."

But in the 1940s the line was just beginning to be drawn. It was
still relatively easy for a liberal down here to skirt the issue of race.
By the late 1950s and certainly by the sixties, it had become impossible to do that. By then the biggest challenge facing a liberal in the
South was figuring out some way to make the voters at home look
away from or see beyond the issue of race alone, so he could find his

way back to Washington and do some work that really meant something on a national level, for blacks and whites alike. If you took a firm stand at home on race—the *wrong* stand—you could be assured you would not be making a stand anywhere else on anything. You'd be out of office.

Albert Gore, one of my Congressional colleagues from Tennessee, told a Birmingham reporter about eight years ago how tough it was to be a progressive Southern statesman like Alabama Senators Lister Hill or John Sparkman or a Congressman like myself in the 1950s and '60s.

"Even though he [the liberal Southern Congressman] recognized the injustices and the discrimination, the horror of the existing order," said Gore, "he also recognized there were limits to what could be done in a given period of time. In other words, I think that while men like Hill and Sparkman pressed the collar for progress, for solutions, for justice . . . they were sensitive to the possibility that if they pressed beyond the limits of public acceptance, then they would be sacrificed . . . but more disastrously, they would be replaced by one who would be a 100 percent reactionary."

Hale Boggs, my Congressional colleague from Louisiana, talked often about this frustrating fact. He didn't like voting the way he had to on civil rights legislation, but he had to. More than once he made the point that he could vote with his conscience on civil rights bills and be defeated, or he could vote against them and vote correctly on nearly every other liberal issue. If he went with his conscience on civil rights, the man who replaced him would vote against every other issue as well, all the economic and social issues that we —Hale Boggs, Lister Hill, John Sparkman, Carl Elliott and everyone else like us—saw would alleviate the suffering of the poor, many of whom were blacks. We may not have been able to do something directly about civil rights, but we knew we could help educate blacks, get medical care for blacks, provide educational opportunities for blacks and *pray* the day would come when we could get political freedom for blacks as well.

I put the situation my own way to the same Birmingham reporter who interviewed Albert Gore:

"Anybody who had a grain of sense," I told him, "knew that

the blacks had to be given their rights. The question was, how were we going to do it? Then the question locally was, what can we do and still live with our own particular situation?"

It was still relatively easy to live with the situation in the mid-1940s, especially when Jim Folsom was elected governor in 1946. After John Sparkman was elected to the Senate that same year, mainly on the strength of his liberal record in Congress but just as largely on the power of his identification with Folsom, the state of Alabama had suddenly moved to the forefront of progressive politics in the South. A 1947 story titled "Dixie in Black and White" in the *Nation* magazine called Alabama "the most liberal state in the South."

But even then the storm clouds were shaping. Alabamians were alarmed after the Supreme Court ruled in 1944 that Texas' all-white primary was unconstitutional, and in 1946 Frank Dixon rallied the state's conservative forces to block any such decision in Alabama. William Barnard, a professor of history at the University of Alabama, in his definitive and detailed book titled *Dixiecrats and Democrats,* described Dixon's game plan to block blacks from getting an effective vote:

> "There should be some definite planning by the best brains in Alabama," Dixon urged, "with the view of setting up a system [to prevent mass registration]which will stand up" in court. If such a system were not devised, not only would the Democratic Party's supremacy in the South be endangered but so also would conservative hopes of dominating Southern Democracy. "It is obvious," Dixon wrote, "that the only thing that has held the Democratic Party together in the South for many years past has been the thing which caused its strength in the first place, namely, white supremacy."

White supremacy. I'll say this about Dixon: he didn't mince words. What he and his boys came up with by the end of that year was an adjustment of the Alabama constitution that would insert what was called an "understanding" clause in the qualifying requirements for registration. Back in 1901 the state had blocked most black voters by requiring them to own a certain amount of property before they could register to vote. By 1946, however, the blacks' lot had improved to the point where most of them owned the required three hundred dollars' worth of property (having an automobile was typically enough to suffice) to register. Most could also read and write well enough to pass the literacy test. So Dixon and his lot added the requirement that a registrant must not only be able to read and write any section of the United States Constitution, but he must also, as Barnard described it in his book, "demonstrate to a local board of registrars a satisfactory understanding of it as well."

It doesn't take a lot of imagination to picture what a local board of registrars looked like in Alabama in the 1940s. You can bet they weren't black. You can bet they weren't liberal. And it's easy to see what they would do with this provision, which would give them complete power to prevent the registration of what one framer of this amendment termed "those elements of our community which have not yet fitted themselves for self-government."

Those elements, of course, were the two hundred thousand Negro voters looming like a dark cloud above the states' righters' heads.

In November 1946 the roadblock to registration framed by Dixon and his boys went before the voters of Alabama as the "Boswell Amendment." The vote was close, but the amendment passed, and the Dixiecrats' first serious shot had been fired across the bow of liberalism in the South.

By 1948 the conservatives in the South, especially in Alabama, were on the offensive. Jim Folsom's short-lived campaign that year as a favorite-son candidate for the presidency, combined with the subsequent accusation that he had fathered an illegitimate son in 1946, made him much less of a force to be reckoned with. Meanwhile, the emergence of Harry Truman's position for civil rights gave the Southern conservatives a focal point to attack.

In February 1948 Truman sent Congress a ten-point civil rights message, asking for an end to Jim Crow laws in interstate transporta-

tion, an end to the poll tax, a federal anti-lynching law and a perma-
nent Fair Employment Practices Committee (FEPC), a temporary
agency established during World War II to prevent racial discrimination in war-industry hiring.

It wasn't only the states' righters who howled over Truman's
bill. Fifty-two Deep South Congressmen declared they would not
support Truman for President in that fall's national election. As
always, the Congressmen in Washington, as well as the conservatives
back home, phrased their opposition to Truman in terms of classic
states' rights political philosophies, like nineteenth-century laissez-
faire and social Darwinism. But when Sam Rayburn called a group
of those Congressmen to a meeting early that year, he cut right
through the rhetoric, harking back to Eugene Talmadge, former
governor of Georgia, who, when campaigning during the 1920s,
repeatedly pronounced, "People of Georgia, you've got only three
friends: The Lord God Almighty, Sears Roebuck and Gene Talmadge. And people of Georgia, you've got only three enemies: Nigger, nigger, nigger!"

Rayburn knew his history. "All your high-flown political vocab-
ulary boils down to just three words," he told those Deep South
Dixiecrats in 1948. "Nigger, nigger, nigger!"

Frank Dixon hardly tried to sidestep the fact that race was at
the core of his efforts. He stated as much in a letter quoted in
William Barnard's book:

> "As a cosmopolitan and a church man I can justify, in theory,
> racial amalgamation. As a Southern man with the normal hu-
> man dislike of foreigners both in space and in blood, I doubt
> my ability to put Christian charity into practice. . . . We are
> behind the times, I admit. The Huns have wrecked the theories
> of the master race with which we were so contented so long.
> Derbies are now being worn by Jackasses and silk purses being
> made out of sow's ears. Blood lines are out. The progeny of a
> cornfield ape blackened with the successive suns of Africa and
> Alabama, mated with a swamp gorilla from the Louisiana rice
> fields has developed promise as great as the sons of the great
> American families such as the Adams clan of New England."

Dixon was disgusted with the developments he saw around him. Truman's civil rights program pushed things beyond the brink. Early in 1948, Dixon and a fellow named Gessner McCorvey, who was chairman of Alabama's State Democratic Executive Committee, summoned the committee into special session and adopted a resolution calling upon every delegate to the Democratic national convention to walk out if Truman's civil rights proposals were adopted.

By then I had become a leader of the Democratic Party in my area. Dixon called me more than once that spring to argue about whether or not I would support him. Each time he called, I told him there was no way I could join him. The bottom line was I couldn't stomach the position he stood for. Enough of the people around me felt the same way that our Walker County Democratic Committee became one of the few in the state to go on record as standing apart from the emerging Dixiecrat line.

In May, in the same election in which I won the Democratic nomination for the fall Congressional election, Alabama's Dixiecrats positioned themselves for the presidential election by sweeping all eleven of the state's Democratic electoral positions. These "unpledged" electors were free to vote for any nominee they chose in the November presidential election, but if that nominee were Truman, they were bound to oppose him.

This put people like Lister Hill on the spot. They had to choose between loyalty to the national party or siding with their state Democratic colleagues back home. Hill chose the former, leading the anti-walkout forces and siding with the national party. But when Alabama's twenty-six delegates arrived in Philadelphia for July's national convention, only thirteen of them were allied with Hill and his "Loyalists." Included among those thirteen Loyalists was a young legislator described in William Barnard's book as "small of stature —almost diminutive—of a rather sallow hue with dark hair slicked down tight against his skull."

That young state Representative was George C. Wallace.

While the Loyalists remained at the convention after a young Senator from Minnesota named Hubert Humphrey proposed a civil rights plank even stronger than Truman's, the states' righters, led by their chairman, a six-foot-six-inch fellow named Handy Ellis, stomped out.

After they were gone, someone heard Sam Rayburn say, "Those Dixiecrats are as welcome around here as a bastard at a family reunion."

They may not have been welcome in Philadelphia, but the swarm of renegade state delegates, presidential electors, national and state committeemen and college students that descended on the Birmingham municipal auditorium on July 17, 1948, for their own Dixiecrat convention was received with open arms.

It was like a circus down there. The hall was filled with Confederate battle flags. Harry Truman was hanged in effigy. Bull Connor, who would later become known around the nation as the man who ordered the fire hoses of Birmingham turned on black protesters, manned the microphone to get the proceedings under way as six thousand people filled the arena with what the Birmingham *News* called "a revival-like fever."

Frank Dixon chaired the conference and was its keynote speaker. Alabama was represented by a fifty-two-man delegation. Louisiana and Mississippi were well represented by local, state and, in the case of the latter, national politicians—Mississippi Senators James Eastland and John Stennis were there, along with Mississippi Representatives Tom Abernethy, Bill Colmer, Jamie Whitten, John Williams and Arthur Winstead. No other state's national representatives chose to attend, but three governors showed up: Fielding Wright of Mississippi; Strom Thurmond of South Carolina; and William Tuck of Virginia.

The quiltwork of attendees from other states was described in William Barnard's book:

> The delegation from the Commonwealth of Virginia consisted of four students from the University of Virginia and a young woman who had stopped off on a cross-country tour. Texas was represented by ten members of the state's delegation to the Democratic Convention, Florida by three nominees for presi-

dential elector. Tennessee, like Virginia, was represented by college students, and Georgia had no official representation. Kentucky's banner was carried aloft by an Alabamian who had formerly lived in Kentucky. North Carolina was not so fortunate. A native Alabamian, with no known connection with the Tarheel state, saw the state's standard standing in its place, grabbed it and plunged into the milling crowd. After all, "somebody's got to carry it."

I can't say firsthand what that scene looked like, because I wasn't there. All that day I got phone calls from Dixon and his group, urging me to throw in my lot, to come down and address the crowd. I told them I wouldn't have anything to do with it, with these so-called Dixiecrats wandering around down there like a bunch of sheep. I thought it was a bunch of damned foolishness is what I thought.

But, as Jim Folsom would say, it was one hell of a show. During his thirty-minute keynote address, Dixon denounced Truman and the national Democratic Party for "trying to force a social revolution in the South." He then went on to define Truman's civil rights program, focusing on the integration of schools:

"Your children are to be required to work and play in the company of and with the forced association of Negroes. Negroes are to teach them, guide them. What will that mean to your children, to your hopes for them? What will it mean in immorality, in vice, in crime? Just what it means in those slum areas of the Northern cities where like conditions prevail, with results fatal to decency."

When Dixon was done, the conventioneers nominated South Carolina's Strom Thurmond for President and Mississippi's Fielding Wright for Vice-President.

In his address to the convention, Thurmond declared, "There's not enough troops in the Army to break down segregation and admit Negroes into our homes, our theaters and our swimming pools."

In his acceptance speech, Thurmond vowed, "The nation will never forget this fight we're making."

He didn't know how right he was. It was not Thurmond's

nomination that the nation would remember—how many people today can recall that Strom Thurmond ran for President in 1948 against Thomas Dewey and Harry Truman?

When Jim Folsom and I went to Washington that October to see what we could possibly do to legally loosen the states righters' hold on Alabama's presidential electoral votes and somehow get Harry Truman's name on the ballot in our state, it wasn't because we thought Strom Thurmond might be elected President. It was because we didn't want Alabama to be permanently torn and scarred by this battle between Loyalists and states' righters.

We did our best, but it wasn't good enough. In the presidential election of 1948, Alabama was the only state in the nation whose ballot blocked its electors from voting for the incumbent President. Folsom protested that "a handful of slickers have tried to take the vote away from three million people in the state," but his words were in vain.

The nation would forget the show in Birmingham and the candidacy of Strom Thurmond. It would forget that Strom Thurmond carried the state of Alabama in that election—as well as Louisiana, Mississippi and South Carolina, where electors pledged to Harry Truman *did* appear on the ballot.

It would forget these things, but what America would be reminded of, painfully and repeatedly, over the course of the next two decades, would be the power of racial fear and resistance that was behind the rise of the Dixiecrats.

I didn't need to be reminded. After what these people were able to do in Alabama in 1948, it was frighteningly clear to me that the fight down here had only begun. But I hoped it would burn itself out. Meanwhile, I had more important things to do—in Washington.

. . . with all deliberate speed.

Brown v. Board of Education of Topeka,
U. S. Supreme Court, 1954

SEVEN

THE THREE R'S

Harry Truman wasn't what you would call happy about the Dixiecrats' behavior in 1948. Before the November election, he had actually seemed charitable to those Deep South defectors for their reaction to his civil rights plank. He told Secretary of Defense Jim Forrestal, "I would have done the same thing myself if I were in their place and came from their states." But once Truman took office, all signs of forgiveness were gone.

He'd come through a tough election, one most people didn't think he'd win. That, of course, was the year the Chicago *Tribune* went to press with the headline DEWEY DEFEATS TRUMAN. His "give 'em hell" aggressiveness had in the end outshone the cautious Dewey, and "give 'em hell" is exactly what Harry Truman intended to do with the Dixiecrats once he'd won the election. The final returns were hardly in before the President ordered Sam Rayburn to purge all states' righters from the Democratic Party in both houses. Rayburn refused, but the chief executive's feelings were clear.

Truman was awfully irked about what had happened, but he knew and appreciated what I'd tried to do, that I'd stuck with him. We got acquainted right to begin with, and I enjoyed his complete confidence—as well as his candor. I arrived in Washington eager to begin building a bill for education, and I told Truman as much the first time I met him at the White House after that election. He just smiled and shook his head.

"Aw, Carl," he said, "you don't want to fool with that. There's no politics in education, no future. You've got to be practical about these things.

"There's probably never going to *be* any federal aid to education in this country, at least not in your lifetime," he said.

"What you need to do," he said, "is get you a dam built down there somewhere. Now *that's* something I can help you with, something that'll do you some good, that'll help you get reelected."

He went on to explain specifically how to go about selling my dam to the people.

"You might not want to be so strong for it upriver from where it's going to be built," he said. "Farmers' fields are there, you know, and a lot of that land might wind up under water.

"But once you get to the site and below, you be just as strong as you can for it. That'll get you a lot of votes. And you'll have none of the problems that come with this education business."

To tell the truth, I was awfully disappointed by what I heard. But I didn't let the President know that. I thanked him for his time and his advice. And, in a way, I knew he was right. Dams—as well as roads and hospitals and housing—were something that paid immediate dividends, in terms both of providing services and creating jobs. These were still hard times in my Seventh District, brutally hard times. There were about 250,000 people living in those nine counties, and for many of them the Depression had not yet ended. This part of Alabama was laden with unemployment. These people didn't speak the language of "states' rights" and "limited government." What they understood was a hungry family, a cold house and the unemployment line. Building a new dam would mean two to three thousand new jobs while it was going up, as well as cheap power once it was finished.

So I took Truman's advice—in a way. With help from the federal government, and with Governor Jim Folsom's support (Big Jim was a great cooperator if you didn't confuse him with too many details), the out-of-the-mud roads and dams I'd promised during my campaign began to be built. So were homes—after the 1949 National Housing Act was passed (for which I voted), more than fifty public housing projects, each sheltering more than fifty families, were built in my district. Hospitals and clinics were built, too—thirty of them rose in those rural hills during my time in Congress. I also helped push through bills and programs for rural electrification, for rehabilitation of the disabled, for support of farmers and of course, being on the Veterans' Affairs Committee, I sponsored a long list of veterans' aid programs.

Representing the veterans in my district meant doing a lot of footwork back home, rounding up evidence of their needs, collecting affidavits for individual cases and gathering other legal details needed to represent these former military men in Washington. Early on, I hired a young attorney back in Jasper to take care of a lot of that work. His name was Tom Bevill.

Garve Ivey didn't care much for Bevill, but his reasons had nothing to do with politics. Really, they had hardly anything to do with Bevill either. Garve's feelings were wrapped up in a wild blend of fate, circumstances and the death of his father.

Back on that rainy morning in 1934 when Garve's father's body was found at the bottom of a train trestle after half the men in the mining camp—including Garve—had spent the entire night searching for him, there were some questions about whether the death had been an accident or not. He had taken a terrible fall, but there were also signs that he might have taken a blow before falling. Although the question was eventually dropped by the law, it never stopped burning in the back of Garve's brain.

On an afternoon in 1951, seventeen years after that horrible night, a man stopped into Garve's café to tell him his father had been murdered. The man was living with a woman who had previously lived with another man. That man, she said, had been a hard drinker. He'd also spent some time in prison. And one night he told her how he had come out of prison and back to Jasper, spent what money he had on some liquor, gotten drunk and desperate and had gone out with a friend to rob a man they knew might have some money in his pocket. The man they robbed was Garve Ivey's father. The robbery became murder when Garve's father put up a struggle. One of the men hit him in the head with a railroad spike, knocking him off the trestle.

Not only had the men never been caught, but they had remained in town. One of them, the one who actually swung that spike, had gone on to work with Garve on the WPA road crew. He knew who Garve was. He knew he had killed Garve's father. And still he was able to work side by side with the son of the man he had murdered.

Showing more restraint than anyone who knows him would have expected, Garve carefully and systematically arranged for the sheriff to arrest the two men. He arranged for the prosecuting attorney to try the case. He arranged for the judge to hear it. And, in the end, he got justice, watching one of the men receive a sentence of twenty years in prison and the other get ten.

A small twist of fate, which meant more to Garve than to anyone else, was that the attorney appointed by the court to defend the two men was young Tom Bevill.

That didn't mean much to me at the time. Neither did the veterans' work Tom did for me early in my Congressional career. The ironic significance of these intersections would only come clear about ten years later, when I wound up meeting Bevill head on in a fight for my political life, a fight wrapped up with the legacy of the Dixiecrats and the gathering lethality of George Wallace.

But that came later. For the time being, in the early to mid-fifties, I went about my business back home, as Truman had suggested, and there were national matters to tend to as well. When the House voted on Alaska's statehood in 1950, I was the only one of Alabama's nine Congressmen to vote for it. When the same vote came up that year on Hawaii, I and Frank Boykin of Mobile were the only two Alabamians to support it. I stayed behind both measures until they were finally passed in 1959.

All that work meant a lot to me, but the work that mattered most was the work Truman warned me against—building a law that would ensure that no boy or girl in America would have to work as hard or reach as far for the rewards of an education as I had had to. There was—and still is—no doubt in my mind that education represents nothing less than the doorway to personal fulfillment, social justice, true freedom and actual equality among all Americans. No political theory could compare to the years I literally sweated for my own education. I always believed the promises America made in those books I'd read as a young boy. Schooling had been the first step toward making those promises come true. It was my ticket out of the hills. As a boy and a young man, education had been my comfort and my source of strength. As a Congressman, it became my crusade.

From the first day I came to Washington, I began working on a bill for federal aid to education. In every session of Congress from 1949 to 1958, I brought up some form of a student aid act, knowing I'd get nowhere for a while, knowing it might be years before my bill would even get a hearing. I knew this would take time, and I was right. But hell, it took me twenty-seven years to get to Congress. I could handle another ten to get this done.

And I took a first big step toward that goal when I was appointed to the House of Representatives Committee on Education and Labor in October 1951.

By stepping into the arena of the fight for federal aid to education, I was entering a battleground littered with nearly two centuries of corpses. Only twice in America's history had the federal government been able to pass laws that significantly and directly provided aid to the nation's schools. The first was the passage of the Northwest Ordinance in 1787, which set aside public lands for elementary and secondary schools. The second came in 1862, when Abraham Lincoln signed the Morrill Act, which provided land grants for state universities.

Other than those two laws, every move by the federal government to aid education in any appreciable way was blocked by forces afraid that their own special interests would be swept aside. By the end of World War II those forces and their interests had become pretty well defined.

First there was religion. Any law that excluded private schools from federal money brought cries of discrimination from the Catholic community, whose school systems were educating thirteen percent of the nation's elementary and secondary students by the 1950s. Of course any plan to *include* Catholic schools brought howls of protest from other religious groups—especially from the Protestant heartland of the Deep South—as well as from people sensitive to the question of separating church and state.

Then, of course, there was the economic issue. One of the best-organized and most consistently outspoken opponents of federal aid to education was the Chamber of Commerce of the United States. That group insisted on the sanctity of local school boards and councils of education to control the teaching of their students. It claimed that federal aid to education would lead to federal control of education. Control was indeed an issue—but it was not as sanctified as the Chamber of Commerce made it appear. Those local school boards and education councils were largely controlled by the Chamber, which of course was largely controlled by the local business community. And that business community did not in the least like the idea of a multimillion- or billion-dollar federal aid program that would ultimately require them to kick in with taxes.

Then there were the issues of Communism and race, which both picked up a lot of steam after World War II. The fear and paranoia that saw Soviet conspiracy and subversion behind nearly every federal program that came down the pike fed the opposition to any aid-to-education bill. There was just a general distrust of the government getting too much control over the country, especially over something so important as the shaping of the minds of its children. I was as concerned as any reasonable man about the threat of Communism in the years following World War II, and there was reason to be concerned. But to play upon those fears for political or any other gain, the way I saw Richard Nixon and, of course, Joe McCarthy do, was far beyond reason. And to use those fears to hold back the best weapon we could ever develop—the minds of our young men and women—made no sense to me at all.

The racial issue made even less sense, but I understood what I was seeing there. As the civil rights movement began to take shape, with integration of schools as a primary focus, segregationists realized that the end of "separate but equal" school systems was coming soon, which meant that any federal aid to white schoolchildren would include federal aid to *black* schoolchildren as well. The segregationists were perfectly willing to sacrifice the futures of millions of poor white children to make sure the blacks were held down.

Nobody denied that this nation needed more and better schools, as well as better salaries for its teachers. The military drafts in both World Wars I and II had revealed how drastically uneducated many young American men were (the same realization arose again after the Vietnam War). School construction had dropped so badly during the Depression and World War II and so many good teachers had left the profession for better-paying jobs in wartime industries that, by the end of the 1940s, the nation's schools were overcrowded and understaffed. Anyone could see things would only get worse with the coming postwar baby boom.

But every time the alarm was sounded, every time any kind of federal law was even suggested, it was blocked by a politically paranoid version of the three R's: Race, Religion and the Reds.

That's the political minefield into which I stepped in 1951.

There were twenty-four members on the House of Representatives Education and Labor Committee the year I joined—fourteen Democrats and ten Republicans. The fifth-ranking Democrat, who was already a friend of mine and became even closer after I joined the committee, was John Kennedy.

I had been attracted to Kennedy from the first time I met him. Part of that was the fact that he walked with a cane when we met, after going through a pretty painful back operation. Maybe it's the fact that I was raised by a man with a crippled leg, but I've always felt an affinity for people with any sort of physical disability, especially when I see them working through and with it the way my father had.

And John Kennedy was a hard worker, which is something else

that attracted me to him. I've heard people run him down for his time in Congress, saying he didn't accomplish much, that the House was just a way station to the Senate for him. There *were* plenty of people who came and went through the House and its committees, just dropping in on their way somewhere else. I'm sure John Kennedy had his plans for the Senate and even the presidency, but while he was in Congress—at least while he was working on that committee with me—he *worked,* by God. He gave it everything he had.

And there was not a smarter man to be found. That was probably one more thing that impressed me about him. He was a reader, and a writer as well. And he had a sense of humor, which can't be overemphasized as a valuable asset for a man making his way in Congress. John Kennedy's wealth was no secret, and I'm sure there were those who resented that fact and mistrusted him for it. Myself, I never held anyone's wealth against him. Just because a man had money didn't make him my personal enemy; and just because a man was poor didn't mean we were necessarily on the same side either. It's always been what a man stood for that mattered to me.

Well, I knew Kennedy was rich, and he knew where I'd come from. And I remember one day he said to me, "Carl, how would you like to have two million dollars?"

I said, "Well, I don't know. I'm not expecting to have it any time soon. But I'm sure if I did have two million dollars today I'd contrive to spend it before Saturday night. That's how folks where I come from are with money."

He chuckled, then he said, "Well, I *have* two million."

I said, "Well, that's great."

He laughed again.

"Yes," he said, "my father gave it to me yesterday."

Now it was my turn to laugh, the point being it was *true.* And it was absurd, because he sure didn't need it. Not only was John Kennedy as unconcerned about his wealth as I was, but he could even laugh at it. Of course his money mattered in terms of financing his career. But he never let it get in the way of seeing himself—and whoever he was with—as a person.

The third-ranking Democrat on that committee was Adam Clayton Powell, Jr., the black Congressman from Harlem. We became good friends, despite the fact that I never thought much of Powell's work habits or his abilities as a legislator, and despite the fact that I was eventually chosen instead of him to head the subcommittee that made my dream of a historic aid-to-education bill finally come true.

Adam Powell was the antithesis of everything I thought a Congressman should be. He was undependable, missing as many committee meetings as he attended. He was irresponsible, rarely doing his homework, showing up at meetings with little or no idea of what was on that day's agenda. And he was unfocused, expounding on every subject that came along, spreading flowery but scattershot comments around the room.

Still, you couldn't help but like him. He was a flamboyant, colorful character, and there weren't many of those in Congress in my day. He liked me, too, which became a mixed blessing by the mid-1950s and certainly by the sixties, with the racial atmosphere in Alabama being what it was. When I made my run for governor in 1966, Powell told me he wanted to do anything he could to help.

"I'll be for you or against you," he said, "whichever will do you more good."

If there's one thing Adam Clayton Powell *did* know, it was politics.

At the time I joined, and during the decade I spent on that committee, the member who meant the most to any plans I had in terms of building a bill was the chairman, Graham A. Barden of North Carolina.

I don't think I've ever heard or seen a reference to Graham Barden that didn't contain the word "crusty." Another term that often popped up with his name was "reactionary." Yet another was "autocratic." Dick Bolling described Barden by saying he "regarded liberals and their legislation as a Moslem regards pork."

Which explains why Barden had little taste for me when I joined his committee. It also explains, in part, why Adam Clayton Powell missed so many committee meetings. Barden had no use for a black man on his committee, and he virtually ignored Powell in meetings. Who could blame Powell for his absence when Barden treated him as if he were invisible?

As for me, Barden treated my education bills at best with amused humor and at worst with complete scorn. He was not about to let any bill like the ones I had in mind get out of his committee. And there was no doubt whatsoever that this was his committee. It would take nothing less than a coordinated, concerted effort by a coalition of members strong enough to stand together against "the Judge" to overcome his iron grip. That stand would eventually come, and I would be part of it, but it was still six years away when I first arrived.

What I saw in the chairman of the Education and Labor Committee was a man as anti-labor and anti-education as could be imagined. When it came to labor, Barden was a union buster from the word "go." And when it came to education, he saw no reason to be spending the government's good money on schools, especially when that money would wind up being spent on Catholics and blacks.

During my first term in Congress, President Truman pronounced that the problems of the nation's school systems were so enormous that only the federal government had the resources to solve them. He was passing the gauntlet to Congress, and the Senate immediately responded in May 1949 by passing a bill authorizing three hundred million dollars a year in grants to states for both public and private schools.

The House version of the bill was in Barden's hands. He chaired the subcommittee in charge of it, and the bill he came out with authorized the same amount of money as the Senate, but restricted it to public schools and made no mention of aid to "separate but equal" schools for racial minorities.

The chairman of the parent Education and Labor Committee at the time, John Lesinski of Michigan, who happened to be a Catholic, publicly accused Barden of creating an "anti-Negro . . . anti-Catholic" bill laced "with bigotry and racial prejudice." Francis Cardinal Spellman, archbishop of New York, denounced Barden as a "new apostle of bigotry." Spellman's comments brought Mrs. Eleanor Roosevelt into the fray as she made clear her own strong opinion that federal aid to religious schools violated the principle of separation of church and state. Spellman shot back that Mrs. Roosevelt's "anti-Catholicism stands for all to see."

By the time all that smoke cleared, the Barden bill—as the Judge knew it would—died in committee.

Once he became chairman in 1951, Barden could effectively choke any legislation that had a liberal smell to it. He called committee meetings whenever he pleased—arbitrarily and often without warning. He adjourned them when he wished—often suddenly if they took a turn he didn't like. If an aid-to-education bill seemed to be gathering some momentum, he would call in a dozen Chamber of Commerce witnesses to kill it with a filibuster. If, on the other hand, witnesses appeared from a group he didn't particularly care for, like the AFL-CIO, he would chide, interrupt and verbally abuse them.

He was a rough, tough son of a bitch, and it was pretty clear from the get-go that it was going to take all the patience and persistence I had to find a way around Barden. You didn't beat a man like that by taking him head on. But if you held your hand, collected your cards, paid attention to the shifts in circumstances that occur with time, and knew when the time was right to make your play, you just might wind up winning a pretty good-sized pot.

And believe me, circumstances were shifting in the 1950s.

The Supreme Court's 1954 *Brown v. Board of Education of Topeka* ruling signaled the beginning of the government's move toward actually making integration the law of the land. The fact that that decision was aimed at integrating schools had a direct impact on our committee. Adam Powell now saw it as his duty to attach a rider to every bill proposed in our committee, an amendment that precluded the use of funds in any institution that practiced segregation. Of course that just about eliminated any institution in the Deep South at that time. And it just about guaranteed that any bill that managed to make it out of committee would be killed on the floor. Only at the end of the decade did the temper and makeup of the House as a whole shift to a point where a bill with a Powell amendment might actually pass, and that terrified the Southerners even *more,* pushing them to retrench even more tightly into the committees over which they still had control. The "Powell amendment" became a byword in Congress. It became his standard oper-

ating procedure, his point of leverage, the only way he had of influ-
encing a committee and a Congress in which at that point in his
career he had little strength and even less sympathy.

As for my own strength, I was looking at that time to buck up
my staff. If I was going to finally push an education bill into law, I
was going to need help. And I had a good idea where I might find it.

A year before the *Brown v. Board* decision, I met a young
woman working on the staff of my Congressional colleague from
Tuscaloosa, Armistead Selden. Actually, I had first met this girl six
years earlier, when I was making my 1948 campaign for Congress
and she was a schoolteacher up in Cullman County at a tiny place
called Cold Springs. They had what they called "all-night singings"
at country churches in those days, and I was invited to come speak
at one in Cold Springs. These things went until two or three in the
morning, so they had me come at midnight, as sort of an intermis-
sion. When I was done, they introduced me around.

Now I've always been known as a man with a pretty good
memory for names and places. Folks down here say the only man
better at it is George Wallace. Well, when I ran into this young
woman on Selden's staff, I remembered her as the piano player at
that all-night singing up in Cold Springs. We got to talking about
Cullman County, about teaching, and the more I saw of this young
woman, the more I learned about her background and her attitudes,
the more I knew this was someone I wanted—*needed*—on my staff.

Her name was Mary Allen. She'd come from Sumter County,
Alabama, down in the heart of the Black Belt. Her father had been a
cotton farmer with a pretty good piece of land, big enough to have
two or three black families living on it and working their own tenant
farms. Mary grew up with those black families, going into their
cabins, sitting on their porches, baby-sitting their infants, playing
with their children.

She was never taught to hate or fear blacks. Her father was also
a local justice of the peace, and more than once Mary watched him
hold arraignments in the living room of their home. It was typical at
that time and in that part of the country that most of his cases
involved white people bringing charges against blacks, for anything
from stealing to murder. The thing that set Mary's father apart is he

dismissed more than half those cases, which was unheard of. It took some courage for a white man to dismiss charges brought by another white man against a black.

It was that background, as well as her clear dedication and willingness to work, that made me call Mary in the summer of 1954. She had been bored stiff in Selden's office, where they had her doing nothing but typing and filing, so she had quit that spring and was back in Alabama looking for a teaching job. I tracked her down, told her I needed someone to help with my footwork up in Jasper and with my legislative work in Washington, and she came on board. From then until the end of my political career, Mary Allen remained my right arm.

Which is not to say she didn't have a lot to learn. Mary was always an idealist—she remains one today, working as director of economic and community affairs for the University of Alabama, traveling throughout the state and to Washington, getting grass-roots development programs started in some of the state's smallest and poorest communities. She's still fighting the same fight today that we were fighting thirty years ago. But politics is a little more complex than simple ideals, which is something I had to teach Mary early on.

I remember sending her down to a judiciary committee hearing on the Voting Rights Act of 1955. I told her I was opposed to the act, and I wanted her to bring back all the information from that hearing, so I could write a statement and put my opposition on record.

Well, Mary went down to this hearing and watched the attorney general of New York, Louis Lefkowitz, give testimony that nearly knocked her off her chair. Not only was he just about the most eloquent speaker she'd ever heard, but to her utter shock and surprise he used Sumter County, Alabama, as an example of a place where blacks were being totally oppressed. She knew what Lefkowitz was saying was true. This was where she *lived.*

So Mary came charging back to my office, all pumped up, absolutely certain that there was no way I would vote against this act once I knew what she'd just learned. When she was finished, nearly out of breath, I told her to have a seat.

"Well now, Mary," I said, "it's time for you to learn something.

"I've made a political decision here, that I am not going to vote for that bill," I said. "If I do, the people I represent are not going to let me stay in Congress, and I won't be able to vote for any of these other bills—not for education, or housing, or libraries, or hospitals, or anything else.

"Your job, Mary," I said, "is not to change my political decision. Your job is to get over to the Library of Congress and make me a statement as eloquent as that of Mr. Lefkowitz."

And she did. And it was.

There was always political maneuvering to be done, but neither Mary Allen nor any of my other staffers nor I ever lost sight of what we called "the cause." I've talked about devotion before, about dedication, and none of us ever lost sight of our ultimate goal, which was the goal of basic justice in educational opportunity. While there were compromises that had to be made on the way to that goal, there were also battles worth fighting along the way.

One, which was in a way a testing ground for the bigger struggle to come, was the fight for the Library Services Act of 1956.

The battle lines were basically the same as those in the fight for aid to education in general. They began to be drawn in 1946, when Lister Hill proposed a rural library demonstration bill in the Senate. In 1950 the Senate approved the measure, but the bill failed in the House, basically because of the same fears about race and religion that crippled any education programs at that time. There was also some skepticism about the need for the federal government to spend any money at all on rural libraries. Even John Kennedy went on record that year against the idea of spending money on a "rural library program."

But there were people who knew how desperately essential such a program was, people who came from a background like mine, who had grown up knowing what it was like to live without any such thing as a library, to know the sense of loneliness and isolation that comes from a childhood without readily available books. Sam Rayburn knew that feeling, growing up in rural Texas.

Carl Perkins knew that feeling, growing up in the hills of Kentucky. Dozens of Congressmen from the Great Plains and the open West knew that feeling. And of course all I had to think of was that box back in Uncle Bob Rea's house up on Gober Ridge to remind me of the hunger a boy or girl living in a remote region of this country can have for a book.

The statistics were there. In 1946, when Hill first proposed a bill in the Senate, there were thirty-five million Americans—more than one fourth of the nation's population—without library service. Most of those people lived on farms or in small communities. A decade later, despite work at local and state levels, twenty-six million Americans remained without access to a library. In 1956, three hundred and nineteen counties in this country had no library within their borders—including twenty-two in Alabama.

Statistics can get real dry real fast. The larger a number is, the more it tends to numb the mind. There's really no number that can match firsthand experience—the sort of experience I had riding around Winston County in a bookmobile in the summer of 1955.

The government wasn't paying for bookmobiles then—that would come with the passage of the library bill I was working on. This particular van had been bought by several women's clubs in Cullman and Winston counties. I knew the sorts of folks it was serving—I'd *been* one of those folks as a boy. But making the rounds in that van reminded me how it still was for people up in those hills.

I remember one old fellow hobbling up to meet us at a place called Poplar Springs. He was well into his eighties, wearing a hearing aid and leaning on a cane. He came up and said he wanted a book on space. "I'll be dead and gone before this outer space business amounts to anything," he said, "but it seems to be comin' and I guess I need to know a little somethin' about it."

That old boy walked away just as serious as could be, with a book on space travel tucked under his arm.

Then there was the lady and her two daughters who came down a railroad bank pushing a wheelbarrow—a wheelbarrow full of books. They'd come from a little neighborhood of seven or eight families over the tracks, and this was how they brought their library books back and forth.

There's no measuring the impact of personal experience like that. I shared those stories with members of the House as a special Education and Labor subcommittee was created in 1955 to hold hearings on a rural library bill. I was on that subcommittee, which was chaired by Phil Landrum, a conservative Democrat from Georgia. It would take some maneuvering to finally pass a bill, but the pieces seemed to be in place.

First of all, we knew we'd need a lot of conservative votes to pass this bill, which is why we got Landrum to take the lead. As for actual sponsorship of the bill, we decided to let Edith Green, an Oregon Democrat in her first term, wear the big hat rather than an earmarked liberal like me. My work was done comparatively behind the scenes.

Much of that work was dealing with the various educational and library associations lobbying for this bill, collecting information and support. The thing about legislative achievement is you've got to forge an instrument to bring it about, and what you've got to start with is your own word. A politician—or a lobbyist—whose word is no good is worse than in trouble; he's useless. Politics is based on loyalty. My word, put together with your word and everybody else's word, is what gets things done.

The problem with too many educators was they didn't seem to understand that process. They had no political training. I was surprised how little political influence or even involvement they had. More often than not they got all tangled up in details, going over everything with a fine-tooth comb. Politics is as much a business of timing as it is of details. You do what you can when you can where you can and how you can.

You've got to *act* when the winds are right, when the iron is hot. Timing. That and a man's word is just about everything there is to politics.

I was amazed how few education lobbyists understood that. But two who did were both women: Julia Bennett, who ran the Washington office of the American Library Association until 1957, and her successor, Germaine Krettek. Again, I don't know what it is about women and politics, but I found on the whole that the women lobbyists I saw in Washington were much more effective than men. I think it's that same dynamic of selflessness and lack of concern for personal power or importance that I'd noticed back in student politics at the University of Alabama.

In any event, Bennett worked tirelessly on this bill we were building in 1956, and it was in part her close relationship with Graham Barden that got him to step back and allow it to get out of committee. The fact that Barden's wife had served as a public library trustee in Craven County, North Carolina, didn't hurt either.

As for the issues of race and religion, the religion question was taken care of by aiming the bill only at public libraries. The racial issue, which was linked so closely to the concept of states' rights, was defused by crafting the language of the bill to give the states the authority to determine how federal money for their libraries would specifically be spent.

I was the first witness to testify for the bill in committee, and when it went to the floor, I spoke on its behalf. Other than that, I was careful to keep myself away from the spotlight, although everyone in Congress realized this was essentially my bill. When the Library Services Act was passed by the House of Representatives in May 1956, and became law when the Senate followed suit by passing it a month later, sending it to President Eisenhower, whose signature authorized the federal government to spend seven and a half million dollars per year for the next five years on building, staffing and stocking rural libraries throughout the nation, I appreciated the fact that Edith Green made a point of spreading the credit around.

"It is true the bill had my name on it," she said, "but because so many of these members have worked on it far longer than I, it could well be called the Carl Elliott bill, the Phil Landrum bill, the Thomas Jenkins bill, or the Frank Smith bill."

There would be more library fights to follow. In 1960, I led the battle to extend the LSA, helping talk both presidential candidates John F. Kennedy and Richard Nixon into making the library issue part of their campaigns. By then Kennedy was sympathetic to the cause, and after I was able to get the renewal of the bill past the roadblock of an uncooperative Rules Committee by leading the floor battle to gather the two-thirds majority in the House needed to override the committee and once again make the Library Services Act law for another five years, I received a letter from John Kennedy congratulating me on my "magnificent fight."

I was proud of that, proud of anything I could do to put more libraries in reach of more people—especially the poor—in this country. But I knew my best fight was yet to come: the fight for the National Defense Education Act.

Upon the education of the people of this country the fate of this country depends.

Benjamin Disraeli to the British
House of Commons, June 15, 1874

EIGHT

"TELL CARL TO TAKE OVER"

In a sense, the unfolding of the 1958 National Defense Education Act set the pattern for the way most of my life would unfold from that point on—both for better and for worse. That is, the NDEA was a fairly significant event with far-reaching ramifications that, for all the work and planning I put into it, would never have come about if not for the stroke of circumstances totally beyond my control.

Circumstances are skittish things. They cut both ways. Sometimes they work for you, sometimes against you. They can be a blessing that settles softly in your lap, and they can be a curse that comes crashing down on your head. In the case of the NDEA, I was blessed by a series of circumstances that came together to create just the catalyst I needed for ten years of persistence to finally pay off.

The first of those circumstances involved Adam Clayton Powell. I didn't realize it at the time, but his decision to defy the Democratic Party and throw his support to Dwight Eisenhower in the

1956 presidential election would directly affect me and my lifelong dream after the Eighty-fifth Congress convened in January 1957.

Graham Barden's grip on the Education and Labor Committee that January was as strong as ever, but some subtle shifting had taken place among the committee's membership, especially among its younger members, who weren't as locked into position—the *chairman's* position—as many of the veterans. Three of those younger members had come on the committee in 1955: Edith Green of Oregon, Frank Thompson of New Jersey, and Stewart Udall of Arizona. Along with myself and Lee Metcalf of Montana, we formed a core of what you might call liberal rebels, a coalition ready to work together to outmaneuver Barden from below and finally get some bills out of that committee. Before that Eighty-fifth session of Congress was through, we would have ourselves a nickname: the Fearless Five. Of course our more conservative colleagues in the House had their own phrase for us: the *Faithless* Five.

With our group doing the steering, and with some fresh blood behind us, including brand-new committee members Ludwig Teller of New York and George McGovern of South Dakota, we were able to gather enough committee votes among the sixteen Democratic and twelve Republican members to force Barden to appoint five education subcommittees at the beginning of the 1957 session. That in itself was a big victory, since a subcommittee is typically the first step—through its research and hearings—toward launching a bill. The chairman of a subcommittee, in his own way, has as much power to decide the focus of that group as the committee chairman has over the committee as a whole. I yearned for the chairmanship of one of those subcommittees, which was awarded according to seniority. But since I ranked sixth among the committee's Democrats (below Barden), and only five chairmen would be appointed, it looked like I was the odd man out.

Until Powell came into play.

From the beginning of their Congressional relationship, Graham Barden had had no truck with the color of Adam Powell's skin, let alone his flashy antics. The flames were fanned even further once Powell began using his integration leverage in the mid-1950s to block whatever bills he pleased (just the year before, in 1956, Powell had killed an Eisenhower federal-aid school construction bill by insisting federal funds go only to integrated schools). When Powell then backed Eisenhower in the November election, that pushed Barden over the brink. He may have been forced to create those subcommittees, but there was no way Graham Barden was going to put Adam Powell at the head of any of them, which made things sort of sticky, considering that Powell was the second-ranking member of the committee, number two in line for one of the five subcommittee spots. But Barden wasn't the only one who wanted to keep Powell out of any of those chairmen's seats. For the Judge it may have been a matter of race but, for me and the rest of the committee members eager to finally get an education bill in motion, it was simply the realization that any subcommittee headed by Adam Clayton Powell was dead in the water from the beginning. He was far too controversial and far too focused on the single issue of integration to have any legislation with his stamp on it get anywhere on the floor of the House—if it ever made it that far.

Once he was branded as a "party bolter"—as all the newspapers were calling him—Powell opened just the door we needed. In the first of a series of decisions that shocked more than a few people (but didn't surprise anyone who looked carefully at what was happening), the Education and Labor Committee (with some convincing from the Fearless Five) voted to permit Graham Barden to ignore seniority in selecting the chairmen of the five new subcommittees. Powell was outraged, telling the press the decision was the committee's way of "punishing me for getting off the plantation."

Sure enough, Barden passed over Powell in making the appointments. The "bumping" of Adam Clayton Powell made headlines across the country. And when Barden named me to head the new Special Education subcommittee of the House Education and Labor Committee, the papers made me out as the bumper. The fact is, Powell was never actually as angry about that whole thing as he made it seem. He had a broader view of things. He knew his constituents in Harlem were going to be sending him back to Congress for a long time, long enough for him to eventually take Barden's place as chairman of the entire committee—which indeed he eventually became. The truth of the matter is this subcommittee flap didn't matter much to Adam Powell one way or the other. Of course he was obligated to raise a ruckus when it happened, if for nothing else than pure principle. That was part of the game. As the most visible black man in the nation at that time (Martin Luther King, Jr., though well known in the South, had not yet emerged as the national figure he would soon become), Powell's role in the game was a unique one, and he played it to the hilt.

As for our own relationship, despite the press playing up my "bumping" him, Powell and I were never the antagonists the newspapermen made us out to be. Powell understood what was happening, and he realized that the subcommittee position meant a lot more to me than it did to him. He also realized how much our goals overlapped, that my push for educational opportunities for poor people included *his* people—although I was never totally convinced that Powell truly cared about his people as much as he did about himself. In any case, we had plenty of conversations about the way blacks had historically been mistreated in this country, and he knew I didn't want to be a part of extending that mistreatment. We were friends before the subcommittee flap happened, and we remained friends after it.

In a way, I'll always think of Adam Clayton Powell as I do of Jim Folsom. Both were larger-than-life characters, and both had larger-than-life flaws. Powell drove most of Congress, especially the Southern bloc, absolutely crazy with his defiant blustering and his mocking humor. Personally, I never took him seriously enough to get too angry about him. I understood his act from the beginning, and most of the time I enjoyed it. And I was sorry to see him finally throw it all away.

It was disheartening to watch Powell's career finally come apart in 1967, when the House decided it had had enough of his shenanigans and voted to "exclude" him from their midst. That was after two House investigations charged him with several misappropriations of taxpayers' money, including taking personal trips to the Bahamian island of Bimini and attributing those trips to his staff members. News of those Bimini trips came as no surprise to me—

Powell had been taking them in the mid-fifties, when we were to-gether on the committee.

What surprised me about the exclusion of Powell was the fight that followed the House vote. Powell hired some lawyers, as did the House, and the next thing you knew, the case was in front of the Supreme Court. The Court ruled against the House and gave Powell back his seat. But by then he'd run out of steam. The House, which grudgingly took him back, stripped him of his seniority and of his chairmanship of the Education and Labor Committee, which he had assumed when Graham Barden left Congress.

It's rare that a man joins a movement in its infancy and lasts long enough to see the fruits of its success. That was true of Powell. He ran for Congress again in 1968, won that campaign, showed up in the House for the swearing-in ceremony, took his oath of office, then immediately went back to Bimini. When he ran again in 1970, he lost an election for the first time in his life. The people of Harlem had had enough.

A year after that, Adam Clayton Powell died of cancer. His ashes, as he had requested, were scattered from an airplane in the skies above Bimini.

When I became chairman of the House Special Education subcom-mittee in February 1957, I knew it was time to make some moves. One of the first, and most important, was to hire the subcommittee's clerk. Every committee and subcommittee has one—the person who schedules all hearings, interviews and lines up witnesses, keeps min-utes of meetings, answers telephone calls and letters about bills, works with lawyers on drafting legislation and does all the footwork when a committee goes on the road for hearings. By the time all that work's done, a clerk is likely to know more about a piece of legisla-tion than the committee members themselves. It's a vital job, and I knew of only one person I'd trust with it: Mary Allen.

There weren't many female clerks in Congress in those days. It was a rigorous job, and the pay wasn't great. The average yearly salary of a clerk in Congress in those days was twelve thousand dollars. When I approached Mary about the job, I couldn't offer her

even half that much. Barden was out to make it as hard as he could
for us, and one of his first moves was to give us the bare minimum in
terms of money. All I could offer Mary was five thousand dollars.
She hesitated, but not about the pay.

"Oh, Mr. Elliott," she said when I approached her about the
job, "I don't know how to do that."

"Well," I said, "I don't know how to be a chairman either, so
we can learn together."

And we did. Mary was beside me every step of the way on this
thing.

There were five of us on that subcommittee: Edith Green,
George McGovern, Republicans Stuyvesant Wainwright of New
York and Donald Nicholson of Massachusetts, and myself. Our responsibilities, under "Special Education," ranged from juvenile delinquency to federal aid to the arts, to education for the physically
handicapped. We were also responsible for higher education, and it
was there, mainly through a program of college and university scholarships and loans for deserving students, that I could see us making
a life-changing breakthrough, not just for the tens of thousands of
young men and women who couldn't afford to go to college at that
time, but for millions more just like them in generations to come.

We got to work right away. I had Mary running day and night
to the Library of Congress, where its Legislative Reference Service
allowed us to study every federal statute dealing with education. We
also began meeting with members of educational lobbying outfits
like the American Council on Education, the National Education
Association and the Association of American Colleges, asking their
advice and gathering information we might need when it came time
to shape our bill.

Another group we spent a lot of time with was the Department
of Health, Education, and Welfare, which early that year had assem-
bled a task force on higher education, aimed at studying what it
called the "waste" of talented but poor youth across the nation who
were unable or unmotivated to attend college. Among the members
of that task force was a newcomer at HEW named Elliot Richardson. In the months to come, Richardson would become a big behind-the-scenes player in our bill, shuttling back and forth between

the White House, Congress and the various other federal and private organizations involved in the creation of this act.

Finally, in August of that year, we took our show on the road, so to speak. Beginning in Washington, and moving on to Wisconsin, South Dakota, Utah and Oregon, we launched a series of hearings to gather testimony and information from high school and college administrators, teachers and students, from professional educators, from businessmen and clergymen, and from anyone else with specific interest, experience or expertise on the subject of the need for a federal scholarship and loan program for college-bound students.

In my own Alabama district, I went into every school to see first hand what conditions they were studying under. I saw high school laboratories whose equipment consisted of nothing more than a five-gallon bucket and a spigot. Some had far less. I'll never forget a school I visited in Pickens County—a black school.

When I arrived, the principal met me with a real downcast, weary look on his face. I could see he was sore in his heart. I asked him to show me his school. We walked past classrooms in which the boys and girls were sitting on the floor because they had no desks. They had hardly any books, and what they had were torn and badly scarred, the covers long gone. There were twenty to thirty children in each of those rooms, with hardly any hope of a decent education, no matter how badly they might have wanted one.

The statement I made to open our subcommittee hearings on August 12 pretty much summed up my feelings then—and now—about the essential need (not to mention the essential justice) of making this nation's seats of higher learning available to any deserving young man or woman, regardless of their resources. In my opening remarks I did my best to get across the sense of urgency surrounding this issue. And the words I said then, I believe, are every bit as true today:

"America's future success at home and abroad, in peace or war, depends on the education of her citizens. Democracy is based on that foundation. Whatever happens in America's classrooms during the next fifty years will eventually happen to America.

"For decades we in this land have exerted every possible pressure to guarantee the preservation and proper utilization of our natural resources. We have dammed our streams, replanted our forests, grassed our hillsides and irrigated our deserts—at a cost of billions of dollars.

"Yet our need for better-prepared personnel has received relatively scant attention. We read about the need in newspapers and magazines. We hear it over the airways. From businesses and professions and from research agencies come constant appeals for educated men and women. Our shortage of engineers, physicists, chemists, teachers, statisticians, doctors, librarians, nurses, executives and other skilled workers has long been described as 'acute' and sometimes as 'desperate.' . . .

"These shortages are not shortages of inborn ability. America is rich in native intelligence. Our capabilities and attainments have long been demonstrated beyond question in every facet of existence. We need only to shape our talents, to educate with discernment, to develop to the utmost the latent endowments everywhere among us, to train each boy and girl to the highest attainable degree, consistent with his or her ambition."

Everywhere we went, everyone agreed something needed to be done about education. There was a vague uneasiness about the strides other nations were making in the fields of science and technology, especially the Russians. But those fears had been simmering for a decade, and still neither the public nor its politicians were willing to actually pay the price needed to substantially encourage the education of America's young minds. I'm convinced you can talk to people until your face turns blue, you can make the most compelling arguments in the world, you can swamp them with statistics, but more often than not they're not going to actually make a move—especially if it involves paying a price—unless they feel they have no choice, unless they feel they *have* to. Sometimes people can be persuaded to do something. But most times they have to be *frightened* into it.

That's where another stroke of circumstance came our way.

It arrived on October 4, 1957, courtesy of the Soviets.

Its name was Sputnik.

It's hard for people today to understand the sheer panic, the utter sense of crisis and doom that gripped this nation once word came across the news wires that the Soviet Union had managed to put the world's first artificial satellite into orbit around the earth.

The thing weighed no more than a man—184 pounds—but the fact that it was up there, circling the planet once every ninety-six minutes, while we sat down here, helpless, with no such capabilities of our own, made it seem as if the sky was indeed falling—or that something deadly might be falling *from* the sky at any minute. The fear of nuclear attack was palpable. The ominous *ping ping ping* of Sputnik's signal, picked up on radios across America as the satellite made each orbital pass, let no one forget what was up there—and what might be coming down.

The response across the nation was immediate.

Senator Henry Jackson of Washington, interviewed in Seattle the day after the Sputnik launch was announced, called it a "devastating blow" to the United States and urged President Eisenhower to proclaim "a week of shame and danger."

Senator Styles Bridges of New Hampshire chastised the American people's priorities, declaring the time had come to be less concerned with "the height of the tail fin on the new car and to be more prepared to shed blood, sweat and tears if this country and the free world are to survive."

Lyndon Johnson, who was chairing the Preparedness Investigating subcommittee of the Senate Committee on Armed Services, gaveled a meeting of that group to order with the announcement, "We meet today in the atmosphere of another Pearl Harbor."

There were some who saw Sputnik as a blessing of sorts. When I heard President George Bush react to Iraq's 1990 invasion of Kuwait by calling it a "wake-up call" for America, it reminded me of what some people had to say about Sputnik back in the fall of 1957.

"We *needed* Sputnik," announced Adlai Stevenson. "It is sure proof that God has not despaired of us."

Secretary of State John Foster Dulles expressed thanks for the "fresh determination" he saw sweeping the country, and said he hoped the "wave of mortification" would spur the "efforts and sacrifices needed to win that struggle."

A *Newsweek* magazine editorial proclaimed:

To every civilization, at some moment in its existence, the mortal challenge comes. Now Red Russia's dictatorship has thrust such a challenge upon the West. The challenge is not simply military; it is total—intellectual, spiritual, and material. To survive, the free world, led by the United States, must respond in kind. Amid a clamor of alarm and self-criticism, America is preparing to shoulder this burden of great historical responsibilities. Technical problems which were long the province of isolated specialists have become the concern of a whole citizenry.

President Eisenhower himself had sounded a warning in the spring of 1957, when he told a meeting of the NEA that "our schools are strongpoints in our National Defense . . . more important than Nike batteries, more necessary than our radar warning nets, and more powerful even than the energy of the atom."

But it took Sputnik to get people to really start listening.

Personally, I was neither as shocked nor as frightened by the news of Sputnik as a lot of people. I'd been studying the issue of American technological know-how for ten years. It wasn't news to me, or to anyone else who paid any attention to the subject, that the scientific manpower of this nation had slipped drastically and that other countries, particularly Russia, had made big gains in the education and training of their own scientists and engineers. The way I saw it, we simply hadn't put enough priority on educational training in this country, and now we were seeing a tangible result. I wasn't afraid of an impending Soviet nuclear attack. It's a big step from firing a small ball of metal into space to actually having the ability to accurately and effectively deliver an intercontinental ballistic warhead. That frightening step was coming, I knew, but I also knew our own scientists weren't far from taking it themselves.

Meanwhile, it was time for me and my committee to strike while the iron was hot—*carpe diem,* as they say. Seize the day. While most of the nation saw Sputnik as an evil shadow, I saw it as an opportunity.

There was no time to waste. Our committee was in the midst of its hearing when the news of Sputnik arrived. I immediately told Mary to get us a flight to Alabama, and we beat it back to Jasper, where we mapped out what to do next.

It turned out Lister Hill and his staff in Washington were doing the same thing. Lister had been trying to get his own education bills together in the Senate for some time, but as long as the House remained dead set against the issue, his efforts were futile. Lister knew whatever he wanted to do for education depended on what I could do, and he knew I had the tougher task on my side of the fence. I wasn't the only one looking for some sort of breakthrough. So it's not surprising that Lister and a lot of other folks involved in this issue saw pretty much the same opportunity in Sputnik as I did. We were all trying to tree the same possum. I was just what you might call the lead hound.

Lister was in Berlin the day that satellite went up. By the time he got back to Washington, his chief clerk, a fellow named Stewart McClure, had put a memo on his desk suggesting they hop right on this thing. Lister was willing, although it was no longer as easy for him to be as eager about this issue as he had been a decade earlier. Race had changed everything, as far as Lister was concerned. The clouds of reaction against integration had begun to roll over Alabama, and it was getting harder to take a step that wasn't shadowed by the issue of segregation. Lister's reaction now was to back off from anything involving race. He was anything but a meek man, but he was getting gun-shy about this racial thing. That was no big secret.

Drew Pearson, the political columnist, was never one of my favorites, although for some reason he took a shine to me from the first year I arrived in Congress. He used to write with a curious kind of affection about my country ways, how I didn't know one fork from the other at a proper dinner setting. Pearson treated me pretty fairly during my career, but I never cared much for his kind of journalism. He shot from the hip, spraying the landscape with his off-the-cuff conclusions. A fellow who fires his rifle as often as Pearson did is bound to hit the target once in a while, but he missed much too often for my comfort.

In the case of Lister Hill, however, Pearson was right on the mark when he described Lister in 1957 as "worried sick" over Adam Clayton Powell and his integration amendments. "The great senator is acquiring the title of 'Fence Sitter Hill' because of his skittishness over the school bill," wrote Pearson in one of his columns.

As for me, I had no bigger fish to fry than this one. This was the battle I'd been preparing to fight for ten years—for all my life, really. If it meant risking my career in the face of race, so be it.

When I called Lister to tell him the time had arrived, that things had come to a head, that we could *pass* this education bill, he was a little reserved.

"You know I've been down this road a few times before, old fellow," he said. "But this time I believe you're right."

By the time my subcommittee finished our hearings in early November, the Soviets had upped the ante by launching Sputnik II, which was six times the weight of the original and carried a dog as well. The reaction was predictable. Not only were the Russians ready to dangle a nuclear threat over our heads, but they were now on their way to sending a man to the moon as well, leaving us hopelessly behind in the race to other planets.

At least that's the way it looked to America, and that was fine with me. When one of our own test satellites launched by a Vanguard rocket blew up on a launching pad at Cape Canaveral in early December, even more fuel was thrown on the fire. The Soviet newspaper *Izvestia* gleefully described America's "hysteria." The United States, it bragged, would never catch up.

All of this was strengthening our hand. But we had to be careful how we played it. The fact is America was nowhere near as far behind the Russians as it appeared. They'd beaten us to the punch, but our scientists were primed to take their own swings soon. If we made too much of Russian superiority, we might turn concern into hopelessness, which would take panic further than we wanted it to go. We didn't mind the public mood to be boiling, but we didn't want it to boil *over*.

We also didn't want people to overreact to the need for more technological hardware and know-how. Although training scientists and engineers was a primary focus, we were looking far past the immediate crisis. We were looking at opening the doors of education across the board, in the humanities as well as the "hard" sciences. The crisis gave us a focal point to get our bill made into law— that's how we came up with the title of the National *Defense* Education Act. But we realized this bill's effects would extend far beyond the current climate of that time. It was education in general, from physics to philosophy, that we wanted to make available to the best young minds of this country.

So both Lister Hill and I spent the months of November and December working with our strategies and points of emphasis with our staffs. Then we got together down in Birmingham over the Christmas holidays to hammer this thing out.

We took a couple of suites at the Tutwiler Hotel—the same hotel outside which the Dixiecrats had hung Harry Truman in effigy in 1948. Lister and two of his staff members, Bill Reidy and Jack Forsythe, joined me and Mary Allen, as we worked pretty much around the clock for close to a week, deciding not just what should but what *could* be part of a passable bill.

From the beginning, Hill kept squirming about what Powell might do. The idea of a Powell amendment had him deeply worried, and it had him combing through everything we did, trying to take out anything Powell might latch on to—which was basically everything in the bill that had any substance. If he'd had his way, Lister would have picked the whole thing apart until there was nothing left. But I wasn't about to let that happen, not when we were finally this close. I'd be damned if I was going to let this thing be watered down.

"The bill is gonna *pass,* Lister," I said. "There's enough people sold on it that we're gonna *see* that it passes.

"And, by God," I said, "we're not gonna let you tear it up."

That made Lister awfully mad. He didn't like having his neck stuck out over this, and it *was* stuck out.

We spent our time hammering out the details of a program that would not just offer scholarships and loans to promising high school students but would also create training centers for teachers and put sorely needed equipment—from scientific hardware to language laboratories—in classrooms all the way down to the first-grade level.

Finally, late one evening, after we'd been at it about a week, we figured we pretty much had this thing ready and maybe we ought to quit for a while to rest up. Just then, the bells across Birmingham began ringing.

It was midnight, New Year's Eve, the beginning of what I hoped would truly be a new year.

When Congress returned from recess on January 4, 1958, the number one item on its agenda was the bill Lister Hill and I announced we would be introducing. Almost immediately, and almost exactly as I had anticipated they would, the battle forces and their positions began to take shape.

There was President Eisenhower, whose aversion to the very idea of offering educational scholarships was summed up in a credo he repeated time and again: "God helps those who help themselves." His version of an aid-to-education program was much more bare-bones than ours.

There was the National Education Association, which, in its zeal to protect and pursue its own interests, proved to be more of a hindrance to us than a help. The NEA folks could never seem to understand that the only way to get some pie is a slice at a time. We considered ourselves extremely fortunate to have a realistic opportunity to pass a specifically tailored bill that would wind up costing the federal government about a billion dollars. The NEA didn't trust a specific-aid bill like ours, believing it took too much control of schools and educators out of local hands and gave too much say-so to the federal government. What they wanted was an across-the-board bill—one that cost about five times as much as ours. To watch the NEA publicly demand a general aid-to-education bill that would pay out nearly five billion dollars a year within five years was more than frustrating. It was enraging.

Then there was Graham Barden. When Eisenhower presented his own special-education bill, with far fewer scholarships and far less spent on testing and counseling high school students than the bill Hill and I would propose, Barden responded with scorn, ridiculing the President's proposal for its message that "the Great White Father in Washington will send kids to college." Of Eisenhower himself, Barden said, "Somebody around him apparently is of the opinion that all you have to do is drop a few million dollars in a slot machine, run around behind, and catch the scientists as they fall out."

Considering that the bill Hill and I had in hand was even more generous than Eisenhower's, we didn't have to imagine what Barden would say about us. In fact, he had some private words for me even before the opening salvos were fired. It was a warning, and there was nothing subtle about it.

"You of course know," Barden told me, "that the Southerners in the House are against the position you've taken on this thing. They're against it all the way, up and down, from one end to the other."

"Of course I know that," I said. "What of it?"

"Well," said Barden, "it's going to cause you *lots* of trouble. You *know* where you ought to be."

I'd been through this song and dance since the day I came to Congress.

"I'm *where* I ought to be, the way I look at it," I said.

"Fine," said the Judge. "Have it your way."

Which is exactly what I intended to do.

And so, on January 27, 1958, began the process of turning this bill into law—a process that would take eight months. A good chunk of that time—nearly all of it—was spent in the Rules Committee, through which all bills in the House of Representatives must pass, and where a good number of them died in those days, thanks to a Congressman named Howard Smith.

Howard Worth Smith of Broad Run, Virginia, member of Congress since 1931, member of the Rules Committee since 1933, and chairman of that twelve-member committee since 1955. Like Barden, Smith was known as "the Judge" (he was a district judge in Virginia before coming to Congress), but Barden's control of the Education and Labor Committee was nothing like Smith's grip on

the Rules. He was a wiry, wily man, sprung from the heart of the
Confederacy (he still lived in the home from which his mother had
watched Union troops march across their farm toward Richmond
during the Civil War), and even more reactionary—if more refined
—than Graham Barden. From the beginning of his chairmanship,
Judge Smith made no bones about the fact that he was bound and
determined to keep any "left-wing, radical, Communist" civil rights,
health, education, labor or housing bills from reaching the House
floor.

And as chairman of the Rules Committee, Smith had that
power—perhaps more power than any other single man in Congress
at that time. Because there was no committee in Congress more
powerful than the Rules. Just as all roads lead to Rome, so all bills in
the House of Representatives pass through the Rules Committee
before being sent to the House floor. The committee's job is to
decide on the rules that apply to each bill: how much debate will be
allowed, whether amendments will be permitted and, if so, what
kind of amendments. Because of their checkpoint status, Rules
Committee members have the power to stall or completely stop any
piece of legislation they choose. It's no wonder that committee was
often referred to as the third branch of Congress, along with the
House and Senate.

With Howard Smith at its helm, the Rules Committee was the
most impenetrable roadblock a progressive piece of legislation—or a
progressive legislator—could face in Congress. It wasn't just his attitude, it was his abilities as well that made Smith such a formidable
force. First, he was as good a parliamentarian as ever held that seat.
He knew the rules inside out, and he knew how to *use* them toward
his own ends. Secondly, he worked as hard as anyone I ever saw in
Congress. If you were up against Howard Smith, there was no time
to rest, because you could be assured that, for each minute you
wasted, the Judge was adding another minute's worth of strategy
and planning.

More than any other committee in Congress, the Rules Committee at that time granted its chairman the power to steer its
course. *He* set the agenda, *he* scheduled witnesses, *he* declared when
an issue was to be put to a vote, and because of the unpredictable

nature of the flow of legislation, the Rules Committee was the only standing committee in the House with no set meeting day. It was up to the chairman to call the committee together, whenever and however he liked.

Or, just as effectively, he could simply *not* call them at all. That was one of Smith's favorite tricks, especially as more and more civil rights legislation was pressed on him in the late 1950s. It seemed as if every time one of those distasteful bills was pressed on Smith, he'd simply leave Washington, drive down to his dairy farm in Fauquier County and ostensibly take care of some chore or other.

In one instance, when Sam Rayburn was pushing him to release a particular bill he was holding hostage, Smith slipped off to visit his cows for a while. When he came back, he explained to reporters that one of his barns had burned down, and that's why he had left so abruptly.

When word got to Rayburn, the Speaker replied, "I knew Howard Smith would do most anything to block a civil rights bill, but I never thought he would resort to arson."

Delivering the National Defense Education Act to the Rules Committee was like sending it into a black hole. If Howard Smith had had his way, it would never have been heard of again. That was no surprise. I was prepared for it to languish there in limbo, under Smith's thumb, for a while. But not even Judge Smith was impervious to pressure, and once the bill went into his committee, my job was to keep the pressure on.

By that time our own American test rockets were being launched successfully, and already you could sense some of the public's mood of urgency beginning to slip. Our job now was to keep the heat on, to keep striking while the iron was still hot, to put this issue in front of America's eyes and keep it there.

Not only did we need to put our program on every Congressman's desk, but we had to get our message out to the newspapers and magazines, radio and television stations across the country. Generating that kind of publicity, simply pulling together the paperwork and the postage, costs money—money we didn't have. Mary

Allen and I did a lot of talking about where we could come up with
some funds. Groups like the NEA were hardly any help at all—they
were our foes as often as they were our friends. If we were going to
find some financial backing, it would have to come from somewhere
else—which it did, in another of those circumstantial sorts of ways.

One Saturday morning Mary was in the office when a woman
named Ada Stough dropped in. Ada was a lobbyist with the American Parents Committee, a group we'd previously worked with on
juvenile delinquency legislation. She just dropped by to chat, and
asked Mary how our education bill was going.

"I don't know," said Mary, picking up a phone message from
her desk. "I wish we could get as much interest from folks on this
bill as the person who keeps leaving these messages. Her secretary
calls just about every day for an update. This message right here says
she's on a boat on her way to Europe, and she wants to know what's
happened when she gets there. Her name's Mary Lasker."

Ada Stough just about fell off her chair.

"Is Mary *Lasker* interested in this?" she asked.

"Yes," said Mary. "Who is she?"

It turned out Mary Lasker was one of the richest women in the
world. She had inherited about eighty million dollars from her husband, Albert Lasker, who had made his fortune in the advertising
business—he was the man who coined the slogan "I'd Walk a Mile
for a Camel."

Mary Lasker was a woman whose concern for public causes
was as big as her bank account. Lister Hill had become a favorite of
hers with his public health legislation in the early 1950s. She continued to donate money to Lister's causes and campaigns throughout
his career. When I learned she was interested in the NDEA, I went
to visit her in New York and came back with a check large enough
to start circulating some "Dear Colleague" letters around Congress
and to begin blanketing the media with word of the NDEA.

The media responded. In March, *Life* magazine published the
results of a survey showing that the American public's number one
concern had switched from inflation to a worry that the Russians
had passed us educationally. "Americans have now turned a sudden
and dissatisfied eye upon U.S. schools and the children who inhabit

them," said *Life.* The survey concluded that a large number of Americans were eager for a program of "state or federal aid for schools, federal scholarships, government direction and financing of scientific enterprise in general."

The same magazine followed with a series of stories comparing two "typical" teenagers, one from Chicago and one from Moscow. While the Soviet student was portrayed as hardworking, determined and driven by an educational system that sent him to school six days a week, where he was faced with a curriculum of rigid, mostly scientific courses, the American student was shown in a much more relaxed setting, free to choose from a wide range of classes and enjoying the pleasures of just as wide a range of nonacademic extracurricular activities.

Similar unflattering comparisons of the Soviet educational system and our own appeared in magazines like *Time* and *U. S. News and World Report,* as well as on several television broadcasts. I didn't want our educational system to become a scapegoat, I didn't want to see people clamoring to replace our system with one as repressive and tunnel-visioned as the Soviets', but I knew those temporary responses might be necessary to get America's attention and to give our bill the momentum it would need to become law.

Meanwhile we did our best to generate that same momentum in Washington, conducting hearings before our subcommittee, where some of the most recognizable and influential minds of the time testified for our bill. We were trotting out some heavy artillery here, voices neither Howard Smith nor anyone else involved with this bill could ignore. And the messages these men delivered and the situations they described, in down-to-earth, straightforward language, still apply today.

Here's what Dr. Lee A. DuBridge, president of the California Institute of Technology, had to say about the particular problem of anti-intellectualism:

"Some of the best students in this country are not being encouraged or do not have the opportunities to get into colleges or universities.

Sometimes it is lack of hearing about the opportunity, lack

of knowledge about it, because of home environment or school environment, sometimes it is financial, and sometimes it is simply a matter of motivation.

"A young high school boy, especially from a rural area, can quite often get himself a quite good job out of high school, and it may not occur to him that there is any reason for going on to a college or university even though he has the ability. Or it may be that he lives in a community or has got in with a gang where intellectual attainments are not highly regarded. There are many areas, many local areas in this country, even in many homes, even in many schools, where intellectual attainment is not particularly encouraged. In fact, in many cases it is just the opposite: The egghead is a despised person, and in many areas the egghead is regarded as anyone who has gone beyond the 12th grade.

"So this anti-intellectual atmosphere, which is found in a number of places, in a number of communities, to a certain extent, in this country, is sometimes a discouragement and prevents a student having the desire to make full use of his intellectual talents."

Dr. DuBridge went on to comment on and present questions about the goals and standards of our high schools and colleges—comments and questions that are being echoed today, in almost exactly the same terms. The concern then about America's students not measuring up to the Soviets is mirrored now by our nation's current alarm over our students' test scores compared to the Japanese and Europeans. The timelessness of DuBridge's words is pretty apparent:

"In other countries the objective of the system of higher education has been to train a very tiny fraction of the people for very specific callings or professions, and so only a quarter or a fifth or even a tenth as many of their students, relatively, go into higher education as in this country.

"We have built a system designed to train, to educate, to give opportunities to a very large percentage of the population, and it is doing that. But when you build a system designed to give opportunities to a very large percentage of the population, there are certain sacrifices, or course, that you make. . . . Possibly we have gone a little too far in some areas in accommodating the large number of students; possibly in certain areas our standards are too low.

"I think, indeed, it is time now for us to take another look at the standards we require for entrance and for graduation from our colleges and universities . . . I think a little toughening process is probably now in order. . . .

"I am afraid it is true that the average high school is not maintaining the intellectual standards that it could and should, and so we face a problem in this country of trying to lift the intellectual level of attainment in our high schools, of trying to drive out the soft and the snap and the nonintellectual courses of study and substitute for them courses which are really of intellectual caliber, which are tough, which are demanding, and which develop the intellect.

"I think, for example, too many high schools have neglected foreign language, mathematics, and science in their curriculums and have allowed too many students to slide through to graduation without taking a tough, intellectually demanding course."

When Rear Admiral Hyman G. Rickover, father of the Navy's nuclear development program and one of the most outspoken, controversial critics of our country's educational system, came before us, he drew plenty of attention:

"I believe that the work of your committee is about as important as the work of any committee in Congress. I further believe that your work should not be predicated on the particular momentary requirements of defense, but that the subject of education can stand on its own feet. In fact, I believe that education is more important than the Army, the Navy, the Air Force, or even the Atomic Energy Commission.

"We really have a much greater problem than defense,

when we consider education, because in this rapidly spiraling technological period, no country can remain a first-class power unless it gives primary attention to education.

"Furthermore, the people of no democracy can remain free and ignorant at the same time. . . .

"We are depending too much on the schools. The parents have a responsibility, too. We cannot send children to school for a few hours a day when the mother and father go off to work, and put the whole load on the schoolteachers. They cannot carry that load, particularly when the average grammar school has about 27 or 30 children in a class. They would have to be superhuman to do anything like that.

"We have gotten into the habit of just throwing the children off to school and depending on the school to perform all of the functions, not only educational, but moral and home training and all the rest of it.

"We must deliberately take the excess things out of the schools and make them places where the children learn, and require the parents to assume their responsibilities as far as the children are concerned.

"Specifically I would throw all of these fringe items out of the schools. For example, in one city in Illinois they have a course on how to tell when you are in love. I think there is a better place than school to find that out. There is a more appropriate place to find out whether you are in love than the school system."

Dr. Wernher von Braun, the German rocket scientist who had become the father of America's space exploration efforts, arrived from the Army Ballistic Missile Agency at Huntsville, in my own Alabama, to make his case. Watching U.S. soldiers recently battle Iraq with a dizzying array of high-tech hardware reminded me of Von Braun's testimony:

"Modern defense programs, such as the long-range rocket systems, ballistic and guided missiles, supersonic aircraft, radar detection systems, antiaircraft and antimissile defenses, are the most complex and the most costly, I suppose, in the history of man. Their development involves all the physical sciences, the most advanced technology, abstruse mathematics and new levels of industrial engineering and production.

"The efficient operation and effective maintenance of such devices require a new kind of soldier, who may one day be memorialized as the man with the slide rule—a 20th-century counterpart of the musket-bearing farmer. . . .

"We must recruit more young people into scientific and technical careers. . . . We must make these careers more attractive to induce more young people to select them. . . . This involves inspiration, at home as well as in school; competent teachers, adequate laboratories and libraries, assistance to those who require it to finance undergraduate study at least, and provision of fellowships or other stipends to encourage graduate study. . . .

"Youth can hardly be blamed for turning to the more glamorous attractions during school years. Scarcely a newspaper in this country does not boast of one or more sports pages; radio and television coverage of athletics is in like proportion. But do you see any science page, or mathematics page? Do you hear any reports of scientific or technical competitions?

"The task of putting things in proper proportion is not exclusively the responsibility of youngsters. What about the service clubs and the parents groups who promote football dinners, basketball soirees and the like? These are healthy expressions of adult interest, but they ought to be balanced with some recognition of and attention to the fundamental disciplines which are musts for tomorrow's citizens."

Von Braun's words were strong, but it was Dr. Edward Teller, the University of California at Berkeley physicist who steered the development of the hydrogen bomb, who explained the notion of studying science and extended it far beyond the mere practical demands of the moment. As Teller spoke, it was easy to imagine we were listening to a poet, not a physicist:

"I would certainly not like to sing the praises of the Russian educational system, certainly not in every respect. They are achieving their results by the onerous methods of competition and the crueler methods of coercion.

"They are driving on their population and they are driving on their young people, too, with the whip. Far from wanting to do the same thing with our own children, I do believe that education is much too beautiful a thing to be crammed down any reluctant throat.

"I think we have to achieve what we must achieve by methods appropriate to our democratic way of living, and I think these results can be achieved. I believe that the highest results always come from spontaneity and not from necessity.

"As a piece of general philosophy, I should like to add, however, that in our democracy we have too often been led by the needs and the desire of the average man. And, if I may use a thoroughly unmathematical expression, this has led to a situation where our average has fallen below the average.

"I believe that it should be considered a normal achievement in any person and in any child that he or she should excel in a particular field, whether it be history or painting or mathematics. The feeling that I can do something much better than anyone in sight is a great source of satisfaction and not the kind of satisfaction that leads to inactivity. . . .

"A child's mind is much more receptive to abstract thinking than the mind of an adult. Abstract thinking is in many ways like a game. It is a fact that many of the world's most outstanding mathematicians and theorists made their great contributions below 30 years of age, some of them when they were younger than 20.

"Among the latter, I should mention the greatest mathematician of all, the German, Gauss; also the great French mathematician, Galois, who was killed in a duel when he was 21 years of age, and by that time had made the most outstanding contributions to mathematics.

"Among other names with which you are thoroughly familiar, although they did their work a little later but still well before their 30th birthdays, I should mention Albert Einstein, Niels Bohr, and Isaac Newton.

"Our educational system does not take advantage of this great propensity of young minds in science. Talent, to my mind, is not something that exists or does not exist. It is not a mental power as some too simple representation of aptitude tests would have it. Talent is something like a very great and specialized interest. It is like falling in love. But if you don't know of a subject, you cannot fall in love with it. . . .

"We are living in a world which is transformed by science from decade to decade. Yet our children remain ignorant, and all of us are largely ignorant about matters which make our society click, at least as far as the material aspects are concerned.

"And we furthermore remain ignorant about the great amusement value which is in a way the same thing as the great intellectual value that you can derive if you begin to look into the details of the working not only of our machines but of this big functioning universe of which we are a part. . . .

"In science we have learned a number of very wonderful things which are important not only because they can produce more practical or more destructive machines, but which are important also because they are most surprising and throw new light on the universe around us. The ideas about relativity, the ideas of the structure of the atom are by no means as difficult and as inaccessible to the common man as they are represented to be.

"I think that these subjects are and should be of great stimulation to the philosopher and, from there on, to many other people in our society, including perhaps, maybe even the poet.

"I believe firmly in the unity of the intellectual effort, and you cannot help one field without helping all of them."

That last sentence could have been the credo of the NDEA, as far as I was concerned. We were hanging our hat on the need for scientists in particular, but our aim was much broader than that.

The forty thousand grant-in-aid college scholarships we were proposing were aimed at the immediate goal of producing scientists,
engineers, mathematicians and linguists. But the program we hoped
to put in place was going to last much longer than any particular
crisis.

That's what most excited me about the opportunity available to
us. Education in general had always been like a religion to me. I
believed totally in its ability to empower every man to explore the
limits of his potential, to allow every person so inclined to explore
the boundaries of his capabilities, to find and fulfill his *self.* Society's
needs are one thing. An individual's are another. An educational
system available to everyone meets all those needs at once.

It was, however, going to take even more than newspaper arti-
cles and all-star witnesses to make my case in the House. Compared
to the Senate, it's a pretty hurly-burly place. Things are comparatively cut and dried in the Senate. The staffs do a lot of the negotiat-
ing, while in the House it's more a member-to-member process,
much more hands-on for the legislator himself. It takes a lot of
ground pounding, a lot of one-on-one discussions, a lot of personal
telephone calls and private meetings, and even then you never know
which way the wind might blow. The mood can change so subtly
and so suddenly, just like the weather. You can almost *see* it sometimes, shifting right before your eyes, and if you aren't able to see it,
you can lose your shirt.

So that's how I spent that summer, playing a sort of political mid-
wife to a very difficult birth. The wave of response we were able to
generate both from the public and from our own political allies
forced Judge Smith to finally release our bill from the Rules Committee on August 4. But we faced another huge hurdle when it was
time to introduce it on August 7 for debate on the floor of the
House.

I wasn't exactly sure what Graham Barden intended to do. As
chairman of the Education and Labor Committee, it was Barden's
prerogative to present the bill to the House. If he did that, he could
damn the thing to hell even as he unveiled it, and we'd be sunk

before we even got started. We had enough of a fight ahead of us as it was.

Graham Barden was the post on which a lot of folks hitched their horses, and he was shrewd. He rarely tipped his hand, and this time was no exception. Mere minutes before our bill was due to be called up for debate, Barden had given no sign whether he intended to do the honors or not. In fact, he was nowhere in the House chamber.

Frank Thompson took me aside, and we decided to play a little game of our own. Frank hunted down Barden and found him back in the cloakroom. The judge was a hot-tempered fellow, so Frank had to play this real carefully.

"Judge Barden," he said, "you don't really want to fool with this bill of Elliott's, now do you?"

The judge just grunted.

"Listen," said Thompson, "why don't you just let him go on out there and make a fool of himself?"

Barden thought it over a minute, then said, "I believe that's just what I'll do."

Another pause.

"Tell Carl to take over."

I swear Frank Thompson was just about skipping when he came back down that aisle to tell me the show was mine.

Who could have known that more than twenty years later Frank would be writing me from prison? He wound up there the same way so many do—because of greed. He'd gotten mixed up in the 1979 ABSCAM affair, in which seven members of the House and one from the Senate were arrested for taking bribes from FBI undercover agents posing as wealthy Arabs.

There are so many strengths a man has to have to make it in Congress, because there are so many ways a weakness can beat him. One of those weaknesses is greed. It's a fact of life in Washington that there are always going to be some crooked sons of bitches drifting around, waving money under a man's nose and hoping he'll bite. Power attracts people like that, and there's no more concentrated place of power in this country than the Congress of the United States.

I knew Frank Thompson well. I liked and respected him. And I knew he wasn't much for writing letters, so it meant a lot to me when I eventually got a piece of mail from his prison address, a letter that filled a couple of legal pages. He talked in there about what he'd heard had become of this person and of that person that he'd known back in Congress, and he said he'd managed to make a couple of friends there in prison but that they weren't the sort of friends you'd seek if you had much of a choice.

Not long after I got that letter, news came that Frank Thompson had died.

But I don't dwell on the way his life wound down when I think of my friend Frank Thompson. I prefer instead to recall the sight of him skipping down the aisle on that triumphant August afternoon.

As if Graham Barden weren't enough to worry about that day, I had to hold my breath while Adam Clayton Powell leaned back by the chamber railing, scribbling something on an envelope. It would only have taken a sentence or two to tack a last-second Powell amendment on our bill and destroy any chance of passing it that session—or probably ever. But as I made my way down onto the floor, Powell stayed put.

By that time the language and specifics of the bill had been so carefully crafted, with the help of Elliot Richardson's folks at HEW, that it was immune to charges of discrimination. No Powell amendment was needed.

In fact, we had anticipated and prepared ourselves for every possible attack. As the debate wore on, every criticism—from the relation of these programs to America's defense, to the fear of federal direction displacing state and local controls, to concerns about inflation and an already swollen national debt—bounced off the bill like harmless pellets. When the rule for consideration of the bill passed the House that day, 266 to 108, we were over the hump. Judge Smith, seeing he was going to lose this one, sputtered to the press that our bill was "half-baked," that it was typical of the kind of "crazy legislation that comes at the end of the session."

After the successful August 7 vote in the House, the Senate, on

August 13, began its own debate. During a fourteen-hour session, Senator Hill and his forces had only to overcome the loud but futile objections of Strom Thurmond, who claimed the bill was "irrelevant" to national defense, and of Barry Goldwater, who pulled out the old saw of the camel getting his nose into the tent. Once you let the nose in, the adage goes, the rest of the camel is bound to follow. Once this bill was passed, warned Goldwater, the federal government would be spending more and more of its money on education with every passing year.

Of course I couldn't admit it at the time, but I prayed Goldwater was right.

The Senate passed the measure, 62 to 26, just before midnight —but only after South Dakota Senator Karl Mundt added a "loyalty oath" provision requiring that all students receiving aid under this act annually furnish proof of their loyalty to the government of the United States. To me, that provision was nothing but a bunch of silly hogwash, a trivial bit of business with no real effect but to appease the hard-core anti-Communists in our crowd.

The loyalty oath proviso raised a real ruckus, however, among the academic community. Administrators from Harvard, Yale, Princeton and every other heavy-hitting university in the country had been howling about this indignity ever since Senator Alexander Smith of New Jersey first proposed it during Lister Hill's hearings on the Senate side. The only real effect was that it gave John Kennedy a chance to score some substantial points with the college and university folks who hadn't been sure up till then whether they could take him seriously. Kennedy was positioning himself for the presidency then, and when he proposed an amendment to erase this loyalty oath nonsense, he had the college folks in his hip pocket.

As for my own feelings about that whole oath business, it didn't bother me one way or the other. Even if the provision stayed on the bill—which it did (Kennedy's amendment failed)—I knew it wouldn't be around for long. And it wasn't. Congress repealed it in 1962.

———

After the Senate vote, what I was most concerned about was passing the final conference report in the House without allowing so much of the bill to be whittled away that it wouldn't mean anything anymore. Every law has to finally be hammered out among the Senate, the House and the President, and very few survive in their original form.

Both I and Elliot Richardson, for example, had hoped to hold on to the concept of outright scholarships. But we had to reconcile the forty thousand scholarships we wanted to award with the mere ten thousand the President was offering. We arrived at a compromise total of twenty-three thousand scholarship grants, but even that was too much for the Republican and conservative Southern bloc in the House. We finally converted the entire scholarship plan to low-interest loans—the concept of a loan was a lot easier for the conservatives to swallow than the "giveaway" of a scholarship, and the effects, as far as we were concerned, were just about as beneficial.

The scholarships were one item I hated to lose, but all in all, the report that came before the House for a final vote on August 23 had enough teeth in it to make me happy—$900 million worth of teeth to be precise. Less than a billion dollars might not sound like a lot compared to the $41 billion the government budgeted that same year on conventional defense spending, but it was by far the most money this nation had ever been asked to spend on its schools.

It didn't hurt to read a New York *Times* account of my efforts on the eve of the House vote:

> This session's champion of the battle for federal aid to education unquestionably is Representative Carl Elliott.
>
> The tall, broad-shouldered, easy-going Alabamian, with a hitherto unheralded skill for calming and coordinating dissident factions, soon will have guided a federal aid to education bill through the House of Representatives.
>
> His will be an accomplishment that has been regarded as impossible for the last twenty-five years.

When House Resolution 13247—as the National Defense Education Act was procedurally labeled—was finally passed by the

House, 212 to 85, on August 23, 1958 (the day before the second session of the Eighty-fifth Congress adjourned), I was as weary as I was elated.

When the President signed it on September 2, making it Public Law 864, I knew that what we'd been able to put in place was going to stay a long, long time—stay and grow. Maybe it was a camel, but I knew this was bound to be one of the most beautiful and bountiful camels this country had ever seen.

There was plenty of press after that, plenty of newspaper and magazine stories hailing both Lister Hill and me as heroes of education. But there was one paragraph buried deep in that New York *Times* article that I should have highlighted at the time, a paragraph referring to the "problems" I had overcome in taking my bill through the floor fight:

These problems were prickly—religious, racial, economic, educational. In his Alabama district, they were also highly political.

And, as I would soon find out, they were only just beginning.

If a man hasn't found something he will die for, he isn't fit to live.
Martin Luther King, Jr.

NINE

∽

THE HORNS OF HATRED

People like to look back at the 1950s and sum it up with scenes of a sleepy American society settling into suburbia, a bland people comfortable with a bland President, white middle-class families watching Milton Berle and Howdy Doody on television.

That's what happens with the passage of time. The complicated, often harsh realities of yesterday tend to get lost in the generalities and superficial summaries of today.

The critical reality of the 1950s, especially in the South and especially in Alabama, was the tension between black Americans—backed by the federal government—rising up to seize their legal rights, and white Americans—backed in many cases by state and local governments—refusing to yield, clinging ferociously to the control they had enjoyed since this nation began.

What a lot of Americans don't seem to realize—or maybe they've just forgotten—is the fact that the racial conflagration of the

1960s began as crackling brushfires in the fifties, white against black, and white against white as well.

In 1974, on the twentieth anniversary of the Supreme Court's May 17, 1954, *Brown v. Board of Education* desegregation decision, a pretty savvy political analyst named Pat Watters stated, "All Southern time must be measured before and after that date because it so changed history, the fabric of life and the very feel of the institutions of government."

Nowhere were those changes more confusing—and more painful—than in Alabama.

I felt that pain—and confusion—personally, watching racial resentment and resistance turn to open violence as presidential orders, federal court rulings and the coalescing civil rights movement of the late 1950s combined to create a climate of open warfare across the Southern section of this nation.

I watched reasonable men to the right and left of me falter and fall as their political careers became casualties of the madness settling over the South—and I knew many more would fall before this thing played itself out.

I had known in 1948 that the Dixiecrats were a warning of worse things to come. One of the best of the South's political historians, a fellow named V. O. Key, dismissed the Dixiecrat revolt as "the dying gasp of the Old South." Key suggested at the time that the Dixiecrat sentiment was limited to "the whites of the Black Belt and little more, at least if one disregards the professional Ku Kluxers, antediluvian reactionaries, and malodorous opportunists."

Unfortunately, he was dead wrong. In fact, it was by both "disregarding" and underestimating the reactionaries and opportunists that the voices of reason and progress in the South were eventually drowned out by the din of angry resistance.

The Dixiecrats weren't about to roll over and die just because the big splash they hoped to make in 1948 didn't amount to much more than a ripple. They might have stepped off the national stage after that, but the white supremacists and states' righters went back home and stayed busy preparing to fight the federal judges and armies of Negroes they were sure would soon be invading their schools, their neighborhoods and their homes.

They were right about one thing: after World War II it was no longer possible to avoid or ignore the demands black people were making for a place in this society. The black soldiers who fought in that war did it in the name of what they called "double victory"— the rights they were defending in Europe were rights they aimed to finally win at home as well.

The creation in 1941 of the Fair Employment Practices Committee, which eliminated wartime discrimination among labor unions and defense-related industries, was a signal of things to come. But to many white Southerners, things came far too quickly.

When the Roosevelt administration gave voting rights through absentee ballots to active-duty black GIs from the South in 1942, white people in Alabama began buying pistols and ammunition to arm themselves for the race war they were sure was on the way. There was talk of it around Jasper, but most of the actual arming was happening further south. Still, even people up in the hills here were worried about it. I was concerned myself. I felt there surely was a race war coming, but I didn't figure it was going to be a war fought with pistols—at least I prayed it wasn't.

As soon as World War II was over, Harry Truman appointed a fifteen-member President's Committee on Civil Rights to prepare a report on the nation's racial situation. The tone of that report, issued in 1947, was clear from its title: *To Secure These Rights.* The civil rights package Truman presented to Congress a year later reflected that goal. Although it was defeated, it set the stage for two decades of continuous civil rights legislation in Congress.

The summer of 1947 also marked the first in a series of home and church bombings in Birmingham, where a twenty-year-old ordinance requiring blacks and whites to live in separate neighborhoods had been struck down. Those attacks earned the city the nickname "Bombingham."

It was Truman's civil rights program that sent the Dixiecrats south from the national Democratic convention in Philadelphia in 1948. After their flashy show that summer and fall, their voices remained largely unheard for a while, and it seemed that Key might have been right. There were a few political outbursts, such as Claude Pepper's 1950 defeat in Florida's Senatorial primary, where

Pepper was beaten in a campaign mounted by a well-to-do developer named George Smathers. The thrust of Smathers' slanderous attacks linked Pepper to Communism (tagging him with the nickname "Red" Pepper), but photos of Pepper shaking hands with black people were distributed as well, reproduced on fliers bearing the phrase "nigger lover." That race-baiting campaign was a preview of more to come throughout the South.

I'd first met Pepper during my last year at the University of Alabama. He was an Alabama native, raised in Clay County at the eastern edge of the state—the same county in which Hugo Black was raised—and he was a graduate of the university. Pepper had just won his first election to the United States Senate from Florida early in 1936 and was back at the university that spring to speak at a student dinner. I had two jobs that evening: as headwaiter, I was in charge of getting the meals on the tables, and as president of the student body, I had the honor of introducing Senator Pepper.

I liked Claude Pepper right from the beginning. I liked him as a man—he was straightforward, plain-spoken and honest, with a good sense of humor sprinkled in. And I liked his politics—he was a liberal, a *real* New Dealer, a Roosevelt man all the way. I was disappointed when he lost to Smathers. Smathers had been a Congressman when I arrived in the House in 1948, but I hardly had time to get to know him. Pepper I knew, and I was sorry to see him lose, especially on an issue as ugly as race and especially to a man whose career he had launched—Smathers' first job out of college was as an assistant U.S. district attorney in Florida, appointed by Pepper, and Pepper had pushed along much of Smathers' early career.

Loyalty counts for a lot with me. I've never traded an old friend for a new one. But I've found that there's plenty who do. Apparently, George Smathers was one.

Claude Pepper was an early casualty of this racial fear. Fortunately his political wounds weren't mortal—he came back in 1962 to win a seat in the House of Representatives that launched an enormously successful second stage to his career. But there were many other men to follow who weren't as fortunate—or resilient—as Claude Pepper.

On the whole, however, the grass-roots populism that had spawned liberals like myself in Alabama and elsewhere in the South during the 1930s and forties was still strong enough into the early fifties to hold back the surge of racists and states' righters.

Until 1954.

When the Supreme Court—with Alabamian Hugo Black playing an instrumental role—issued its *Brown v. Board of Education* decision that May, ordering the nation's schools to be desegregated "with all deliberate speed," the first shot was fired in the real war for civil rights, and the remainder of the decade saw the casualties mount as the fight got uglier.

Lynching, which had almost disappeared since the early part of the century, began rearing its hideous head again in 1954.

In 1955 a black seamstress named Rosa Parks refused to give up her seat to a white man and move to the back of a Montgomery city bus. The games the white bus drivers played with black passengers in those segregated days were humiliating. Not only did they taunt them with racial slurs, but they would force them to climb in the front door to pay the fare, then climb back out and enter the bus by the rear door. "The game," wrote a woman named Janet Stevens in a book called *The Montgomery Bus Boycott,* "was to wait until a black passenger got outside, slam the two doors, and drive off, leaving him standing on the curb without a dime."

When Rosa Parks said, "Enough," so did the rest of black Montgomery, and so began the first true expression of a unified movement among blacks.

That same year a black minister named George Lee was murdered in Belzoni, Mississippi, for trying to register blacks to vote. Another black man named Lamar Smith was gunned down in broad daylight in Brookhaven, Mississippi, for trying to do the same thing. And a fourteen-year-old Mississippi boy named Emmett Till was beaten to death and dumped in the Tallahatchie River for allegedly whistling at a white woman.

These were horrifying stories, no matter which side of the fence you stood on. Everyone, white and black, liberal and conservative, could feel the screws getting tighter and tighter.

In February 1956, three months into Montgomery's bus boycott, a black woman named Autherine Lucy, represented by a black Birmingham attorney named Arthur Shores, became the first Negro to enroll in classes at the University of Alabama. Outraged Tuscaloosa townspeople and students responded with demonstrations and protests, burning crosses in the streets and attacking passing automobiles driven by blacks. The university's board of trustees reacted by first suspending Lucy for her own safety, "until further notice," then they expelled her after she publicly protested the university's delay in readmitting her and questioned their motives for the suspension. When a court upheld that decision, Autherine Lucy left Alabama—not just the university but the state.

Meanwhile, the crises in Montgomery and Tuscaloosa sparked an almost overnight flood of Alabama membership in something called the White Citizens' Councils. Created in Mississippi in 1954 to organize leading community citizens against racial integration, the group was considered a sort of highbrow Ku Klux Klan. They were coat-and-tie racists, reactionaries with money, organizing and carrying out their segregation behind the scenes, using cash and influence. The Montgomery *Advertiser* described them in an editorial at the time:

> The manicured Kluxism of these White Citizens' Councils is rash, indecent, and vicious. . . . The night-riding and lash of the 1920s have become an abomination in the eyes of public decorum. So the bigots have resorted to a more decorous, tidy and less conspicuous method—economic thuggery.

The *Advertiser* sneered at the Councils' existence in Mississippi, but it only took the events in Montgomery and Tuscaloosa to bring the group in full force into Alabama. At the end of 1955 there were only five Citizens' Councils established in the state. By February 1956—after the uproar in Tuscaloosa—there were twenty-six Councils in seventeen Alabama counties, with a total membership of forty thousand "citizens."

And the flames kept spreading. In 1957, Arkansas Governor Orville Faubus refused to allow nine black students to enroll at Little Rock's Central High School. Faubus ordered National Guard troops to block the blacks, and when President Eisenhower sent troops from the 101st Airborne Division to enforce the law in Little Rock, American soldiers faced one another with fixed bayonets for the first time since the Civil War.

That same year, six white men in Birmingham abducted a black veteran named Edward Aaron, emasculated him with a razor blade, dressed the wound with turpentine and left him on the side of a dirt road, where he bled to death.

These nightmares were part of a swing in the South from a mood of populism based largely on economics to a feverish reactionism based almost entirely on race. It really wasn't far to swing, since both fed on an emotional rawness that has always seemed to be more open in the South than in any other part of the country.

I'd seen and felt the rawness of Alabama's politics all my life, the visceral emotion that spilled out of my neighbors as they watched Cotton Tom Heflin spew his venom, the anger that swelled among desperate crowds gathered in Tuscaloosa and Russellville and Jasper during the Depression, the defeat and despair felt by my relatives and friends who still called themselves Confederates a century after the Civil War.

It doesn't take much for emotion like that to spill into violence. There are few things more dangerous than backing a desperate man into a corner, and that's how Southerners clinging to the way of life they'd always known felt when that way of life was threatened in the 1950s: they became desperate.

Another astute Southern political historian, a fellow named George Tindall, described the bulk of Dixie's political leaders in the 1940s and fifties retreating "back within the parapets of the embattled South, where they stood fast against the incursions of social change."

But the racists weren't simply retreating. They were attacking as well. And their victims were not just the blacks and whites who were beaten and killed in the streets as the racial war wore on. Politicians and statesmen fell as well, some after resisting, and others even after compromising.

Jim Folsom held out for a while. Even after the *Brown* decision, he kept his sympathetic views toward blacks. In the summer of 1955 an interracial gathering at Southern Union College in Wadley was interrupted by an armed and hooded gang of whites who threatened to "blow the place up" if the college's president did not "get these niggers out of here." Folsom responded by ordering in the Alabama Highway Patrol to enforce the state's anti-masking law—a law Folsom had pushed through the legislature during his first term.

But Adam Clayton Powell's visit to the statehouse in November of that year was the death knell for Big Jim. By the end of the decade his career was, for all intents and purposes, finished, partly because of liquor but largely because of race.

Hugo Black, too, was hung on the horns of racial hatred—at least in his home state. After the *Brown* decision, he was called a "nigger lover" and "a traitor to the South"—the same phrases that would be thrown at me a decade later. When his University of Alabama law school class of 1906 held its fiftieth reunion in 1956, Black was not invited. His son, who tried to pursue a political career of his own, was finally forced to leave the state in 1961 after his family was harassed by Alabamians who, as Hugo Black, Jr., put it, treated his father "like a leper."

Respected by the rest of the nation as one of the outstanding Supreme Court justices of all time, Hugo Black could not be forgiven by his own people for his sins against segregation. Reviled early in his career for his association with the Ku Klux Klan, he was ultimately scorned for standing against them.

This was the same no-win situation anyone other than an extremist faced in the South at that time. There was no room left in the middle anymore. A course of reasoned moderation had become a tightrope almost impossible to walk. Lister Hill, who captained filibusters against civil rights even as he guided some of the most progressive social reform bills in this nation's history through the Senate, wound up mired in the middle, finally frustrated that his career hadn't gone as far as he hoped—and many expected—it would.

"The reactionaries didn't think Lister was enough of a racist," said Hugo Black, summing up Hill's career, "and the liberals thought he was too much of one."

What I saw as the 1950s unfolded was a South that seemed to be slowly losing its senses. Someone has written that it was as if "a steel cage had snapped shut on the Southern mind." Well, a caged mind is a tough one to deal with.

Still, if you were in the position I and the rest of Alabama's Congressional delegation were in, you had to do what you could to somehow connect with the people, to find some way to appease them without sacrificing your own principles. Not only did you face that challenge with your constituents at home, but you faced it as well with your colleagues in Congress—at least with your colleagues from the South. In the same way that state and local leaders back home seemed to be circling their wagons, so too were the leaders of the Southern bloc in Congress throwing up fences against the forces of inevitable change.

One of those fences was the Southern Manifesto.

They officially called it a "Declaration of Constitutional Principles." That's the name Harry Byrd and Howard Smith and their crowd came up with when they decided it was time to draw the first of what would become many lines in the suddenly swirling sands of the South. In direct response to the *Brown* ruling, it was a symbolic document declaring that "meddlers" and "outside agitators" had acted "contrary to the Constitution" to upset the "Southern way of life." Issued on March 12, 1956, it was signed by 101 Senators and Congressmen from the Deep South, including the entire delegations of Arkansas, Georgia, Louisiana, Mississippi, South Carolina, Virginia . . . and Alabama.

Yes, I signed it. I can say now it was an evil thing, but I could not say it then. And I honestly did not feel it then as strongly as I do now.

My feelings about the integration process that had begun with the *Brown* decision were nothing like the rabid reactions of Byrd, Smith, Richard Russell of Georgia and the other men who wrote this declaration that came to be called the Southern Manifesto. I was nowhere near the reactionary most of these men were when it came to the issue of race.

But I did have reservations about the meaning of the phrase "with all deliberate speed." I was concerned about the pace of this process, how carefully it would unfold. I could see the whole situation already coming apart at the seams, and that's what worried me most. I knew things had to change, that the time had come for blacks to be given their rights—I'd always believed they deserved their rights. But I was afraid things were happening too quickly, too fast, with too much force.

Congressmen outside the South considered me a moderate on this issue of race—which made me radically liberal compared to most of my Deep South colleagues. When this Manifesto came along, neither those colleagues nor my constituents back in Alabama cared about moderation. You were either with them or against them. And if you were against them, you were gone. Voted out. Politically excommunicated.

There were a select few Southerners who refused to sign the thing, men such as Lyndon Johnson, Sam Rayburn, Albert Gore and Estes Kefauver. Truth be told, these men all had more political power and a stronger base than me—strong enough to stand against something like this and survive. I knew there was no way I would survive, and I hadn't yet achieved what I came to Congress to do. It was that knowledge, along with my own personal concerns about the pace of the integration process, that guided me as I decided to add my signature to the others.

It's been almost forty years now since this all took place. It's hard to remember how tenuous everything seemed at that time. It was as if the ground itself was shaking beneath our feet. Those of us trying to somehow hold things together were fighting against the crosscurrents of time. I believed, for example, that the aid-to-education bill I was working on was something that could heal and strengthen us all, black and white, as we let go of the past and built toward the future. But I also knew time was slipping away, that this bill and any others like it had to be passed before things busted wide open, or they might never pass at all.

It was in the swirl of these circumstances, two years before the NDEA actually became law, that I signed the Southern Manifesto. I don't want to sound like I'm making any excuses. Given that time, that place and those circumstances—with none of the knowledge that comes after forty years of hindsight—I'd probably make the same decision again.

When the NDEA was finally passed in 1958, any sense of triumph I might have felt was tempered by the knowledge that there would be prices to pay back home. By then, anything a man in the South did that could be construed as helping black people was cause for retribution. A citizen on the street faced censure and even physical violence. A Congressman in Washington faced scorn and political defeat.

Both Lister Hill and I were heaped with praise in Alabama's newspapers after the passage of our education act, but it would not be long before many of those same papers referred to that same act in language that damned the both of us.

I didn't help myself any by taking center stage the very next year in what *Time* magazine called "the roughest, bitterest brawl" of the Eighty-sixth Congress—the fight over the 1959 Elliott "anti-labor" bill.

At first glance, it seems crazy that someone as linked with labor as I was, someone whose constituency back home was the working-man, who was carried to Congress on the sore backs of hardworking coal miners—hard-core *union* men—should have his name put on a bill that would cut back the power of those unions. But there are a lot of situations in this world—political and otherwise—that take more than a glance to understand.

The chain of events that led to that bill began in 1957, when the Teamsters Union was expelled from the AFL-CIO on charges of internal corruption. A year later a Senate committee assigned to investigate the nation's sixteen-million-member trade union movement shocked the country when its hearings revealed corruption and mismanagement of funds among many local and national union leaders.

The attorney for that Senate committee was Robert F. Kennedy. His brother John, who was then chairman of the Labor subcommittee of the full Senate Committee on Labor and Public Welfare, reacted to the hearings by sponsoring a bill requiring public disclosure and reporting of certain aspects of labor union operations. The Kennedy-Ives bill, as it was called, was passed by the Senate in 1958 but failed miserably in the House, where our Education and Labor Committee was split the same way as the House at large—between conservatives who wanted a bill with even more anti-labor teeth than Kennedy's and labor-minded liberals who wanted no bill at all.

When the Eighty-fifth Congress adjourned soon after the Kennedy bill's defeat, we all knew this was not the last we'd see of this sticky subject. The American people were alarmed about labor racketeering, and they were demanding that something be done. When we came back to Washington in January 1959, the lines had already been drawn—the forces of management on one side and the "lib-lab" lobby, liberals and pro-labor people, on the other.

As was the case so often in my career, I found myself among the few trying to steer a course in the middle. While that might seem the most sensible place to be, it's not always the safest. When you're in the middle, you've got bullets flying at you from both sides.

Which is exactly where they came from that session. On the Senate side, Kennedy came up with another bill, this time in partnership with Sam Ervin of North Carolina. The Eisenhower administration also leaped into the fray, with a bill even tougher on unions than the Kennedy-Ervin version. And the American public was clamoring for something to be done.

By the time the Senate passed its bill and sent it to the House, management and labor lobbyists were crawling all through Congress. Anti-labor forces, backed by public opinion, wanted something tougher than what the Senate had passed. Labor wanted the Senate bill softened up, or they wanted no bill at all. This was one of those times when the House was like a storm center, buffeted by strong winds, its opinion seeming to swing this way and that, almost from day to day. After a while, though, it was clear the House was moving in an anti-labor direction.

It was up to our Education and Labor Committee to set the course. The bill we reported out would be the one considered by the House. Of the thirty members we had then—twenty Democrats and ten Republicans—twelve were pro-management, ten held the AFL-CIO position, and eight were sympathetic to the unions but saw that a hard-line position would get nowhere and could wind up losing the whole ball of wax.

I was among those eight, along with the rest of our "Fearless Five" left from the previous Congress—Stewart Udall, Frank Thompson and Edith Green. We all realized we'd feel some heat from our home folks for backing any sort of bill at all. But we also knew we had to do something to save what we could. There was no way labor was going to get what it wanted—which was no bill at all. The other side was poised to choke the unions with some pretty severe laws—and they had momentum and public opinion going their way. We needed to come up with a bill that could be accepted by the country and swallowed by labor as well—no matter how bad it tasted going down.

Whenever there's a close fight in Congress, one factor that counts in the strength of a bill is the member whose name is attached to it. By this time I'd established a pretty good reputation in the House as someone who could take the heat, stay the course and still keep my head. I'd earned a good deal of respect after the NDEA fight, and my fellow committee members were counting on that—along with my ability to fight for votes once this thing hit the floor. So the decision was made to put my name on the bill, a bill that was strongly anti-racketeering but nowhere near as harsh as the President's.

No sooner was our bill sent to the floor than Phil Landrum of Georgia and Robert Griffin of Michigan introduced their own version, much closer to what the President was after. I was set for the struggle to follow when another of those circumstances came along that changed the entire course of what had been up to that point a well-planned, well-executed fight.

It was my gall bladder.

I'd been feeling bad for some time, but by May it had gotten almost unbearable. I woke up each morning feeling like someone was pressing a two-by-four piece of lumber against the back of my stomach. The pain was excruciating, the worst pain I think I ever felt. But I didn't say anything to anyone because I wanted to see this fight through. I felt that was the only chance we had of winning.

I held out for three months, keeping this thing to myself. I didn't want the newspapers to get hold of it and say I was unable to proceed—until I knew damn well that I truly *was* unable to go on. Several times a day I'd slip out of a committee session and go down to the bathroom on the fifth floor of the Old House Office Building, where I'd sit and sweat for a while. Often as not I'd vomit as well, hoping no one would wander in.

I almost made it, but not quite. By early August it was too much to take. I went to Sam Rayburn and told him I thought it was about time to go to the hospital. He couldn't believe it. "Oh no," he said, "you can't do that." But when I explained what I'd been through, he saw there was no choice. Dick Bolling, who had been steering this thing from the start, told me to get myself to some doctors as fast as I could, that he and Rayburn would take care of everything.

The doctors took one look and told me my gall bladder was not only swollen, but it was infected with gangrene as well. I called Jane, and she came on up with the children. They took me over to Bethesda Naval Hospital, where I stayed for the next thirty days, after going into surgery.

And that pretty much did it. My colleagues were counting on me to lead this fight, and there I was, on my back in a hospital bed on the sixteenth floor of Bethesda Naval Hospital, from where I watched the whole thing go down the drain. When Eisenhower went on national television and backed the Landrum-Griffin proposal, we had no ammunition with which to answer. Dick Bolling and Sam Rayburn did their best to rally the forces, but when the vote came on August 13, Landrum-Griffin became law by a margin of 229 to 201.

So I had another strike against me with some of the folks back home. I'd lost a few more friends, but I was used to that. Losing friends is part of this business—and business was real brisk by then.

Still, as hot as it got for a while, the labor issue meant nothing compared to race.

By 1960, with sit-ins and student protests sweeping the South, with groups like the Southern Christian Leadership Conference and the Student Nonviolent Coordinating Committee rallying blacks into organized and effective action, and with Martin Luther King, Jr., having established himself as the powerful focal point of a relentless crusade, more and more Southern whites no longer felt part of a "nation." It was "us against them," whites against blacks, the South against the North, the states against the federal government.

The NDEA, which had been hailed by Alabamians two years earlier for its *national* significance, was now attacked for its "nigger-loving" taint. That hateful phrase hadn't been directed specifically at me—yet—but it was being spoken a lot by 1960. And by then, there was more to hate in the South than just "niggers."

There was John F. Kennedy.

Kennedy was a Catholic.

That single sentence was enough to nail him in Alabama, and during the summer of 1960, as Kennedy was running for President, people down in these parts were spitting out that sentence as if it were the worst of curses. It was bad enough that he was a Yankee, bad enough that he looked like he might be more liberal than anyone down here could bear.

But worst of all, Kennedy was a *Catholic.*

The feelings down here about Catholics sprang from some of the same roots as the feelings about blacks. That is, they stemmed from a mixture of fear, competition and control.

The first great numbers of Catholics to arrive in Alabama were immigrants from southern and eastern Europe who came in the 1800s to work in the coal mines and in the steel mills around Birmingham. A lot of Alabama's native farm people were making that same move at the same time, seeking the same jobs. They were Protestants, of course—mostly Baptists and Methodists—and to them these strangers were a threat, intruders out to take their jobs and replace their religion.

It was largely those native-born steel workers who came to form the foundation of the state's largest Ku Klux Klan klavern—Birmingham's Robert E. Lee Klan No. 1. By the 1920s, Klan membership in the state had peaked at about eighty-five thousand, and its chief target then was not blacks or Jews; it was Catholics.

The whole country at that time was consumed with a concern about Catholics. There was talk everywhere about a conspiracy, about Roman Catholics taking control of this nation, and when a fellow named Alfred E. Smith made a run for the White House in 1928 as the Democratic nominee—as a *Catholic* Democratic nominee—those feelings were inflamed.

There were plenty of politicians eager to fan those flames. Tom Heflin was one. Invited by the Klan to speak at rallies across Alabama during the 1920s, Heflin warned everyone who would listen of a Catholic plot to bring the United States into war with Mexico. When he attacked Smith's candidacy in 1928 as a threat to everything the South stood for—namely, segregation, prohibition and Protestantism—the party punished old Cotton Tom severely, making him run as an independent in the next election. He lost his Senate seat in that 1930 race, but Tom Heflin continued to hold the hearts of many Alabamians who remained terrified of the Catholics.

The issue never disappeared in Alabama politics. If a man couldn't be beat on the issues, and if he couldn't be cornered on race, a few well-placed rumors that he was a Catholic would be enough to do him in.

Lister Hill faced those rumors throughout his career. He was always able to maneuver around them, which took some doing since Lister *was* a Catholic.

His mother's side of the family had converted from the Jewish faith to Catholicism in the nineteenth century, and Lister's mother had raised him as a Catholic. But by the time he decided to make politics his career, he knew he didn't stand a chance as a Catholic. So he made a point of being a visible Methodist, and during the forty-five years he held elected office in Alabama, he never publicly acknowledged either his Jewish ancestry or his Catholic upbringing. That took some fancy footwork, but Lister was able to do it.

Only after he died in 1984 on December 20—my birthday—

were Lister Hill's Catholic roots finally openly acknowledged. As he was laid to rest in a Montgomery cemetery, an Episcopal rector read passages from Scripture, assisted by a curate . . . and a Catholic priest.

As long as he was simply a Congressman and Senator from Massachusetts, Kennedy's Catholicism was no problem. His constituency up there was largely Catholic, just like him. But once he declared himself for the presidency in 1960, his faith became an issue, a big, big issue. There were plenty of people in the party who were dead set against Kennedy's nomination for just that reason, as well as for the fact that he was so young.

Sam Rayburn was one of the people who initially opposed Kennedy's candidacy. Rayburn didn't think the country was ready for a Catholic President, and he didn't think Kennedy was old enough to be taken seriously as presidential stock. The Speaker had a habit of referring to Kennedy as "the boy," but that stopped once it was clear Rayburn's own preference for the candidacy, Lyndon Johnson, was not going to get it.

Personally, I thought a lot of Kennedy. He was bright, he could think for himself and he had some ideas of real substance, which is better than what this country had had for a while. I never thought much of Dwight Eisenhower, never thought he had too many ideas that amounted to much. He was everybody's papa, but so what? All that means is you've got a large family.

The way I felt, this country was in a crisis that had nothing to do with Communism—although the Soviets were certainly something to be mightily concerned about. But there was a broader shifting going on as well among Americans at a grass-roots level, a turn in *direction,* in the purpose and attitude of this entire nation. You could *feel* it. It wasn't just race that was shaking everybody up. This country was restless, it was ready to take some big steps, to turn away from the past and step toward some sort of future. It was ready to *move.*

And I couldn't see too many men better prepared to point the way than John Kennedy.

So I leaped whole hog into his campaign. I made more than two hundred and fifty speeches for Kennedy during the late summer and early fall of 1960, throughout the South but mainly in Alabama. I worked his campaign hard, not just in my district but throughout the state, and I needed a lot of help. Some of the best of it came from a young college student who would soon become as close to my own cause as Mary Allen. His name was Julian Butler.

Julian was another of that seemingly endless line of University of Alabama student body presidents that wind up very involved with the direction of this state. I first met him in May 1960, when I was invited down to speak at the dinner at which Julian took the student body reins from the outgoing president, a young fellow named Max Pope. Max and my son, Carl, Jr., were fraternity brothers at the university.

What I saw in Julian Butler was a smart young fellow with a background that made for a good Democrat—*my* kind of Democrat. He grew up in Birmingham, but his parents were from the northern hill country. His father had worked his way through the university, the same way I had. And his father had gone into education, working as a school principal before taking a job with the federal government. Julian's parents were both Roosevelt New Deal Democrats, so their son came by that philosophy naturally.

But it was Kennedy who had become the man of the moment for Julian and his generation. In the same way that young liberal Democrats in my day had worshiped Franklin Roosevelt, I saw this new generation completely smitten by JFK. The Kennedy campaign recognized this same wave of the future across the country, and they seized on it by putting together a national Students for Kennedy organization, getting college student body presidents to organize campaigns on their campuses and in their communities. Although only a small percentage of college students could actually cast a ballot—the legal voting age then was twenty-one—they provided a valuable source of energy and manpower.

Julian became the Students for Kennedy man in Alabama—in fact, he was the only college student body president between Virginia and Texas who allowed his name to appear on the organization's letterhead. Anti-Kennedy sentiment was strong enough in the

Deep South to keep the rest of the campuses away from the Kennedy cause.

Julian's job—and he took to it with relish—was to set up some sort of Kennedy organization on every campus in the state. But beyond that, he also got carloads of these college boys and girls and carried them up to the rallies we were staging throughout my district that September and October. At Jasper, Haleyville, Fayette, Carrollton, Sulligent and every other county seat in these hills, Julian and his crowd would meet Mary Allen and me at a courthouse or school, and they'd work as our crew for the rally.

It was exciting, watching the enthusiasm of these young men and women. I felt like I was looking at some of the country's future. There was certainly some of Alabama's future in that crowd. One of the regulars in those car pools was a boy named Bill Baxley, who later became attorney general of Alabama and who ultimately tried and convicted the bomber of the Sixteenth Street Baptist Church in Birmingham, in which four black children were killed. Baxley established probably the greatest record anybody's ever had in this state for making the dreams of black people actually come true. It was Baxley who hired the first black assistant attorney general in the state, a fellow named Myron Thompson, who is now a United States district judge in Montgomery.

Bill Baxley made a lot of changes, but then there are some things that seem like they'll never change. Baxley eventually ran for governor of Alabama twice, in 1978 and in 1986, on a progressive platform and philosophy that could have been my own, and he lost both times because of a racial backlash against him.

The racist bandwagon is still rolling along in this state, and those who don't climb aboard continue to get crushed beneath its wheels.

But during that campaign of 1960 things seemed to really be changing. Few of even the most liberal of those college students was out and out for integration at the time. Most of them were attracted to Kennedy by his views on almost everything else. Still, as the campaign went along, Julian Butler later pointed out, these young folks couldn't help but be affected by Kennedy's views on everything—including race.

"For those of us in the South who believed in Kennedy," said Julian, "he made us *begin* to deal with the race issue. We were backed into a corner by the people who were against him, and in defending him we began to adopt his views on other subjects, including the subject of race."

But it was the issue of Catholicism that mattered most in Alabama that season, and that's the issue we tackled by giving our own little twist to a tactic the Kennedy crowd had used in earlier campaigns up in Massachusetts. They called them Coffees for Kennedy, and we gave them an Alabama flavor.

The idea was to have people themselves host a gathering in their home, in a more intimate, more comfortable setting than for a rally or a formal speech, and in a format more face-to-face than radio or television. In the living room of the hostess—and in almost every case these were hosted by women—a crowd of anywhere from a dozen to as many as a hundred gathered, all invited by the woman of the house. There'd be coffee and fixings, provided by the hostess, and we'd provide the show, with either me or one of our campaign staff giving a little talk and answering questions.

Something like this was made to order for the way I'd always liked to do things. The crowds were almost all women, at least at the beginning. Women weren't often as involved in this man's game of politics as they might like, so they jumped at a chance to get close to the process. And what they saw and felt they naturally took home to their husbands. The result—at least what we were hoping for—was a ripple effect. And I think that's what we got.

Pretty soon we had more scheduled than we could get done in a day. The thing just caught fire. I remember going into Blount County in late October, and by then the fellows had the fever as much as their wives. This one old boy had ninety-eight homes in his precinct, and he knocked on the door of every living last one of them, inviting them to his house to a Coffee for Kennedy. And almost all of them came.

I didn't drink the coffee, of course, but either I or one of my staff spoke to at least two hundred Coffees for Kennedy in that campaign. That was the first and only time anyone used that idea in this state—until I used the same setup six years later in my own race for governor.

With those coffees, we were basically preaching to the choir. The people who were invited were almost all good Democrats, the point being to spread the word and build a good base, an *active* base, among our own party. There was no real tension in the air, not like there was at the traditional rallies and speeches that I and my Kennedy campaigners spoke at that summer and fall. One of those campaigners was a close friend of mine from Jasper, a circuit judge named Roy Mayhall.

I had no more loyal personal friend and political ally than Judge Mayhall, and when I appointed him Kennedy campaign manager for my district, he faced the Baptist backlash against Kennedy head on. Which took some courage, since the judge was Baptist himself, both a deacon and Sunday school teacher for his church. The sermons he listened to that summer were as likely as not to contain unkind references to Kennedy and the Catholics.

The judge hit the campaign trail hard, saying that the preachers should confine their sermons to spiritual matters and leave politics to the politicians. He also included a short history lesson on the contributions Catholics have made to this country. As he went along, the judge saw more and more preachers filling those front rows, staring him down for his attacks against them and his defense of the Catholics. Mary Allen was traveling with the judge then, and one afternoon, on the way to a speech at Susan Moore High School in Blount County, Mary told him that if he weren't a little more lenient in his lectures there might not be a preacher left in the state to bury him when he died.

Well, the judge thought that was pretty amusing, and he repeated Mary's warning in that night's speech at Susan Moore. As usual, there was a row of preachers up front, and one in particular got increasingly agitated as the judge talked on.

When Mayhall got to Mary's warning, this old fellow could contain himself no longer. He leaped up and hollered out, "By God, I'll be *glad* to bury you!"

Through mid-September, there was great fear in the Kennedy camp that this Catholic issue might indeed bury their candidate. Something had to be done, but what Kennedy himself proposed sounded like suicide to a lot of his advisers. He wanted to walk right into the teeth of the enemy and tackle the issue in Texas, at a speech he was scheduled to make to an association of ministers in Houston.

His people warned him against it, but Kennedy's instincts were that it was time to make his move, and this was the place to make it. As was more often the case with Kennedy than not, his instincts were right. The speech, which was telecast the night of September 12, contained just about the most complete and eloquent summary of religion and its relationship to politics ever made in this country:

"While this year it may be a Catholic against whom the finger of suspicion is pointed, in other years it has been, and may someday be again, a Jew, or a Quaker, or a Unitarian, or a Baptist. It was Virginia's harassment of Baptist preachers, for example, that helped lead to Jefferson's statute of religious freedom. Today I may be the victim, but tomorrow it may be you, until the whole fabric of our harmonious society is ripped at a time of great national peril.

". . . I believe in an America where religious intolerance will someday end, where all men and all churches are treated as equal, where every man has the same right to attend or not attend the church of his choice, where there is no Catholic vote, no anti-Catholic vote, no bloc voting of any kind, and where Catholics, Protestants and Jews, at both the lay and pastoral level, will refrain from those attitudes of disdain and division which have so often marred their works in the past, and promote instead the American ideal of brotherhood.

". . . This is the kind of America I believe in, and this is the kind I fought for in the South Pacific, and the kind my brother died for in Europe. No one suggested then that we might have a 'divided loyalty,' that we did 'not believe in liberty' or that we belonged to a disloyal group that threatened the 'freedoms for which our forefathers died.'

". . . If I should lose on the real issues, I shall return to my
seat in the Senate, satisfied that I had tried my best and was fairly
judged. But if this election is decided on the basis that forty million
Americans lost their chance of being President on the day they were
baptized, then it is the whole nation that will be the loser, in the eyes
of Catholics and non-Catholics around the world, in the eyes of
history, and in the eyes of our own people."

As much as any other single factor, that speech in Houston
turned the tide for Kennedy. By October we felt he was going to
win, and we thought we had a pretty good chance of carrying Alabama for him.

It was late that month that I got an urgent call from Sam Rayburn. He said, "I need to see you," and told me to meet him at a
little town in Tennessee called Pulaski, in an old law office, at ten
o'clock the next morning.

I got there, and Rayburn led me back into the stacks of this
firm's large library. The books on those shelves went back to the
Revolution. They'd been practicing law there a long time.

Rayburn was real secretive, and very intense. He put his hand
on my shirt, grabbed my collar and pulled me close to him.

"We're in a hurry now," he said. "John F. Kennedy's going to
be elected President."

I said, "I think so."

He said, "Yeah, yeah, he's going to make it. Not big, it'll be a
squeeze, but he's going to make it. And he has a right to have his
program put before the country, before the people."

He said, "We'll be the majority party after this election, and
we'll have the President. If we don't have the strength to give his
program a hearing, it would be a disaster."

I said, "I understand that."

Then he told me he was going to put three new members on
the House Rules Committee. There hadn't been a word in the papers about this. No one knew a thing. But Rayburn was ready, and
he told me he wanted one of those three new members to be me.

"This is going to be tough," he said. "It's going to be the
toughest thing you've ever been through."

Then he looked me hard in the eye.

"Will you serve?" he asked me.

I saw the dilemma, that this was all about breaking the choke hold Howard Smith held on that committee, and that I'd be the point man for breaking that grip. I knew the issue of race would somehow or other become central to all this, no matter what else was involved. But the way I saw it was we had to do something to move this country forward. I believed it could happen, but to give it a chance—to give not just John Kennedy but this *country* a chance —someone had to do what Sam Rayburn was asking me to do.

"Yes," I told him. "I'll serve."

Rayburn was right. That 1960 presidential election *was* a squeeze, but Kennedy won. And he carried Alabama, despite never setting foot in the state during that campaign.

It was Lyndon Johnson who made the ticket's big campaign visit to Alabama, working his way through the state on a train carrying Lady Bird, Alabama Governor John Patterson and the state's entire Congressional delegation along with him. Stopping and greeting crowds along the way, we got to Birmingham that evening, where the whole shebang was taken to the top of Red Mountain, for an appearance in the mountaintop studios of a local television station.

Now protection for politicians in those days was a different matter from what it soon became with the violence of the 1960s. There was no such thing as a Secret Service escort for a mere vice-presidential candidate, so it was up to us to provide security. You rounded up what you could, and in this case what we had was Mary Allen and Julian Butler.

I'd sent the two of them up ahead to the station with orders to allow no one in the building. They took those orders in earnest. When a man came banging at the front door, hollering that he was a reporter who needed to call his office, Mary and Julian wouldn't let him in. The man insisted, saying he had to call Washington, that it was urgent. They finally relented, still very suspicious, and they watched the man's every move as Joseph Alsop, one of the top political correspondents in the country, put through a collect call to the Washington *Post* and filed his story.

Not long after Alsop was done, there was a commotion at a back door. Mary and Julian rushed back, saw the door beginning to open, and put their shoulders against it, holding their own until it finally began to give way. Something strong was pushing on the other side. When Julian peeked around the corner, he saw the burly figure of Lyndon Johnson leaning against the thing with all his might, as Lady Bird and the entire Alabama delegation, including me, looked on.

Mary and Julian let the door go—and hid behind it, praying no one would see them as the group poured past.

I know my Seventh District made a big difference in that election, going more heavily for Kennedy than any other in the state. And Kennedy knew it too. He won only five of Alabama's eleven electoral votes—the Dixiecrats had collared the other six back in May and cast them in November for Harry F. Byrd—but Kennedy knew who his friends were down here, and he knew I was among the best.

So he didn't hesitate to show his appreciation when I sent his inauguration committee a list of every person in my district who had hosted a coffee—folks like Henry Box, who ran a general store at a little place called Locust Fork. The day before Kennedy's inauguration, more than a hundred people from those north Alabama hills climbed on trains and buses headed to Washington, each of them with an inauguration invitation in hand. Some of them had never made a trip out of the state in their lives. Some of them had hardly been out of their respective counties. Henry Box had never been to Washington, and there was twenty inches of snow on the ground when he got there, but he said he wouldn't have missed it for the world.

Neither would the kids from Carbon Hill. The tradition at every presidential inaugural parade is that each state sends a marching band to represent it. Typically the bands come from colleges or large high schools. But when I let President Kennedy know that these boys and girls from Carbon Hill were largely the sons and daughters of coal miners, and that it was the votes of those miners and their wives that had helped him over the hump down here, his people made sure that the band from little Carbon Hill High School was at the front of the line that cold January afternoon, marching in the name of the state of Alabama.

"It's a perilous business for a nation to thrust by force great social changes upon a part of it determined to resist."

Howard W. Smith, chairman of the
House Rules Committee, 1956

TEN

∞

WINNER TAKE ALL

By the time the Carbon Hill marching band made its way down snowy Pennsylvania Avenue on January 20, 1961, I was well into the struggle Sam Rayburn had prepared me for and Dick Bolling had warned me about the day that year's session of Congress convened.

Bolling, who by then had moved to the heart of Rayburn's inner circle and who was a key member of the House Rules Committee, took me aside that first day of Congress and echoed Rayburn's concern with a question I'll never forget.

"Can you *fry* for thirty days?" he asked me.

That turned out to be almost exactly how long it took to win the most intense political battle I was ever involved in during my career on Capitol Hill—the "packing" of the Rules Committee.

This was one political poker game in which the pot was about as big as it gets. Not only were the players risking their own reputations and careers, but the course of the entire country was at stake as well.

There was Sam Rayburn, in the twilight of his reign as Speaker of the House and near the end of his life, laying his power and influence on the line in a winner-take-all showdown with Howard Smith.

There was Smith, never more secure in his own strength, surrounded by his loyal sons of the South, tapping his cigar with disdain and sneering at anyone who might question his authority.

There were the young Kennedys, John and Bobby, poised to launch a barrage of legislative reforms that would sweep America into their vision of a "New Frontier," but knowing they couldn't make a move until this fight was finished.

Then there was me, Rayburn's ace in the hole. If this hand played out as planned, I would wind up as the card the Kennedys were counting on to win.

If they did win, I would wind up on the most powerful committee in Congress. I would be in a position far beyond what I had aimed at when I first came to Washington. I would have the opportunity to do even more than I ever dreamed for the people in this country who needed a helping hand. I would have reached the apex of my Congressional career.

And I would have more hell to pay back home.

This battle had actually been brewing since 1958. That's when a collection of liberal party members called the Democratic Study Group confronted Sam Rayburn and laid down the gauntlet. They'd had just about all they could stomach of Howard Smith. For years he had bottled up every piece of housing, labor, education and civil rights legislation that had come his way, storing it on the shelf and settling back with one of his long black stogies.

Now this team of 125 House liberals, which included me, was telling Rayburn they were ready to roll up their sleeves and move for reform—a drastic process with some possibly high political costs. What the Study Group had in mind was restoring a measure called the "twenty-one-day rule," which Rayburn had enjoyed for two years during the Truman administration. The rule allowed the chairman of any standing committee to bypass the Rules Committee and bring a bill directly to the floor if the committee failed to act on it within twenty-one days. That would keep a man like Howard Smith from sitting on a piece of legislation until he smothered it, but passing that rule would be a severe test of the liberals' strength in general and of Rayburn's in particular. Only the Speaker's personal promise that he would make sure things changed in the coming Congress kept the DSG from revolting.

But Rayburn couldn't keep that promise. No sooner did he give it than his closest ally on the Republican side, Representative Joe Martin of Massachusetts, was replaced in the vote for House minority leader by a fellow named Charles Halleck of Indiana. While Martin had been someone Rayburn could work with—a personal as well as a political friend he could count on in the clutch—Halleck was much more partisan, one of the hardest, meanest political street fighters in the business and a man who made no secret of his general allegiance to the conservative line and of his particular alliance with Howard Smith.

When Halleck replaced Martin, Rayburn lost his trump card, and Smith spent the next two years using a steady string of 6-to-6 stalemate votes on his Rules Committee to put almost every piece of important liberal legislation into a coma. He and another Democrat, William Colmer of Mississippi, sided with the committee's four Republicans to form a conservative coalition with absolute control on almost every issue. Rayburn's failure to beat the Landrum-Griffin bill with my own "moderate" labor-reform bill was an example of the gap that had grown between the Speaker and this coalition.

By late 1960 things had come to a head. At that year's national Democratic convention in Los Angeles, in which John F. Kennedy was nominated for President, the party's platform included a specific commitment to do something about the Rules Committee. The issue became part of the presidential race when Kennedy singled out the Rules Committee coalition as the cause of several legislative defeats, while Richard Nixon, the Republican nominee, pledged to keep the committee as it was.

Even as Kennedy was campaigning for President, Rayburn and

Bolling, under pressure both from House liberals and from the Kennedy camp, were positioning themselves for the fight to come. And if there's one fellow you want on your side in a fight like that, it's someone like Dick Bolling. He never got the lion's share of publicity. That's not how he operated. He didn't care about headlines; in fact, he avoided them. What he cared about was results, and he knew how to get them.

After the smoke eventually cleared from this particular fight, there were some reporters smart enough to realize Bolling's central role in the whole thing and how he played it. One of those reporters, in a story for *Harper's* magazine, described Bolling as "a kind of unsung field commander in a great war between the generalissimos, Mr. Sam and old 'Judge' Howard Smith of Virginia," and praised the Congressman from Missouri as "an occupational, professional anticipator of difficulties; a smoother-out of ruffled feelings; an estimator of the human weaknesses and strengths of other Democrats; a worker of small and sometimes large miracles."

If anyone ever had a mind to sum up my own political career, those are the kind of words I'd hope they'd use. Dick Bolling earned them long before 1960, but he showed how true they were as he worked tirelessly throughout that fall and winter, moving literally from coast to coast, collecting information, opinions and strategy.

In October, Bolling spent several days in Los Angeles, discussing the Rules situation with Bobby Kennedy, who was very protective of his brother and very concerned about this Rules Committee roadblock. Then Bolling came back to Washington, where three liberal Democrats—Chet Holifield of California, John Blatnik of Minnesota and Frank Thompson—were pulling our side of the House together even as Smith and Halleck were shoring up Southerners and Republicans.

There was no question the Rules Committee would be attacked. But the decision on how to attack it was still up in the air. There were basically two choices. One was for our own Democratic leadership to "purge" Bill Colmer, to vote him off the committee and replace him with a man who would give the liberals a 7-to-5 edge on committee votes. Colmer had jumped parties and supported Richard Nixon in the November presidential election, so there was the basis for a purge.

The trouble with purging Colmer was that the racists, along with everyone else aligned against us, could cry foul, pointing out that Adam Clayton Powell, a *black* man, had not been purged after he backed Eisenhower in '56, so how could a white man be booted out for the same offense? Never mind that the Dixiecrats went unpunished for their sins in 1948.

The other choice, rather than replace Colmer, was to expand the size of the Rules Committee from twelve to fifteen members, adding two Democrats and one Republican. That would put an end to those 6-to-6 deadlocks, but it would be a riskier, and more costly, course than a purge. While a purge was strictly a party matter, settled among the Democrats themselves, an expansion of the Rules Committee would require a vote among the entire membership. The whole House would be pulled into the fray, and the fallout from that sort of a fight can last long after the punches are thrown.

We knew Smith would scrap tooth and nail against expansion, but we also knew there was precedent for that plan. In 1933, as part of their strategy to pave the way for Franklin Roosevelt's first-term reforms, House Democrats were able to expand the Rules Committee to speed up the "crash program" their new President had in mind. Their ability to expand that committee opened the doors to what became the New Deal. The new Rules Committee member added at that time was none other than Judge Howard Smith.

Funny how what goes around always seems to come around sooner or later. When Dick Bolling traveled down to Palm Springs, Florida, near the end of 1960, it was to attend a gathering of Democratic leaders much like a conference Franklin Roosevelt had called in Warm Springs, Georgia, twenty-eight years earlier. In both cases, a President-elect with big plans in mind needed to map out strategy on how to put those plans into effect. The single most important strategy discussed in Palm Springs was how to handle the Rules Committee.

John and Bobby Kennedy were there, of course, as were Vice-President-elect Lyndon Johnson and Mike Mansfield, who had replaced Johnson as the Senate's majority leader.

Sam Rayburn was there, too, along with Bolling. The decision hadn't yet been made whether to "pack" or "purge" the Rules Committee, but Kennedy made it clear this issue was a priority. Without some sort of change, he told Rayburn, his whole program would be "emasculated."

Whenever a crisis closed in on Sam Rayburn, once he had listened to everyone around him and gathered all the information he could, he had a habit of pulling into himself, taking his own counsel and tipping his hand to no one.

That's the position he was in by then. He assured Kennedy he would settle this thing, he asked the President to "stay out of the fight," and he headed back to Washington, where the Eighty-seventh Congress was about to convene and the battle was set to begin.

There was never a thought in Howard Smith's mind that he wouldn't win this thing. He was cocky, dripping with confidence as he held court for reporters in the days before that Congress began, flicking the ashes off his cigar and waving away questions about his heavy-handed way of doing things.

"My people didn't send me to Congress to be a traffic cop," he crowed.

When Rayburn returned to the Capitol on the last day of 1960, he was met by Democratic leaders pushing for a purge. The Democratic Study Group, led by John Blatnik, reminded Rayburn of his failure to keep his promise in the last Congress. The DSG favored a purge. So did Lyndon Johnson, who suggested me as a replacement for Colmer.

But Rayburn didn't commit. Instead, he called Howard Smith to his office on New Year's Day and offered the Judge a choice: purge Colmer or allow three new members to be added to the committee. Smith curtly refused both choices and left.

The next day Rayburn pushed the ante by telling the press he was for purging Colmer. Smith came back with an offer: if Rayburn let things alone, Smith promised to allow five key Kennedy bills go to the floor. But Rayburn wasn't about to make a deal like that. The point of this whole fight was to establish that one man did not have the right to interfere with the ability of Congress as a whole to make and pass the laws of this land. There are plenty of compromises to be made in Congress, but there are also points where a stand has to be taken. For Sam Rayburn, this was one of those points.

When the Speaker called the Eighty-seventh Congress to order on January 3, he was three days shy of his seventy-ninth birthday. You could see the fatigue on his face. On the surface he seemed a different man from the one who had greeted me when I'd first come to Washington a dozen years before. He seemed a little more weary, a little slower on the draw. No one knew it, but Sam Rayburn had cancer pretty bad by then, bad enough that it would kill him before the year was out.

But as the 1961 session began, the Speaker was steeled for the fight. After sitting silent for four days, he decided against purging Colmer and instead committed to enlarge the committee, scheduling January 26 as the date for the House vote.

My name had already come out in the newspapers as Rayburn's personal choice, should a purge occur. For that alone, I had received letters from back home calling me "a traitor" and warning me not to commit "political suicide."

"The next year will probably be trying for you both in Washington and here at home since your district will no doubt be involved in reapportionment and you may have to run against one of the other congressmen," wrote a doctor in Jasper, in a pretty pitiful attempt at being subtle.

"I'm not telling you how to vote," he wrote, "but as a friend I'm letting you know how many of us feel."

When Rayburn committed to "packing" the committee, I got even more attention from the newspapermen speculating on who would fill the new seats. And I got even more hate mail from home. I'd been used to getting those sorts of letters from elsewhere in the state, and I'd always been secure that my own district was behind me. I'd gotten used to running unopposed in recent years, including in 1960. But now I was seeing a sharp increase in unhappy mail from people in my own district. Something was happening down there, and it wasn't good.

Still, I wasn't about to turn against my party, my principles and my word because of rumblings back home. I had no doubt I could take care of things back there once I was done with the job at hand —or rather, once Rayburn and the rest of the Democratic leadership were done with the job. I was in the peculiar position of having to stay away from the center of the fight, since my position both as a Southerner and as a prime candidate for one of those seats demanded discretion and a little bit of distance.

It was the Southern Democrats—99 of them—and the moderate Republicans who held the key to this thing. Rayburn knew he had 164 liberal Democrats he could count on. If he could get half the Southerners to side with him—a tough job in itself—he would still need a good number of Republicans—maybe two dozen—to vote for enlargement.

When Charlie Halleck started playing rough, announcing that he would not make committee assignments for Republicans until *after* the Rules Committee vote, the vises began getting tighter. As usual, lobbyists were swarming all over Capitol Hill, trying their best to push and prod things their way. In Congress, the pressure is always on to some extent, but this was about the most intense I'd ever seen. The Washington *Post* reported that one Congressman had already changed his decision four times. Most of the 99 Southerners had made this a civil rights fight, which left fewer on Rayburn's side than he had hoped for.

On January 25, Smith's Rules Committee voted the question out for House consideration the next day. Then Rayburn dropped a bombshell, surprising his own supporters and outraging the opposition by announcing that he was delaying the vote until January 31.

It wasn't like Sam Rayburn to waver, but that just shows how tough a struggle this one had become. His cancer couldn't have helped any, but that's the wisdom of hindsight speaking. We didn't know at the time how sick Sam was.

When the delay was announced, Charlie Halleck screamed bloody murder. He was hungry for the kill, and he was real upset at having to wait. But old Judge Smith, he was enjoying it all. He hadn't had many chances to see Sam Rayburn squirm, so he was soaking this for all it was worth. When the reporters came to ask him what he thought about the delay, the judge just shrugged.

"They must be afraid they haven't the votes," he said.
And he was right.

Up to this point, the President and his people had stayed on the sideline, just as Sam Rayburn had asked them to. It wasn't easy for them to sit and watch, especially when things started looking like they were going the other way.

Three days after his inauguration, President Kennedy called Dick Bolling to talk specifically about how things looked. Bolling was honest, saying it was going to be extremely tight, whichever way it went. Within a day, Bobby Kennedy called Bolling, and he was not happy. He said his brother had been convinced by Rayburn and Bolling to do things their way and now the President was set up for an embarrassing defeat in the first Congressional test of his term. Bobby Kennedy was tough, no doubt about it. John Kennedy couldn't have found a fiercer friend than his brother.

With five more days to rally, after postponing the vote, Rayburn relented and called in the Kennedys.

But they had to be careful about this. The issue of interference from the executive branch is always a sticky one. And the Kennedy forces carried it off just right, coming in carefully, quietly combing the ranks of the House, probing to find out just where each member stood. Everyone from Bobby Kennedy to White House aides, from Lyndon Johnson to a variety of influential Democrats on the Senate side, sought out House members in their offices. The pressure was so strong that some members actually hid out. A rumor even began that the House leadership had sent cases of whiskey to several Deep South Democrats, hoping they might get too drunk to show up for the vote. I can't say whether this was true or not, but I wouldn't have been surprised.

Finally the President himself made his move. Speaking at a press conference, he carefully acknowledged that this was an issue for House members to decide among themselves, but he went on to say that, strictly as an "interested citizen," he hoped no small group would be allowed to stand in the way of the will of the American people.

Apparently there were some members who heard the President's message. When Sam Rayburn walked into the House chamber at noon on January 31, the entire membership rose and applauded, both with respect for the fight the Speaker had waged and with relief that this awful battle was finally about to be decided.

The debate, as defined by the Rules Committee, was limited to one hour. When Rayburn himself left the Speaker's chair to make a rare speech from the floor, it was clear how much this meant to him. He referred to the fact that Howard Smith had been put on the Rules Committee by the very procedure he was now protesting, and Rayburn went on to share with the nation the same message he had given me back in that law library in Pulaski: that America had elected this President as well as these Congressmen, and that the President's program deserved a hearing from Congress as a whole, not just from a select group of men on a single committee.

Then the vote began, with everyone sweating out the twenty-five minutes it took to call the roll. People under this sort of pressure can waver even at the last second. As Rayburn put it more than once, there are some situations that make it hard for a man to "stay hitched."

When the count was completed, the vote stood 217 for enlargement to 212 against. They don't come much closer than that. We'd beaten Howard Smith, but I'll have to say he took it pretty well. No sooner was the vote finished than he was gone to the cloakroom, where someone tracked him down and asked him how he felt.

"Well," said the judge, "we done our damnedest."

We'd done our damnedest too. We'd thrown everything we had at Smith, and still we won by only a microscopic margin. Although the newspapers and more than a few House Democrats were rejoicing after the victory, assuming the doors were now open for the President's New Frontier program to just roll right on through, there were those who knew better. Kennedy himself, noting the slim margin by which we'd won and realizing the Republicans and that bloc of Southern Democrats would remain tough to deal with, was cautious.

"With Rayburn's own reputation at stake," said the President, "with all the pressures and appeals a new President could make, we won by five votes. That shows what we're up against."

As for me personally, I was up against the spite of a man who was less magnanimous in private than in public. Howard Smith wanted no part of the three new members on his committee—Democrat B. F. Sisk of California and Republican William Avery of Kansas were the other two—but he especially wanted no part of me. I'd been a thorn in Smith's side for a long time. Our politics were completely different, and since we were both from the South, he considered my deviant behavior nothing short of treason. He knew that among the three newcomers on his committee—and it was still *his* committee—I was the one the Kennedy administration was counting on to bend things their way. The judge was not about to take that sitting down. In fact, the first flap we had was over the subject of sitting down.

It was a silly incident, just the sort that makes great headlines for the newspapers and political hay for the man who plays it right.

The Rules Committee meeting room consisted of a long conference table surrounded by soft leather swivel chairs. When I and the two other new committee members joined the group, we had three hard straight-back chairs waiting for us. After two weeks, a reporter noticed the setup and needled the judge about it, asking him what was going on.

"Those chairs are good enough for them," he sneered. "They'll be around for only this session anyway."

Well, when that quote hit the newspapers, there was an explosion of outrage, especially from the people in my district back home. The next thing I knew, they had literally passed a hat down there, collecting eighteen hundred dollars, much of it in quarters and dimes from schoolchildren, bought me a chair—a nice, brown leather model—and shipped it up to Washington.

When that chair arrived, reporters came out of the woodwork to take photographs and chuckle at the judge. Smith was livid, just about beside himself. He ordered the piece of furniture taken away and locked in his private office—which prompted a photo of me in my chair in *Time* magazine, along with even more unwanted headlines in newspapers across the country. One of those headlines read "Salt in the Wounds for Old Judge Smith." Beneath it was a reporter's account of the judge's anger:

> "I'm not," he said, "going to have a picture made of any chair some damn fool sent up here."
>
> We told him the chair was sent by children, among others.
>
> The lawmaker studied his long unlit cigar and his jaw muscle worked.
>
> "I don't," he said, finally, "care who blankety-blank it was."
>
> He didn't exactly say "blankety-blank."

A day later, three Congressional-issue swivel chairs arrived at the Rules Committee meeting room.

As for the chair my constituents sent me, it became the centerpiece of my own office, a reminder that there were still some folks back home who believed in me.

But things were getting pretty turbulent by that time. The Rules Committee remained a rocky place for the Kennedy agenda, even after the shake-up. The landslide of liberal legislation a lot of people had predicted never came about. The close vote on the expansion of the committee showed that Howard Smith wasn't the only member of the House standing against the Kennedy program. And on some particular pieces of legislation, even the President's friends stood against him.

That's what happened with Tip O'Neill not long after I joined the committee. Tip had come to Congress from Massachusetts in 1952, and he'd been on the Rules Committee six years when I came on in 1961. He was normally part of the liberal bloc allied against Smith, but when the President tried to extend the National Defense Education Act that spring, Tip and another liberal committee member, Jim Delaney of New York, voted *against* it, on the basis that it did not include parochial schools in its benefits. The act eventually wound up getting extended, but that particular version of the bill

was killed in an ironically twisted fashion: it was beaten by two
Catholic Congressmen voting against a Catholic President.

But it was back home that things were getting more twisted
than I'd ever dreamed. While I'd been pitching all these battles up
in Washington, the storm clouds had been building thicker and
thicker. Race had become just about everything, and there was no
getting out of its way. Sam Rayburn had chosen me for the Rules
Committee precisely to avoid that issue. It was understood that
while I would vote for just about every liberal reform Kennedy had
in mind, when it came to specific civil rights legislation, I would side
with Smith and his crowd. That was understood, but it did little to
appease the judge. And it was totally ignored by the segregationist
crowds back in Alabama. An editorial written that spring in the
Alabama Journal was typical of the race-focused reaction to my place
on the Rules Committee:

> The effect of the victory is this: Stuffing the committee with
> three more members is acknowledged as a blow to the South. It
> is thought to mean more and stricter civil rights laws. It is
> supposed to permit a great expansion of spending which may
> bring in a panic through inflation of our money. It was a
> wicked bill now being nationally condemned.
>
> Alabama has special reason to resent this blow against the
> South, this liberalism run wild and turned loose to foist all sorts
> of alien schemes upon the nation. It is a pro-Negro plan, a
> strictly political thing to carry out some of the wild schemes put
> into the Democratic national platform at the Los Angeles con-
> vention.
>
> Four Alabama members of Congress voted for this iniqui-
> tous scheme. . . . It is therefore fair to say that four Alabama
> representatives are responsible for the victory of this anti-
> South, anti-white man, anti-business man, anti-conservative
> monstrosity.
>
> One of Alabama's four, Elliott of Jasper, was rewarded
> with one of the stuffed committee memberships. It is not stated
> what could have induced the other three to vote so harshly to
> betray their own people. But they must come home and answer

for it. Rains of Gadsden, Roberts of Anniston and Jones of Scottsboro, along with Elliott, must face their own people next year and explain why they deserted their own people in an hour of crisis.

They made their bed and there is probability that they will have to come home and lie in it from now on.

I'd taken the biggest step of my career in Congress that year, but it was pretty clear the other shoe was about to fall.

When it did, it would be worn by a fellow I hadn't paid much attention to till then—a man named George Wallace.

At the least, he is a simple primitive natural phenomenon, like weeds or heat-lightning. He is a mixture of innocence and malevolence, humor and horror. . . . he represents the dark side of the moon of the American democracy. . . . he is a consummate political and cultural articulation of the South, where life is simply more glandular than it is in the rest of the nation.

From Wallace, by Marshall Frady

ELEVEN

THE SWELLING STORM

I reckon America got its first good look at George Wallace in 1963, that hot, hateful year that ended with the murder of John Kennedy.

That was the year Birmingham Police Commissioner Bull Connor turned his police dogs and fire hoses on the blacks in that city's streets. That was the year four children's lives ended in the bombing of Birmingham's Sixteenth Street Baptist Church. It was in June of that year that NAACP leader Medgar Evers was shot to death outside his home in Jackson, Mississippi. And it was only twelve hours before Evers' death that the new governor of Alabama took on the Kennedy brothers themselves by keeping his campaign pledge to block the path of any black student who tried to enroll at the University of Alabama.

It was his "stand in the schoolhouse door" that finally got George Wallace the spotlight he'd been seeking all his life—the *national* spotlight. It's a safe bet most Americans had never seen a man like this before, a state governor sticking his chin out at Washington and daring the President's men to take a swing. People from beyond Alabama probably couldn't understand how a man could stand in the middle of all that hatred and heat, with his state burning up around him, with the force of the federal government staring him in the face, and not only stare right back but look like he was actually *enjoying* himself.

And he *was* enjoying himself. Lord, he was just eating it up. That's one thing all of us down here knew about George Wallace. Those who loved him, those who hated him, those who respected him, those who ridiculed him—everyone in Alabama knew there was nothing Wallace loved better than a good fight. Hell, he'd been throwing punches all his life, both literally and politically. I knew how much George Wallace loved to scrap, and I knew he was one of those fellows that likes it even better when the gloves come off.

There are plenty of those kinds of people around, not just in politics but everywhere. You're as likely to find them in business boardrooms as in bars. They're street fighters, fellows who will do anything it takes to win. They're clever, and they're dangerous. They'll reach for whatever weapon they can find, and if there's no weapon within reach, they'll just grab whatever they can get their hands on and turn it into one.

That's the way George Wallace was. With him, everything was a fight. You were either on his side or against him, and if you were against him, he was going to keep coming at you with everything he had—and you never knew what it might be—until he knocked you down. If you were ready to cry "Uncle," he'd let you back up to join his side. If not, then he'd do all he could to put you down to stay.

I knew George fought that way. I'd watched him punch his way through state politics in the 1950s, making a name for himself by staging showdowns designed to build his reputation and push himself up a notch. I knew he didn't stand for anything that was constant, that he was as likely to be for something as against it, depending on which way the wind was blowing, depending on what would get him the most votes. As the saying goes in these parts, he'd become anybody's dog that would hunt with him. Votes were just about all George Wallace cared about, and when he latched onto the racist whirlwind of the late fifties, well, he had himself just about all the votes he could imagine.

The thing I never imagined was that that whirlwind would take him as far as it did—and that it would eventually blow me away in the process.

Wallace-watching was a pastime in this state for twenty years before the national press joined the game in the 1960s. There were plenty of people who had been looking at George a lot more closely than I was during his rise to power. If you sift through what some of those people have to say, you can find some pretty good observations about what makes George Wallace tick.

A fellow named Wayne Greenhaw wrote a book, published in 1976, titled *Watch Out for George Wallace,* in which he quoted a former Wallace associate talking about the then governor:

> "He has always played the game ruthlessly. He has played it without regard to principle or philosophy. He's a racist, that's the one thing you know about him; but after that he might be liberal one day and conservative the next, according to the shifting tides of public opinion. George Wallace has no political principles. He has no political philosophy. He believes in helping George Wallace. Every move that he makes is motivated with self-interest in mind. Of that you can be sure."

On the more poetic side is a fellow named Marshall Frady, whose book *Wallace* came out the same year as Greenhaw's. There's a passage in there that comes as close as any I've seen to getting at the core of George Wallace's fearsome magnetism:

> In a sense, Wallace is common to us all. That, finally, is his darkest portent. There is something primordially exciting and enthralling about him, and there still seems to be just enough of the wolf pack in most of us to be stirred by it and to answer to it. As long as we are creatures hung halfway between the cave

and the stars, figures like Wallace can be said to pose the great
dark original threat.

George Wallace didn't seem like much of a threat when I first
met him, outside that dining hall on the University of Alabama
campus back in 1941. In fact, the eager student I saw that night
seemed, on the face of it, a lot like me. It's funny that two fellows
who looked to have so much in common could be as completely
different as George Wallace and me. But I thank God we were.

There's a lot to be learned by looking at the differences between Wallace and me. I don't think anyone can say they truly
understand George Wallace, but by looking at how he worked his
way up the ladder—a ladder a lot like the one I climbed—some
things come clear about how he wound up with as much power as
he did and about what he did with that power once he had it.

Like me, Wallace came from the country, down in the wire-
grass region of southeast Alabama, with its flat peanut fields and
shady pecan trees. Most of the folks down there have traditionally
been as far from the Black Belt seats of power as their hill country
counterparts up north. Most of them are just as poor and just as
proud as the people I grew up with.

But while my kinship with the common man came from my
roots and my rearing, George Wallace created that kinship by exag-
gerating the hard times he'd come through. Some folks call it "low-
rating" your past. George always encouraged the impression that he
was sprung from rock-hard poverty, but the fact is his was one of
the more well-off families in the little town of Clio, down in Barbour
County. His grandfather was the town's leading doctor, and while
Wallace's own father had a hard time with this business or that, the
grandfather was always there to bail them out.

Wallace got his political start sooner than I did, when he was
hired during high school as a page in the state Senate. He was savvy
even then, making political connections he'd use later in life. One of
the legislators Wallace met at that time was a man named Eugene
Connor—"Bull," his friends called him. Years later Connor would
chuckle about the "lil feller in short pants" who'd caught his eye
way back then.

By that time, Wallace was already pretty good with his hands. He was fighting all over the state in boxing tournaments and wound up winning two Alabama Golden Gloves titles in the bantamweight division. But he was a boy who'd just as soon box outside the ring as in it. His brother Gerald told a reporter one time how it was, growing up with George. "We fought all the time, but he'd always whup me," said Gerald. "He was just mean as hell. I got a six-inch scar today on my right leg where he spiked me once slidin' into second base. He did it on purpose, too. We had a fight right there. I threw down my glove and we went to it, but he got the best of me. He was a helluva fighter."

And not just with his little brother. Folks in Clio remember young George Wallace bringing kids over to his house to play, then putting on the gloves and beating the tar out of them. "George wasn't brutal about it," said one neighbor. "He just wanted somebody to practice on."

In the fall of 1937, the year after I left the University of Alabama, George Wallace arrived on campus much the way I had—carrying nothing but a cardboard suitcase. Like me, he worked a lot of jobs to pay his way; like me, he leaped right into campus politics; and, like me, he went after the non-Greek vote, beating the fraternity political machine to win his freshman class presidency.

But the way Wallace went after votes even then was just about as different as it could be from my way. I was a persistent campaigner, no doubt about it, but I was never one for pushing people. I always believed in patience, in coaxing and convincing people with solid ideas that made sense. I always had faith people would respond to sense. George, on the other hand, relied more on emotion, on the sheer force of his presence and his personality. He campaigned the way he boxed—aggressively, feverishly. He overwhelmed people. And he was transparently ambitious even back when he was at the university.

"Actually, nobody took him too seriously at first," one of his college classmates once said. "He always gave the impression of injecting himself into every possible crowd, like he was never there for the main purpose, but for purposes of his own. He seemed to be a misfit who was always scrambling, scratching, trying to find a place. He wanted to run for everything."

Another classmate said Wallace's reasons for standing against the fraternities had more to do with power than with principles: "Anything he was in he had to run, or he wasn't interested in belonging to it."

"We all knew of his ambition to be governor," said one schoolmate. "Everybody knew he was planning to be governor, even back then."

That's something to understand about Alabama politics—that there are two almost entirely separate political tracks in this state. One leads to the governorship, the other to Congress. More often than not, those paths don't cross. The road to Congress rarely runs through Montgomery, and vice versa. Basically, a man who's on the federal track stays there. Same with the state track.

That's another point where George Wallace and I diverged. My eyes were never on anything but getting to Washington. Wallace's, on the other hand, were always on Montgomery—until, eventually, they veered toward the White House.

We both enlisted in the service once the war began, but again there was a difference. While I went on to become an officer, Wallace, although he was a college graduate, made a point of remaining an enlisted man in the Army Air Corps. One of his friends from that time later put the reason in pretty simple—and strategic—terms: "George didn't want to be no officer. He had it figured out that when he got back to the county, there would be a heap more enlisted men voting than officers."

Everything George Wallace did was geared to getting votes. He'd do and *be* whatever he needed to get them. When he made his first run for the legislature in 1946, it paid to be progressive, so that's what George was. He pushed for trade schools and for luring out-of-state industry, which upset the Black Belt businessmen, but so what? This was the era of Big Jim Folsom, so Wallace rode that wave.

By 1948 things had shifted a bit, so Wallace did the same. He stayed with the loyalists after the Dixiecrats walked out of the national Democratic convention in Philadelphia that year, but he made

points back home by fighting the convention's civil rights plank and
nominating Richard Russell of Georgia for Vice-President.

In 1952, Wallace ran for circuit court judge back in his home
county against a state senator named Preston Clayton. Clayton had
served eight terms in the legislature, compared to Wallace's three,
but George shifted the voters' attention away from experience. Clayton—unfortunately, as it turned out—had been a lieutenant colonel
during the war. "Now, all you officers vote for Clayton," Wallace
said in his campaign speeches, "and all you privates vote for me."

That was not a new ploy. Politicians in these parts had been
using it since the Civil War, appealing to the underdog soldier's
resentment against the more privileged men who commanded him.
Wallace would use the same theme with a little twist ten years later,
seizing on the fear and anger of Alabamians unlucky enough to be
either poor or uneducated or both, and turning their resentment
against the "liberals and intellectual morons" running the country
up in Washington.

Wallace was an easy winner in that 1952 race for the circuit
court seat, and a year later he was sniffing the racist breeze by
becoming the first judge in the South to issue an injunction against
the removal of segregation signs in railroad terminals. He was
bound by a previous promise to support Jim Folsom in the 1954
gubernatorial race, during which he worked as Folsom's south Alabama campaign manager. But within a year after that, after Folsom
had shared his disastrous drink with Adam Clayton Powell, Wallace
had completely broken with Big Jim, claiming the governor was
"weak on the nigguh issue."

Years later, Folsom talked about that break with Marshall
Frady:

> "George wasn't no race bigot either back yonder. Me'n'George
> was always close. My uncle and his granddaddy were Populists
> together. George ain't nothin' but an old Populist himself. . . .
> He just wanted to get elected to things, that's all."

Wallace's next election was as a delegate to the 1956 national
Democratic convention, where he represented Alabama on the plat-

With some Alabama Democratic leaders during the 1960 presidential campaign, of which I was a leader in Alabama. From left: my longtime political and personal friend Judge Roy Mayhall, an unidentified man, state Senator Hugh Moses Hamilton, me, Alabama Governor John Patterson, and state legislator Bryce E. Graham.

With presidential candidate John Kennedy and vice-presidential candidate Lyndon Johnson at a national Democratic meeting in New York City, September 1960.

With the storied chair my constituents gave me after Rules Committee Chairman Judge Howard Smith denied me a chair of my own.

A Greyhound bus on its way to Birmingham carrying "freedom fighters" was set afire outside Anniston, 1961.

State Democratic leaders surround gubernatorial nominee George Wallace in September 1962. To Wallace's left are Judge Roy Mayhall and me.

Carl Elliott, Sr., September 1963.

Anti-Kennedy campaign literature, 1960.

CANDIDATES IN 9-8 CONGRESS RACE

ROBERT E. JONES JR.
Dist. Pop. 383,628

CARL ELLIOTT
Dist. Pop. 236,216

ARMISTEAD I. SELDEN JR.
Dist. Pop. 251,765

FRANK W. BOYKIN
Dist. Pop. 441,490

GEORGE M. GRANT
Dist. Pop. 386,075

GEORGE HUDDLESTON JR.
Dist. Pop. 634,864

ALBERT RAINS
Dist. Pop. 305,941

KENNETH A. ROBERTS
Dist. Pop. 315,817

GEORGE W. ANDREWS
Dist. Pop. 310,947

Mobile Press Register Sunday May 27, 1962

Candidates for the 1962 "low man out" Congressional primary.

George and Lurleen Wallace leaving the statehouse after Wallace's unsuccessful attempt to amend the law barring an Alabama governor from succeeding himself, September 1965.

Campaign literature from the 1966 Alabama governor's race.

Some of the opposing candidates during the 1966 gubernatorial campaign were Bob Gilchrist, second from left; Charles Woods, fourth from left; and Richmond Flowers, fifth from left.

A campaign speech at Talladega during the 1966 race.

The caption below this May 1966 Birmingham *News* photo read, "Don't look now, but somebody's peeping."

Vandalism plagued my campaign in 1966. The Ku Klux Klan defaced billboards and intimidated campaign workers with threats and gunfire.

From one Wallace to another, during the 1966 governor's race.

Former U.S. Senator John Sparkman, former Governor Jim Folsom, and me in 1980 at a Jimmy Carter presidential rally in Tuscumbia.

form committee and fought successfully to water down the party's civil rights plank. But two years later he suffered the first loss of his political career when he ran for governor against the state's attorney general, John Patterson.

Patterson had a pretty flamboyant background himself. His father had won the Democratic nomination for attorney general in 1954, after making a campaign promise to clean out the organized criminals who were running gambling operations in a southeast Alabama town called Phenix City. But before he could keep that promise, before he could even take office, he was gunned down in a contract killing. His son then took his place and wound up finishing the job his father had started. They even made a movie about it, called *The Phenix City Story.*

But by 1958 Patterson needed more than the Phenix City cleanup to put him in the governor's seat. And he found it. While George Wallace ran on his anti-civil rights record—at the same time seeking the support of black voters—Patterson went him one better by blatantly going after the racists and receiving the public endorsement of the Ku Klux Klan.

Years later Patterson explained his tactics in purely practical terms:

"Alabamians are gullible for that kind of thing. . . . Give the people something to dislike and hate, create a straw man for them to fight. They'd rather be against something than for something. As long as our people are of that frame of mind and like their politics with that brand, then we're going to have people to take advantage of that kind of situation."

Patterson took advantage, whipping Wallace by sixty thousand votes. It was after that election that Wallace let drop one of his legendary quotes, reportedly telling a circle of political friends, "John Patterson out-nigguhed me. And boys, I'm not goin' to be out-nigguhed again."

I heard about that vow at the time it was made, but I had no idea how directly—and how soon—it would involve me.

Wallace wasted no time keeping his word.

Early in 1959 the United States Civil Rights Commission sent agents into his judicial circuit to investigate complaints that black people there were being denied the right to vote. When the agents asked to see the district's voting records, Wallace refused to hand them over, setting up just the sort of headline-grabbing showdown for which he'd earned nicknames like the "Barbour Battler" and the "Fightin' Lil Judge."

That particular fight was significant because it was the first of many more that would pit Wallace against an old friend of his—and mine—a federal judge named Frank Johnson.

Frank Johnson came out of the same hills I did. He was raised in Winston County, the old "Free State" that remained Republican a hundred years after the Civil War. I knew Frank's father well. He was a Republican, but I didn't hold that against him. He had started out as a schoolteacher in a Walker County village called Dog Town, then he got into the grocery business before receiving a Winston County postmastership in 1921 as a reward for his devotion to the Republican Party. Frank Johnson, Sr., was an honest, intelligent man, and he raised his son the same way.

I wasn't surprised to see Frank, Jr.'s career climb like it did, from his graduation from the University of Alabama's law school, where he was a classmate and a pretty close friend of George Wallace, to his return after the war to Walker County, where he began law practice in 1946 with a fellow who was a law school classmate of mine and personal friend, Herman Maddox. Herman, who went on to become a long time mayor of Jasper, was as deeply Democratic as me, but that didn't keep him and Johnson from becoming partners and fast friends.

Frank was an open-minded, scrupulously fair man, with a fine sense of humor and an ability to slice through the smoke and get right to the heart of an issue. Those are just about perfect qualities for a judge, and that's what he became in 1955, when he was appointed chief judge of the United States District Court for the Middle District of Alabama, located in Montgomery.

He was thirty-seven at the time, making him the youngest federal judge in the nation. And he was immediately put on the hot seat, dealing with the Montgomery bus boycott and drawing the wrath of the racists by ruling in favor of desegregating the buses. A cross was burned in his yard and his family received threatening phone calls, but Johnson stayed steady. He was asked once about his open-minded attitude toward the issue of racial segregation, where that perspective had come from, and his response could have been mine:

> "I wasn't confronted with it like I would have been had I been growing up down in the Black Belt, in Lowndes County or Macon County or someplace like that. I grew up there in the hills of northwest Alabama, and there were maybe fifty or sixty blacks in Winston County. Two or three of them at the most voted. Those that lived there in Haleyville where I grew up as a kid, their parents worked on the railroad, or some of them worked as domestics in the homes that could afford domestics, and there weren't many of those. But we didn't go to school together, we didn't socialize, and it never occurred to me that that was good or bad. It was just there."

It was inevitable that Wallace and Johnson would run up against each other. After his 1958 defeat, Wallace was committed to a campaign of "fed-baiting," pitting himself as the champion of states' rights against the "evil forces" of the federal government. When Wallace refused to comply with the Civil Rights Commission's request in 1959, it was Johnson who stepped in to order George to turn over the records or face jail for contempt. The idea of becoming a martyr sounded good to George—as long as the price wasn't too high. He paid a personal visit to Johnson and asked his old friend to put him away for a week. Johnson was not about to make a deal, telling Wallace the jail term would be a lot longer than that. George stalked out, wound up turning over the records, then scalded Johnson with one of those trademark George Wallace phrases. Judge Frank Johnson, he said, was a "carpetbaggin', scalawaggin', integratin' bald-faced liar."

He hadn't gotten exactly what he wanted, but Wallace still had won by losing. The 1962 gubernatorial race was three years away, but already crowds gathered around him wherever he went, wearing "Win with Wallace" buttons. He was the chosen commander of the states' righters, the general they'd need as the federal forces moved in.

And there was no doubt the federal forces were moving in. Events began unfolding in earnest in 1960. That's when four black students refused to budge from the all-white counter of a Woolworth's store in Greensboro, North Carolina. Their "sit-in" sparked a wave of similar protests throughout the South. When Martin Luther King, Jr., was jailed that October during a sit-in at a department store in Atlanta, John Kennedy, in the midst of his presidential campaign, called Mrs. King to share his concern and support.

People in Alabama weren't too happy about that. They were even more upset when the "Freedom Riders" arrived the following summer. These were white and black civil rights protesters from the North, organized by the Council on Racial Equality (CORE) to ride into Southern states on public transportation, desegregating buses and bus terminals as they went. They rode through Virginia, the Carolinas and Georgia, meeting little resistance. But when they got to Alabama things exploded.

First, a gang of whites in Anniston attacked a Greyhound bus with clubs and iron bars, then when the bus broke down outside town, a bomb was thrown into it and, as the passengers poured out, they were beaten by the mob.

Soon after, on Mother's Day of that year, a Trailways bus carrying Freedom Riders pulled into the downtown Birmingham station, where they were greeted by a crowd of forty whites, including some with Klan connections. No police were in sight. For twenty minutes the mob freely attacked the passengers, injuring nine of them seriously. When the police finally arrived, a reporter asked Bull Connor, who was by then the city's police commissioner, where his men had been. "Visitin' their mothers," answered Connor with a sneer.

Governor John Patterson announced from the statehouse that he could not guarantee the safety of these "rabble-rousers" and suggested they just turn around and go on home. Two days later I was at the University of Alabama to give a talk. When I was done, Julian Butler, who was near the end of his term as student body president, drove me to the Birmingham airport for my flight back to Washington. As we got near the airport, we found ourselves in a long line of police and state trooper vehicles heading in the same direction. When we got to the terminal, I sent Julian in to see what was going on.

It turned out that some of the more seriously injured Freedom Riders from the Birmingham attack were inside, amid heavy security and surrounded by newspaper and television reporters, waiting for a flight back north—the same flight I was scheduled for.

"Julian," I said, "I don't believe the best thing for me to do this afternoon is to be filmed climbing onto a planeload of Freedom Riders and accompanying them to Washington."

We went back to town, had a cup of coffee and waited an hour or two for the next flight.

I was sickened by the attacks in Anniston, in Birmingham and, later that month, in Montgomery, where an agent sent from the Justice Department by President Kennedy to monitor the Freedom Rider situation was beaten unconscious after he announced to an attacking mob that he was with the federal government. That prompted Kennedy to order National Guardsmen to escort the riders on the last leg of their trip, into Mississippi.

But as much as I was repelled by the violence I saw spreading around the state, I also resented these "activists" coming into Alabama from other places, fanning the flames that were already frighteningly high. James Farmer, the leader of CORE, explained the strategy of the Freedom Rides by saying, "We were counting on the bigots in the South to do our work for us."

Well, I resented that approach. I can look back now and say maybe it had to be so, maybe things never would have changed if they hadn't been shoved along. But at the time I felt that a lot of these protesters, especially the more aggressive ones who eventually melded into the movement Martin Luther King had been so careful to keep nonviolent, were opportunists eager to provoke and bring out the worst side of the white South. Up to this very day, the image many Americans have of Alabama remains the snarling racists they saw on the evening news thirty years ago.

And that's a shame. It's a shame because it ignores the fact that there were and *are* so many good, sensible people in this state who were just as sickened and sorry at what they were seeing as the rest of America. It's also a shame because those people's voices—not to mention their votes—were swamped by the rising tide of fear and hatred encouraged by people within our own borders who were as opportunist as the outsiders they attacked.

By 1962 the biggest opportunist of them all was set to take control of Alabama in a way no man's ever taken control of any other state at any other time in this nation's history. George Wallace's day had finally come, and the timing couldn't have been worse for me.

The funny thing is, even by then I wasn't real worried about Wallace. I just never considered him a very big factor, and I'll probably go to my grave regretting that. I just never took George Wallace seriously enough. While he was mounting his campaign for governor in 1962, I was more concerned about holding on to my own Congressional seat in the face of a challenge that had nothing to do—at least not yet—with Wallace.

That challenge was the 1960 census, which showed that Alabama's population had slipped enough during the previous decade that the state's membership in the U. S. House of Representatives had to be cut from nine seats to eight.

It was up to the state legislature to figure out how to make that change. The normal thing to do in this situation would have been to redraw the district lines throughout the state, reshaping nine districts into eight. Naturally none of the nine current Congressmen, including me, wanted his district to be the one that was chopped up. And each Congressman had enough state legislators behind him to block any plan that would make his district the one that was killed.

Making the situation even more muddy was the fact that, at the time, there was an almost perfect balance among the nine of us, split basically along the traditional hill country versus Black Belt lines.

Four were liberals, all from the northern section of the state, of course: Bob Jones, Albert Rains, Kenneth Roberts and me. Roberts had made his mark by leading the investigation of automobile safety standards, Rains was a legislative leader in the field of housing, and Jones was a power on the Public Works Committee, pushing through bills for federal construction of everything from roads to dams.

Four other members of Alabama's Congressional delegation—Armistead Selden, Frank Boykin, George Grant and George Andrews—all from districts in the central and southern sections of the state, were more standard Southern conservatives. The ninth Representative, George Huddleston in Birmingham, was sort of a swing man.

The delegation couldn't have been more balanced. But suddenly the scales were about to be tipped, and no one could figure out how to do it. Neither side wanted to give up the edge to the other. While this issue was being batted around, I got a call from a *Newsweek* magazine reporter, who had picked me, for some reason, as the focus of a story on an "average Congressman" home in his district during Easter recess. After weathering the storm of the Rules Committee fight just three months earlier, and with no idea that the Freedom Riders would be converging on the state within a month, I was happy to get back home and just breathe easy for a few days. I invited the *Newsweek* reporter along, with no idea how ironic his story, which appeared April 17, 1961, would become in the coming months. I had no idea that these would be just about the last easy breaths I'd be taking for a long time.

From Jasper, Ala., correspondent Joseph Cumming reports on Rep. Carl Elliott, a Democrat serving his seventh term:

At 6:30 one morning last week, Carl Elliott's petite wife, Jane, already dressed for the day, shook her husband and told him it was time to get up. Reluctantly the 47-year-old congressman heaved his massive frame (6 feet 4 1/2 inches, 227 pounds) out of bed and groped his way toward the shower. Later, when he came out for breakfast, in blue serge suit and cheerful red tie, he was bursting with hearty energy.

Over sausage and eggs (and for non-coffee-drinking Elliott, two glasses of iced tea), he discussed the day's schedule with his secretary, former schoolteacher Mary Allen. First to the coal-mining area of Carbon Hill, where surplus food was to be distributed; then to the town of Brilliant to discuss a new post office; a look at newly completed Lewis Smith Dam; back to Jasper in the evening for a banquet, speech, and dedication of a new laboratory at the Walker County High School; and, finally, a late meeting with a group of doctors to discuss a new hospital wing.

Strenuous as it was, the day was typical of Elliott's week at home. From the time he arrived until he returned to Washington, he was crisscrossing his nine-county district in Northwest Alabama, either in his own Ford or Mary Allen's. He is a man of tremendous popularity in his district. His liberal voting record sits well with the depressed areas. But conservative businessmen also have a high regard for him. He is fortunate, too, in not having an acute segregation problem in his largely white area. He is more concerned with matters like Carbon Hill.

A thin drizzle veiled the town when Elliott and his party drove up to Carbon Hill's little City Hall. "Hello, there, Vernon," Elliott called to Mayor Vernon Cook, and the two walked together up the ragged dirt road leading to the corrugated metal shed where the surplus food was being distributed.

About a hundred men and women were standing outside. Elliott went along the line, reaching for people's hands and saying: "I'm Carl Elliott." Most, at first, looked bewildered. Then word got around. "Hey, looky thar," one after another said, "that's Carl Elliott. Thought I recognized him."

Inside the shed, lit by naked bulbs, Elliott talked at greater length to the old men and women waiting their turn at the counter where the cans and boxes of food were stacked. One elderly woman wanted to know about disability benefits for her husband "who got blowed up in the mines last August."

"You write all that down in a letter and send it to Carl Elliott, Washington," he told her. Now and again he would whip out a piece of paper and jot down a name—or ask Mary Allen to make a note.

It was like that all day long, except that most other constituents were better off than Carbon Hill's. Other days were much the same—there was precious little time during the week for Elliott to spend with his children (two boys, two girls) or in the green rocking chair on the porch of his modest, one-story house in Jasper. That has always been Elliott's way of politicking—even though in recent primary contests he was unopposed.

What impression had the week at home given him? "I have a renewed feeling that my [liberal] votes express the hopes and ideals of a great majority in my district."

Unfortunately, by the end of that year it was no longer my district alone that would determine my fate. The state legislature, unable to decide what to do about the problem of the lost Congressional seat, finally decided to turn the whole thing over to the voters. In lieu of redrawing the district lines, the legislature passed what became commonly known as the "Nine-Eight" plan.

According to that plan, the Democratic Party would hold two primaries the following May (the state's Republican Party nominated its candidates by convention rather than primary, so this was no issue for them). In the first Democratic primary, each of the state's existing nine districts would elect a candidate for Congress. Four weeks later, a statewide election would be held, with all nine candidates' names on a ballot. Voters throughout the state would select *eight* of those nine as the Democratic nominees for that fall's general election.

The ninth-place finisher would be, as they say, the "low man out."

It was a situation tailor-made for targets, as people from far beyond a Representative's district would be free to determine his fate. And it set into motion a scramble like I'd never seen before, as men who had spent their careers carefully building a constituency in a particular section of the state suddenly had to find a way to win votes in places they'd never even visited. An editor with the *Ala-*

bama Journal named Dan Dowe wrote a column that pretty well summed up the scene during that time:

> Half a decade from now, when one of Alabama's eight congressmen wakes up screaming in his Washington bed, chances are his troubled dreams will have returned him to 1962 and his being smothered in fractions.
>
> The state's unique method for reducing its congressional delegation from nine to eight has been termed everything from "Russian Roulette" to "low man out."
>
> But as far as the nine incumbent congressmen are concerned, the "9–8" plan presents a nightmarish problem in political arithmetic: How do you conduct one-half of a campaign against one-ninth of an opponent?
>
> Attempting to find a solution, nine groggy veterans of the U. S. House of Representatives have fanned throughout the state, shaking the hands of voters who have never seen their name on a ballot before.
>
> Each candidate has won acceptance in his own district. Now each is conducting a one-sided statewide campaign in his own behalf. There are no battle lines drawn. Each of the nine must sell himself as a bill of goods one-ninth more desirable than an unnamed colleague. . . .
>
> Whatever his support at home, each congressman must depend on a half-million voters in other districts to provide him the critical one-ninth margin over somebody else.
>
> As one representative put it: "It doesn't matter how many votes you get. What counts is how many you lose."

No one was racing to finish first. The race was to avoid finishing ninth.

That didn't suit my situation well at all. I'd made a lot of headlines for my work in Congress—headlines across the state, not just in my district. While those headlines might have pleased the majority of voters in my own district, they didn't make the rest of the state too happy. In an election where people are looking for one name *not* to vote for, the publicity I'd gotten put me in a bad position.

It didn't help any that my district was the least populated in the state. What *did* help was that the George Wallace machine, while well formed, was not yet in place. In its hands, this "Nine-Eight" setup would become a powerful tool. But in 1962, when Wallace was still focused on getting himself into the statehouse, the Congressional race was left as a battleground among the traditional factions in Alabama's state legislature—basically between the hard-line conservatives and the dwindling number of progressives.

The first round of in-district primaries that May were no problem for me, since no one ran against me. That was encouraging, but I had no idea what would happen as I stepped onto the statewide stage. Of course, neither did any of the others. The message I tried to put out, through newspaper ads and appearances at as many places as I could get to, was that I'd worked my way into a very influential position in Congress, a position that gave this state a voice it had rarely enjoyed at the national level—only two Alabamians besides me had ever served on the House Rules Committee: Oscar Underwood and Will Bankhead. I tried to make it clear how long it takes to get into that position, and how much Alabama itself would lose if it voted me out.

There did wind up being a target in that '62 statewide race, but it wasn't me. Frank Boykin, from down in Mobile, had spent twenty-eight years in Congress and had little to show for it but a lot of long speeches (his motto, which nobody ever quite figured out, was "Everything's made for love"), a huge appetite (he was known for eating enormous breakfasts and he once hosted a dinner party for Sam Rayburn at which a thousand guests were served salmon, elk, venison, bear steaks, turkey, antelope and possum), a large personal bank account (he was by far the wealthiest of the state's Congressional delegation) and some questionable business dealings.

It was those dealings that finally did Boykin in. He wound up as the Congressional casualty in that May's statewide primary. A year later, a federal jury convicted him of receiving a quarter million dollars from some savings and loan people in Maryland who were paying him to step in and stop the Justice Department from prosecuting one of their executives. Boykin got a pardon from President Johnson two years after that, and four years later he died.

As for me, I survived that '62 campaign, I was going back to Congress for another term, but I felt far from safe. First, I finished seventh in that statewide balloting, which was not too comforting. Second, it didn't look like the legislature was getting any closer to redistricting and getting rid of the "Nine-Eight" nonsense. And finally, George Wallace was on his way.

I'd been able to basically avoid Wallace so far. I knew where he stood, and I didn't want to be seen standing too close to the same spot. There were times we had wound up on the same stage together here or there, as fellow Alabama politicians. I'd grin and bear it, and be gone as soon as I could. He might have impinged on my presence, but I made sure George Wallace never touched my politics. I'd spent my career in Congress building a record I could be proud of, one I could look back on without regret until the day I died. And I was not about to let that record be sullied by shifting toward the likes of Wallace.

Until 1962 I had been able to pretty much step around him, but at the end of that year we finally had our own showdown.

Wallace had been through a fight of his own in the gubernatorial primary that May. He faced seven candidates, but only two of them really posed a threat. One was Jim Folsom, who still had enough support left over from his heyday to make him a force to be reckoned with. The other was a relatively new fellow on the scene named Ryan deGraffenried, from Tuscaloosa. His father, Edward deGraffenried, was elected to the U. S. House of Representatives at the same time I was and served two terms. Ed deGraffenried had a drinking problem that kept him from making much of a mark in Congress, but his son was set to make a much bigger splash, having built a strong following as a state legislator among the Black Belt's young, professional silk-stocking crowd, a group that was beginning to emerge by the early 1960s and would eventually be the backbone of what came to be known as the "New South." I think they're called "yuppies" these days.

Wallace went about that campaign with his sleeves rolled up, keeping the vow he'd made after losing to Patterson four years earlier. He told a crowd in the town of Warrior, a coal-miner, steel-worker suburb north of Birmingham, "the worst thing that's happening to our chillun is this integration mess," and he pledged, "I'll stand in the schoolhouse door to keep them out!" He assailed the "lily-livered liberals" in Washington and said, "It's about time somebody told those big shots up there where to get off." He had boiled his racial philosophy down to a simple credo by this time, one he'd repeat when he later ran for President: "Nigguhs hate whites, and whites hate nigguhs. Everybody knows that deep down."

The night before the 1962 gubernatorial primary, Folsom still looked like a formidable threat, strong enough at least to force Wallace into a runoff. But then Big Jim went on television for a state-wide broadcast they still talk about today. His supporters later swore he had been drugged by the Wallace people. Most folks assumed he was simply drunk again. In either case, Folsom stumbled on camera with his family, slurring his words and forgetting the names of his sons as he tried to introduce them. He described his opponents as "Me, too!" candidates and began chanting that phrase like a cuckoo clock: "Me, too! Me, too! Me, too!"

My children and I were watching that night in our living room, and my mouth was hanging open as widely as theirs. By the time that broadcast was done, Folsom was finished. It was deGraffenried who came in second the next day, forcing a runoff in which he collected a respectable forty percent of the ballots but still lost to Wallace by seventy thousand votes.

So George finally had the stage. Winning the Democratic nomination meant he had won the governorship. November's general election would be merely going through the motions against a Republican Party that barely existed. But he still needed to consolidate all the power he could get. He still needed to gather all the allies he could for the battles he knew he'd be fighting soon from Montgomery.

And that's what brought him to the doorstep of my house in Jasper early that September.

He arrived that evening with a couple of his people. One of them was a fellow named Bill Jones. Jones had worked for me for a while, as a member of my Congressional staff, but when the Wallace train started picking up steam, he'd done what so many others were doing—he jumped ship and climbed on board. A couple of years later he wound up writing a book about—actually, *for*—Wallace. It was called *The Wallace Story,* published in Alabama, paid for in Alabama and written by Bill Jones, who was by then Wallace's press secretary—a job more challenging than just about any I could imagine. His book was transparent propaganda, and I'm sure Bill Jones didn't believe half the words he wrote in there, but he knew where his bread was buttered. That's what had brought him to Wallace in the first place, and that's what brought them both to my door that night.

George was pretty heady by that time, giving orders and telling the people around him what to do. He was especially full of himself that night, striding into my living room and scattering all this poppycock about how I had to join him. All I could think to myself as I watched him strut around was what an upstart he was, blowing into my home and telling me what I had to do.

I went ahead and listened to him just as politely as I could for a pretty long time, until about two o'clock in the morning, while he told me all about why he needed me and why I needed him. Finally, I said, "No, George, you don't need me, because I don't agree with your stand on most everything you've talked about. You don't want me."

He said he did want me, that I had character and intelligence and so on. It didn't sound that much different from the way he'd approached me twenty years earlier, back on the university campus. Eventually it got to the point where I just cut him off.

"George," I said, "you don't want me because I don't want *you.*"

That pulled him up short.

"You and I are on completely different sides," I said.

He tried to go on talking. Then I stopped him and ended the evening with just about the last statement of any substance that would come between us.

"George," I said, "don't piss on my leg."

So that was basically that. When he stepped up on the Alabama Capitol portico on January 14, 1963, to take the oath as governor, George Wallace delivered a speech that not only etched itself in the consciousness of 1960s America but was a battle cry aimed directly at me and anyone else who stood against him:

"Today I have stood where Jefferson Davis stood, and took an oath to my people. It is very appropriate then that from this Cradle of the Confederacy, this very heart of the great Anglo-Saxon Southland, that today we sound the drum for freedom as have our generations of forebears before us time and again down through history. Let us rise to the call of freedom-loving blood that is in us and send our answer to the tyranny that clanks its chains upon the South.

"In the name of the greatest people that have ever trod this earth, I draw the line in the dust and toss the gauntlet before the feet of tyranny. And I say: Segregation now! Segregation tomorrow! Segregation forever!"

That speech was like pouring gasoline on a fire. The racists and every other right-wing group down here went wild. It was as if all the stops had been pulled. People's patriotism was suddenly questioned right and left by outfits who wrapped their hatred and racism in the red, white and blue of the American flag or in the Stars and Bars of Dixie, groups like the John Birch Society and the White Citizens' Council.

I just couldn't stand it, and I finally said so, in a speech I made that March to the Walker County Young Democrats at a Jackson-Jefferson Day dinner—a speech that was excerpted the next morning in just about every newspaper in Alabama, under headlines like the one chosen by the Montgomery *Advertiser:* ELLIOTT WOULD HORSEWHIP BIRCHERS.

My words focused on the John Birch Society, but they were clearly meant for every one of the extremist groups that were sprouting like ugly weeds across the American landscape—including those crowding around the heels of George Wallace:

"This organization, as you will know, is composed of a motley crew of malcontents and troublemakers who deserve the scorn and contempt—if not the pity—of every responsible American.

"Pretensions aside, the John Birchers and their stooges actually are loud-mouthed know-nothings whom Thomas Jefferson would have dismissed as intellectual nitwits and whom Jackson probably would have horsewhipped.

"And I am not at all sure that even today a good horsewhipping might not be the best way to dispose of these political delinquents. . . .

"The extremists do not strive to offer constructive and well-intentioned criticism, the type to which no one could reasonably object.

"These extremists cringe from the fact that ours is the richest, most powerful nation in the history of mankind, that our people have a greater and more abiding degree of personal liberty and freedom than the people of any society since time began.

"The extreme right wing ignores the fact that only in the United States is there no ceiling on the hopes and aspirations of the people, that even the most remote goal and ambition is within reach of every industrious citizen.

"These malcontents did not come to praise the United States. They came to condemn and carp, to smear and slander, to exaggerate our weaknesses and to ignore our strength and our decency."

The reaction was pretty predictable. Up in Washington, a correspondent for the Birmingham *News* named Edgar Allan Poe (now *there's* a tough name for a young reporter to live up to) wrote a story describing the reaction in Congress:

A few days ago Rep. Elliott baffled some of his colleagues not only from the South, but from other parts of the country as well.

Some cloakroom talk on Capitol Hill the past several days

described Elliott as either a "courageous statesman" or a "terrible politician."

I guess it's possible to be both. In fact, at that time, in my place, one sort of necessarily went with the other. Anything that took courage was going to hurt you at the polls. The Montgomery *Advertiser* tried to make that point when it ran an editorial questioning my judgment:

> There are a lot of John Birch Citizens about [it read], and as a class they are upper. Elliott has invited their hostility. . . . What has impelled him to alienate so many voters needlessly is not visible on the face of things.

Actually, it seemed pretty simple to me. I didn't *want* those people's votes. Not only that, but I thought someone should answer back just to let it be known that these loud, braying voices weren't speaking for everyone in this state. Maybe that was a political misstep—probably so. But it felt damn good to get it off my chest.

Something I've noticed, looking back after thirty years, is that I'm proud of most of the things I did that hurt me politically—and I'm sorriest about some of the things I did that were supposed to help.

The rest of 1963 unreeled like a bad dream.

First there was the ugliness of Birmingham that May—the brutal retaliation of Bull Connor's men to black marchers, followed by a night of riots in that city touched off by the bombing of a motel in which Martin Luther King was supposed to be staying.

Then came June, with Wallace responding to the enrollment of two black students at the University of Alabama by setting up a personal confrontation between himself and the federal government. His "stand in the schoolhouse door" on June 11 was another of those overblown Wallace face-offs that have become the stuff of his legend—and it's one I could have been a part of if I'd chosen.

Both the Kennedy administration up in Washington and the

Wallace forces down in Montgomery had been carefully mapping out their strategies for this showdown long before it happened. Both sides knew that two black students, Vivian Malone and James Hood, planned to enroll for summer school classes and that the day for that enrollment was June 11.

What a lot of people don't realize is that Wallace tried as hard as he could to get someone to stand *with* him in that door. He even tried to get me.

In the days just before that showdown, I started receiving telegrams from Wallace's staff asking me if I would join him in this gesture. I mailed back my response, and my message was pretty brief. I'd refused to symbolically stand with Wallace the previous fall, and I certainly was not ready to stand with him literally now.

What finally transpired in Tuscaloosa that day boiled down to nothing but a four-and-a-half-hour delay. Rather than force their way past Wallace when they first arrived at eleven that morning, the two students, escorted by Deputy Attorney General Nicholas Katzenbach, went back to their dormitories and waited while the Alabama National Guard, which had been federalized by President Kennedy, arrived at three-thirty that afternoon to ask Wallace to step aside. He did, the students came back, went on in and registered and that was the end of the "stand."

This was a show hardly different from the charade Wallace had staged against Frank Johnson four years earlier. In both cases Wallace made a dramatic appearance of facing down the federal government, in both cases the federal government got exactly what it wanted, and in both cases Wallace walked away claiming victory.

There were reports that summer as I went about my work on the Rules Committee that the turmoil back home had frightened me away from my liberal leanings. Drew Pearson wrote in his column that I was "blocking" the Administration's bills and that I had "turned against Mr. Kennedy." The fact was that I'd done exactly what had been expected when the move was made to put me in the committee's new swing-vote position: my votes were consistently in favor of every piece of liberal legislation that came along . . . *except* civil rights legislation. It was understood before I joined the committee—understood by Sam Rayburn and everyone else involved—that this would be the one area where I would have to vote with the standard Southern position. And I did.

There was a lot of civil rights legislation coming through the committee that year. Mine was the key vote that killed a bill to create an urban affairs department, which President Kennedy had indicated would be headed by a black fellow named Robert Weaver. I also made headlines that summer with my statement that the President was "dead wrong" to assume civil rights legislation would settle the racial turmoil in the South. My comments went on to call for a "cooling off" on both sides. "The delicate problems of race relations cannot be solved overnight," I said. "The proposed civil rights bill can only add to existing tensions." But all people saw was the phrase "dead wrong."

That became the focus of folks like Pearson. They didn't mention that, far from turning against Kennedy, I made speeches for him throughout that summer, urging Alabamians to stay with the Democratic Party and with the President rather than deserting them. In the face of the anti-Kennedy hysteria that was getting more intense back home every day, I committed myself to supporting the President if he ran for reelection in 1964.

When Kennedy visited Alabama that summer, coming to Muscle Shoals to dedicate a new TVA headquarters building, he invited me to come with him. We, along with others, flew to Nashville in the President's plane, U. S. Air Force 1. After the President spoke to a crowd of thirty thousand people at the Vanderbilt stadium, we all boarded the presidential helicopter to make our trip on to Muscle Shoals. Just before landing, we got a message that a threat had been made on the President's life and we were to stay aloft. When I mentioned that the place I'd grown up was only thirty miles south of where we were hovering, Kennedy suggested we fly on down there and take a look, since we had a little time to spend.

So we did. We flew over the little cabin I was raised in, flew over the old farm my father had worked, and when we got to Vina I said, "Now this little town, Mr. President, there's hardly anybody living here, maybe three hundred people. And there's nobody living here that has ever had a bath in water drawn from a central water system."

Well, that really impressed him. He looked over at me and said, "Now, Carl, this trip hurts you politically, I know it does. I'd like to find a way to show my appreciation."

I said, "Well, I was hoping you'd bring that up, Mr. President. This little town right below us could sure use a water system. It'd cost about two hundred thousand dollars. And down the road there is a place called Russellville. It's a little bigger than Vina, and it needs a water system just as badly."

He listened, then he said, "Larry, come up here," calling Larry O'Brien, his administrative assistant, from the back of the helicopter.

"Larry," he said, "I want two hundred thousand dollars for Carl for a water system in Vina, Alabama, and I want seven hundred and fifty thousand dollars for one in Russellville, Alabama."

"Well, my God, Mr. President," O'Brien said, "we don't have a quarter to give. The money that we've appropriated for this kind of thing was used up long ago. It was allocated just the way you wanted it."

Then the President said, "Yes, but, Larry, the hand that allocates can *dis*allocate. I want you to have on Carl's desk tomorrow a telegram saying water systems have been approved for these two towns and that the funds are available."

Larry O'Brien seemed pretty overcome by that. He said, "Well, Mr. President, if you say so." Then he said, "There's going to be an awful lot of disallocation going on around here."

That was by no means the end of the day's events. When we finally landed at Muscle Shoals for the ceremony, George Wallace was there to greet the President. After the ceremony, Wallace rode with us in the helicopter on over to Huntsville, where the President was to make a short speech before leaving the state. When we arrived in Huntsville and took our seats on the stage, I noticed Tallulah Bankhead sitting in the audience. Of course I'd known Tallulah a long time, since her early days in Jasper. I also knew she had a mind of her own and wasn't afraid to speak it. So I wasn't surprised by her response when the President, after a word from me, asked me to invite the actress to join us up on the stage.

"Well, dahling," Tallulah told me, "you tell the President of the United States that I would be honored to join him, but I refuse to sit on the same platform with George Wallace anywhere."

And so Tallulah stayed put. And President Kennedy had all he could do to keep his laughter to himself.

It was early that year that President Kennedy called me to the White House to talk about the racial situation down in Alabama.

"Carl," he said, "the time has come. We've got to do something about civil rights and the black people of this country. It won't stand as it is anymore."

He said, "I'm calling you and two or three others, and I'm talking to you first. I want to know if I have overlooked any chance of accommodation with the leaders of the South. Is there any way by which we can move this thing forward a little?"

I said, "No, Mr. President, there isn't. I'm sorry to say I've recently finished a campaign in Alabama and there is absolutely no spirit of accommodation there on civil rights at all."

He said, "Is there any chance that, if I walk half a mile, your folks will walk a hundred yards?"

I said, "No, there isn't."

He looked terrible. I can see his face right now. He said, "Your answer is one of the saddest things I've ever heard. I just wish I was smart enough to do this thing without the country becoming disrupted over it. But there is no choice. It's either respond to the desire and insistence of these people to have their rights or have the country face revolution."

We visited for about half an hour, just the two of us in the Oval Office, then I left.

In August of that year, my mother passed away up at a place called Burnout, not far from Gober Ridge, on the farm I'd bought her and my father before I went to Congress. She was seventy-five years old.

Four months later—the day after Christmas—my father followed her out of this lifetime. He was seventy-four.

And in between them both, John Kennedy died in Dallas.

I was in a committee meeting that November afternoon, when

the chief counsel for the House Committee on Public Works, a fellow named Richard Sullivan—we called him "Big Six" Sullivan—came breaking into the room to tell us there'd been a report the President had been shot and had been taken to a hospital. I told him to just go ahead back and gather every detail he could get and bring some specifics for us as soon as he could.

It wasn't too long before Big Six returned. This time he told us two priests had been reported entering the President's hospital room. Sullivan was an Irishman from Pennsylvania. He knew what it means when two priests arrive like that.

"It's over," he said.

We all just folded our books and sat there. Within minutes it was announced that the President was dead.

I adjourned the meeting and called Jane with the news. She hadn't heard. I caught a plane out of Washington that afternoon and spent the next week at home with my family, watching the events unfold on television, just like the rest of the country did. That was a horrible week.

I tried to think clearly that week, but it was hard. It was hard to see where everything was headed. Events were piling up so fast it was real difficult to predict what would happen next, which direction we'd be going, what the next step might be, and the step after that. I felt a deep disturbance swelling up from somewhere, almost like a tremor.

But I also felt a basic faith that we would make it through, that we would endure as a people. This is a hell of a country. I'm the last person to be clinging to the glimmer of the Civil War, but I've always believed that any nation that could come through a conflict like that and come out head up and feet firmly planted on the ground can make it through just about anything.

I knew I still had that faith. But I also knew it had yet to receive its sternest test.

I would rather lose in a cause that will some day win, than win in a cause that will some day lose.

Woodrow Wilson

TWELVE

LOW MAN OUT

There's something about the two-year term of a Congressman that's a lot like the old story of Sisyphus, the Greek fellow who spent his life pushing a boulder up a mountainside. Every time he got to the top, the rock would roll back down and he'd have to start all over again.

That's pretty much the way it is with a Congressman and elections. Unless he's lucky enough to run unopposed, a Representative spends about half of each two-year term—maybe even more—working at winning reelection. If he's fortunate enough to win yet another term, he's scarcely settled in before yet *another* campaign is staring him in the face.

It's a tough situation in the best of times, but in 1964, with my state—and the nation—in crisis, with George Wallace firmly in control, with the Republican Party making its loudest noise in a long time, and with the state legislature still paralyzed on the redistricting question, I knew I was facing a battle far more brutal than what I'd been through two years earlier. In 1962, I'd seen a skirmish. This was going to be a war.

And I wasn't about to wait for the fight to come to me. Even before the new year began, I was shuttling back and forth from Washington to Alabama, trying to shore up the strength I'd need when the bullets began flying. A columnist for the Montgomery *Advertiser* named Tom Johnson caught up with me in November 1963 and wrote a pretty good account of how manic the pace had become by that time. His story was headlined LIFE IN THE 9–8 WORLD:

> Apart from the convulsive effort that voting has become, the congressmen-at-large have found their work enlarged proportionately. Congressman Carl Elliott's mail sometimes runs as high as 2,000 letters a day and his long-distance telephone calls as high as 75 or 100. Because his office is geared to represent a district-sized constituency, Elliott has to do what is disagreeable to any politician—answer some of the mail with obviously mimeographed replies and let some of the phone calls go unacknowledged.
>
> Nobody is working harder for re-election than Elliott. . . . He has missed but one weekend this year coming back to Alabama, and every weekend at home means a grind of trying to get around the state to set up something for next spring's primary.
>
> Last Thursday Elliott flew out of Washington at 4 P.M. and was in Montgomery at 8 to address the Alabama State Nurses Association. At 10 he checked into a local motel to make some phone calls and meet with friends. At midnight, he decided to drive back to Jasper, stopping at Tuscaloosa on the way to see his son, who is a law school student.
>
> Finding his son asleep, Elliott slipped a letter under the door and resumed his drive at 3:30 A.M., getting home at 6.
>
> The rest of the weekend proceeded at the same urgent pace. He drove to Haleyville Friday and then on to Vina to visit with his father and his brother and some constituents who dropped by. Back home at 1 A.M.

Up early the next morning, he saw other callers, who included a delegation wanting help in getting an area redevelopment loan and two visitors who wanted to be mail carriers. That afternoon, to Tuscaloosa for the Alabama-Mississippi State game. More visiting. Back home about midnight.

Sunday morning more visitors, plus preparation of a post office dedication speech to be made that afternoon in Spruce Pine, 65 miles away. After the speech, more constituents to be heard.

Back in Jasper at 7 P.M. Sunday, Elliott found a stack of phone calls to be made. He explained to one caller that he couldn't talk because he had to make his plane in Birmingham. The caller volunteered to drive him in order to discuss his business on the way.

At 11:20 P.M. Sunday, Elliott was back on the plane, arrived in Washington at 4:30, grabbed three hours sleep and was in his office at 9.

As Elliott arrived at Washington Airport, he was given a plaque from United Airlines saluting him for his "valued contributions to airline progress"—in response, no doubt, to the fact that Elliott had flown 1,000,000 miles and forks over $110 every week for a roundtrip ticket to Alabama.

Sometimes a friend or a relative contributes the plane fare, but mostly it is Elliott's money—and "the till is running dry." His campaign costs in the state-at-large election last year were five times what they are in a district race. Elliott campaign committees still owe $21,000, about what it used to cost him to wage an entire campaign.

Raising money is hard because voters outside his old district have their own congressmen to elect and don't have any money to contribute to a congressman who won't be able to help them if redistricting is passed.

Elliott himself is gloomy about the chances of redistricting before the next election. He expects no such "balm for a weary traveler in Gilead."

To the extent that Elliott's activities are typical, the life of an Alabama congressman today is one of long hours, little sleep, meals caught on the run, frustration, campaign debts and a ceaseless effort to ingratiate himself with Alabama voters, most of whom don't care whether he wins or loses unless he happens to be their own congressman.

For some if not all, there is the additional grim prospect of tough opposition in their own districts. If they get by that, they must survive the 9–8 cutoff. And if they get by the cutoff, Republicans are waiting further down the calendar with long knives.

Elliott is a big, powerful man but he feels the pressure physically. In 1948, his first campaign, he made 16 speeches in as many towns on the Saturday before election. A few weeks ago he tried again and almost didn't get through the last one.

"I'm 50," he says, and quotes the Latin phrase *res ipsa loquitur*—"the thing speaks for itself."

I was right about the redistricting. The legislature ended its 1963 session still deadlocked. A bill proposed late that year that would have left my own district—along with Albert Rains's and Bob Jones's—untouched was attacked as "obviously a Kennedy-backed bill" by a fellow named James Martin. The fact that Jim Martin had become an influential voice in Alabama politics shows just how turbulent the state had become by this time.

A year earlier Martin had been a gasoline distributor in Gadsden best known for being married to a former Miss Alabama. At the time, he was a political nonentity. He had been a Democrat, but the anti-Kennedy sentiment boiling throughout the state made the time ripe for some disenchanted Democrats to turn Republican. As Alabama's GOP state chairman, a fellow named Claude Vardaman, put it at the time: "Under Ike it was respectable to be a Republican; under Kennedy it is an honor."

Martin accepted that honor and switched parties. Then, basically out of nowhere, he announced in 1962 that he was going to challenge none other than Lister Hill. Even with the unrest across Alabama, no one thought Jim Martin stood a ghost of a chance to unseat the fifth-ranking member of the United States Senate.

Lister apparently didn't think so. Rather than come home to

campaign that summer, he stayed in Washington working on legislation. It was incomprehensible to him that anyone, much less a *Republican,* could unseat him. And with all the racial unrest rocking the state, he was just as happy to stay away.

Meanwhile, Martin, bankrolled by a suddenly ambitious GOP, mounted a furious campaign, telling voters that time had passed their senior Senator by, that Hill was holed up in Washington, totally out of touch with the people. "Listless Lister," they called him, and stickers proclaiming KENNEDY AND HILL, WE'VE HAD OUR FILL began plastering billboards and bumpers across Alabama, paid for by "Rebels for Martin."

By the fall, Lister realized he was up against a genuine threat. He hurried home and rallied all the support he could muster, squeezing the last ounce of strength he could still find among the old-line Depression-era New Deal Democrats in the state. When the final returns were in very late that election night, Lister Hill had held on to his Senate seat, but just barely—he beat Jim Martin by a margin of one percent.

That 1962 Senatorial campaign was Lister Hill's last. It left him severely shaken, and it shocked the rest of us into realizing no one was safe anymore.

I certainly knew I wasn't.

There was talk as early as the summer of 1963 about who the targets might be if there were another Nine-Eight race in '64. Bob Jones, Albert Rains and I were mentioned more than any others, which didn't surprise me. But when word started getting around late that year that someone was ready to run against me in my own district, I knew the Wallace people were putting the pieces in place. The man getting set to face me was the floor leader of the state House of Representatives, who had become a close ally of George Wallace. His name was Tom Bevill.

It didn't seem that long since Tom had been working for me. But this Wallace machine had become a magnetic thing, practically irresistible. It was going to take whatever loyalty was still left around me to turn back the tide. The first place I looked was back up to

Washington. Mary Allen had left my staff a year earlier to join a Kennedy commission on vocational education, and Julian Butler had finished law school and was working on Lister Hill's Senate staff. I called them both on a cold December night and asked them to join me at a restaurant on Pennsylvania Avenue.

We talked about the situation back home, about how hard it was going to be to fight through two elections—first against Bevill and then throughout the rest of the state. I needed them both, and I told them so, proposing that they each go in the next morning, quit their jobs and head back to Alabama with me.

Julian, half joking, turned to Mary and said, "If you do it, I'll do it."

Mary shocked us both by saying, "I'll do it."

I think Lister Hill was pretty shocked as well. It's almost unheard of for a staff person to switch from the Senate to the House. But, for Julian, his job with Lister was just that—a job. He enjoyed it, he learned a lot from it, and he had nothing but respect for Lister Hill. But Julian always said it felt more like family with me, like a *team.* He was needed now, and he answered the call.

They both did. By Christmas Mary and Julian were living at the new Holiday Inn that had just been built in Jasper, and we began working every day to map out our strategy for the spring.

It still wasn't certain that I'd face a Nine-Eight race at all. There was a big push, not just among the eight incumbent Congressmen, but among the public, for the governor to call a special session of the state legislature to come up with a redistricting plan. Wallace, however, was in complete command at this point. As far as this question went, he held all the cards, and he played them to the hilt.

In early January, our Congressional delegation visited Wallace's office in Montgomery for a meeting that got us nothing but hoots from newspapers like the Tuscaloosa *Graphic,* which printed the following account, written by a reporter named Bob Ingram:

> It came a little late, but Gov. George C. Wallace got about as nice a Christmas present as he could hope for.
>
> It didn't come until Jan. 3, but the present he got was a

visit from Alabama's eight congressmen. They came humbly, hats in hand, asking forgiveness for past transgressions.

Their contrite hearts were motivated out of necessity. . . . Wallace enjoyed the meeting immensely, as one congressman after another gave pro-Wallace testimonials. Several of the men probably had to swallow hard to do so. They did everything but sing "Dixie" and had Wallace asked for a chorus of that tune from the octet he probably would have got it.

Making the scene all the sweeter for Wallace was the fact that he knew full well that at least a majority of the men present had not voted for him for governor. He also knew, thanks to his superb underground organization, that several of the congressmen felt the governor had made a fool of himself in his segregation fight with the feds.

Yet despite all of this, the eight were dancing a jig to Wallace tunes.

It ate at my insides to attend that meeting. It was humiliating. And it was all for nought. No special session was called.

To make matters worse, Congress had convened that year with one item at the top of its agenda: civil rights. The push for a Civil Rights Act had reached a head, and with my seat on the Rules Committee, I found myself in the strange position of being cast as Howard Smith's *ally,* as we voted the same way on that bill. In the spin of circumstances, Dick Bolling, who had become the leading House advocate for the Civil Rights Act—the same Dick Bolling who had been so instrumental in getting me on the Rules Committee —went on the "Today" show and denounced me for "obstructing and stalling" consideration of that legislation.

I had made my commitments, and I knew what they were. Dick had made his as well, and we both understood. But still, so many things seemed to be getting turned inside out, it was almost enough to make the head spin. Any way I turned, I was stepping off a cliff. If I went with the Wallace crowd, I'd lose everything I ever stood for or worked for. If I went against them, I'd lose any chance to stand for or work for anything more.

I stood against civil rights, believing it was too much too soon, hoping this Wallace madness would pass away, having faith that some less confrontational steps toward integration could then be taken, and knowing I wanted to be around when they were.

I also believed the law was the law, no matter how you felt about it. It's one thing to fight a piece of legislation before it becomes law, but once it passes, I believe it has to be obeyed. I stated that belief time and time again throughout my life, beginning with the 1954 *Brown v. Board* decision and on through every piece of desegregation legislation that followed.

Simply stating that belief set me apart from the segregationists.

A historian named C. Vann Woodward—a real smart fellow—did a pretty good job of summing up the outlook shared by Wallace and the rest of the segregationists toward an attitude like mine:

"A 'moderate,' " said Woodward, "became a man who dared open his mouth, an 'extremist' one who favored eventual compliance with the law, and 'compliance' took on the connotations of treason."

I guess that made me a traitor.

So that's how things stood when I officially announced my candidacy in February. Six of the other seven incumbents did the same— all except Albert Rains, who decided he had had enough of this insanity and announced he would not be running for reelection. Albert Rains was a smart man.

That meant there would be first-round primaries in Rains's open district and in Frank Boykins', which had been unrepresented since Boykins' defeat two years earlier. And there would be two incumbents facing in-district, Wallace-backed opposition: Bob Jones was opposed by a fellow named David Archer, and Tom Bevill had announced his candidacy against me.

Bevill's candidacy was clearly a can't-lose proposition for the Wallace machine, the same as Archer's was against Jones. If Bevill beat me, so much the better. If he lost, I still would have spent thirty days and untold amounts of money and resources simply getting on the statewide ballot.

There was no more guessing about targets. It was clear by then that either Jones or I would become the bull's-eye. Wallace's plans were obvious, not just inside Alabama, but beyond. Rowland Evans and Robert Novak, the Washington *Post* columnists, described the situation in a March 30 edition of their "Inside Report":

> Alabama's Gov. George Wallace is trying harder to convert his state into a feudal principality than any politician in any southern state since Louisiana's Huey Long. . . .
>
> Wallace's "plan for Alabama" is simple and direct: liquidate the state's elected moderates and replace them with Wallace men.
>
> Thus, Wallace is running David Archer against Rep. Bob Jones of the 8th congressional district in the Democratic primary. He's running Tom Bevill, the Wallace-owned floor leader of the State House of Representatives, against Rep. Carl Elliott in the 7th district. . . .
>
> Wallace is now extending his political hold in the state to every nook and cranny, riding the twin issues of racism and hate-Washington. So much a symbol of hate has the "central government" become that the mere presence of Rep. Elliott, an Administration man, on the powerful House Rules Committee is being used against him. Elliott, it is said, is part and parcel of the Washington power structure.

That's what Tom Bevill was saying as he launched his campaign that month. For our part, we decided to use the same tool that had been so effective in working for Kennedy—the coffees. Again, the point wasn't to win converts so much as to shore up the people who were already with us, to make sure they got out and voted and that they got their spouses and friends out to vote as well.

I remember those coffees as one of the few bright spots of that summer, working our way through as many as ten a day. Oh, we had it down to a science. Julian would ride ahead, carrying a coffeepot and a case of Coca-Colas in the trunk, and in the back seat he had a film projector, a screen and a little movie we'd made summing up my politics and my career. He'd arrive at a house, set up the refreshments, show the movie and be on his way out just as Mary and I arrived. While I was giving a little talk and meeting with the crowd at that house, Julian would be setting up the next coffee at a house down the road.

One afternoon we wound up a long day with a coffee over in Cordova, at a housing project called Carl Elliott Heights. A woman there had volunteered to be a hostess, and we jumped at her offer. The press was playing it up pretty big, since this was one of the projects I'd gotten built early in my Congressional career. We had a huge crowd there, people squeezed wall to wall in this tiny apartment, with an even bigger throng gathered outside, peering in through the windows.

Since this was the last stop of the day, Julian was back in the kitchen, winding down with his own cup of coffee while I entertained the crowd out in the living room. As he sat there, the hostess came up and grabbed a chair.

"Mr. Butler," she said, "I hear you're a lawyer."

Julian had gotten his degree the previous spring, but he hadn't practiced a day of law in his life. He was not, however, about to admit that to this woman.

"Yes ma'am," he said, "I'm a lawyer."

"Well," she said, "I've got a little legal problem I'd like to discuss."

"That's fine," said Julian. "What's the problem?"

"I got in a little trouble with a woman at work," she said.

"What kind of trouble?"

"Well, she accused me of running around with her husband, and we wound up sort of getting into it on the job."

"Into what?"

"Well, when she said those ugly things about me, I picked up some scissors and I stabbed her."

Julian stopped sipping his coffee.

"Then what happened?" he asked.

"The sheriff arrested me. The case is set to go to trial in two weeks."

Julian set down his cup.

"What are you charged with?"

"Assault with intent to murder."

I had finished my speech and was shaking hands with a long line of people when Julian slipped up behind me and whispered in my ear, "Mr. Elliott, I just found out your hostess is under indictment for assault with intent to murder."

"The hell you say," I whispered back, still smiling and shaking hands. "Let's get the hell out of here."

Luckily, none of the reporters in the crowd heard about—or from—our hostess that afternoon.

I beat Tom Bevill by about two to one in that election, carrying every county in the district. But it cost me, just the way Wallace's people hoped it would. It cost me time, and it cost me money. I hit the statewide campaign trail a month behind most of the others (Bob Jones was also late getting started, after beating Archer), and what I found when I started getting around was a racism even deeper and more widespread than I had sensed two years earlier.

I stopped into a barbershop one afternoon down in Demopolis, south of Tuscaloosa, and here came an old Southern colonel-looking kind of a fellow, who stopped in and sat a minute while I was getting my hair cut. He was just sort of looking me over, then he finally spoke.

"Do I understand that you're a member of Congress?" he asked.

I told him I was.

And he said, "Well, when on earth are you people going to learn some sense?"

He said, "When will you learn that God put these niggers on this earth to serve God's children, and that *white* folks are his children?"

He went on like that for a while, then he left. I said to the man cutting my hair, "Hell, does everybody around here think like this fellow?"

"Naw," said the barber. "Not more'n eighty percent of 'em."

It was on the wave of that kind of support that George Wallace went out to test the national waters that same month, entering presidential primaries in Indiana, Wisconsin and Maryland, to "take the

Alabama story to the people of this nation," as he put it. He warmed up by speaking at some college campuses in the North, where the reception was less than warm. Of course that put George right in his element—confrontation. He traded insults with picketers and hecklers almost everywhere he went, giving the reporters more material than they could handle. They'd never seen anything like George Wallace up there in New England.

But after losing by two-to-one margins in both Wisconsin and Indiana to favorite son stand-ins for Lyndon Johnson, Wallace decided he needed some reinforcements and a little more legitimacy when he moved on to Maryland. So, in mid-May, he sent for Alabama's Congressional delegation to join him on the stage at College Park, where he was scheduled to make a speech to an audience of University of Maryland students.

Of course that put those of us who weren't on Wallace's side on the spot. To openly defy him at that point, in the midst of the statewide primary campaign back home, was to put a nail in our own coffins. The only one of us with nothing to lose was Albert Rains—and he wound up being the only one who didn't go.

That was one of the lowest points of my life. Simply sitting on that stage, lending any kind of validity at all to George Wallace, made me realize how desperate I had become. It physically hurt. When I got back to Alabama the next day, I went right home to Jasper. That was the only day during that race—in fact, it was the only day during any race in my life—that I did no campaigning at all. I just couldn't.

As election day came closer, it was hard to tell what was going to happen. Trying to gauge that situation was like groping around a dark room. The Klan and the Birchers had been speaking out against me, but the full force of the Wallace machine hadn't been aimed at me—or at anyone else. Yet.

Then, ten days before the June 2 election, an outfit called the United Conservative Coalition held a meeting at the old Jefferson Davis Hotel in Montgomery. This outfit was the core of the old-line Dixiecrat states' righters, a reactionary think tank, part of the heartbeat of the George Wallace machine. A banker named Wallace Malone, from down in Dothan, pulled the meeting together, with the express purpose of deciding who they wanted to beat in this election, Bob Jones or me. I was nowhere near Montgomery that day, but it didn't take long for word to reach me about what went on down there. That bothered me, of course, but what hurt worse was finding out that Bob Jones, my ally and friend through a lot of long years, had been registered in a room at the Jeff Davis Hotel that same day.

I don't know if Bob Jones had anything to do with that meeting. I have never wanted to find out. But I do know that three days before the election the state was flooded with more than a million sample ballots, printed and paid for by the United Conservative Coalition, distributed in every county across the state by Alabama state troopers, each ballot bearing the Wallace slogan "Stand Up for Alabama," and each ballot listing the names of all candidates in that Tuesday's Democratic Congressional primary election . . . all except me.

Sample ballots are often used in elections, to familiarize voters beforehand with what they'll be seeing when they step into the voting booth election day. In this case, voters saw the slogan they recognized as George Wallace's. They saw eight names beneath that slogan. The ninth name, mine, was nowhere to be seen.

By the time the newspapers wrote about the "Drop Elliott" ballots, the damage had been done. Wallace, at a "hastily called news conference," as the New York *Times* described it, denied any connection. I called him the day before the election and confronted him about it.

"Who do you accuse?" he asked me.

I said, "I'm not being funny with you, Governor. I'll tell you who did this." And I gave him the names, as if he didn't know.

But it didn't matter. Neither did the last-minute television time I bought to try undoing the damage of those ballots. When the Birmingham *News* arrived on my doorstep the morning after the election, its front-page headline told me what I'd known before I'd gone to bed at three the night before: ELLIOTT DROPPED IN 9–8 BALLOTING.

I'd finished ninth, the low man out.

My career in Congress was finished.

If there was any consolation in that defeat, it was the fact that some people, not just in Alabama but across the country, recognized the threatening significance of what had happened in this election. In one sense, I had made the bed in which I was buried. The Montgomery *Advertiser*'s Bob Ingram made that point:

> Congressman Carl Elliott of Jasper has been called a lot of different names in his political career.
>
> But nowhere in the files is there any evidence to suggest that anyone ever accused Elliott of straddling the fence.
>
> Elliott has distinguished himself as a man who spoke his piece, letting the chips fall where they may. On Tuesday they fell on him.
>
> He found out what history has frequently recorded—a candid candidate is not always a successful one.

But there was more to this particular election than the simple hard-knocks lessons of politics. Something disturbing was afoot not just in Alabama but in the mood of the entire country, and George Wallace had seized on it. The willingness of a large portion of the public not only to embrace a hateful philosophy but also to accept and endorse the foul tactics that came with it frightened more than a few folks both inside this state and out.

The Tuscaloosa *News* had this to say:

> Morality is not always an element in political situations, but that is one thing wrong with politics. And if we expect those who hold political position to be honest, why should we, their constituents, be any less demanding in our relationships toward those in office and those who seek office? Those thoughts arise in connection with the experience of Representative Carl Elliott of Jasper. . . .
>
> What have we done to ourselves by joining in a campaign by some group offended by Mr. Elliott, to scalp him? We have turned a congressman out to pasture. But haven't we also

helped to point up the unnecessary sacrifice we sometimes require of honest men seeking to serve?

The Nashville *Tennessean* was a little less restrained in its outrage:

The fate of Congressman Elliott leaves an ugly scar on the image of democratic government and gives frightening insight into the vicious methods of extremist groups.

Mr. Elliott had served his district well and served the nation well. Because of his refusal to accept contributions with strings attached, he usually operated on a thin campaign budget.

With the reshuffling of the Alabama congressional districts, Mr. Elliott had to leave his district and run as an at-large candidate. This left him exposed to the tactics of those who would misrepresent his record to those not familiar with it.

Mr. Elliott had drawn the opposition of the United Conservative Coalition of Alabama—a group that includes members of the White Citizens Council, Ku Klux Klan, and the John Birch Society.

In the campaign last June Mr. Elliott was blacklisted from the group's approval. To combat this he was forced to go on television in a last-minute effort to straighten out his record. But the damage had been done. Mr. Elliott lost. The television time had cost him $15,000 paid in advance, running up most of his debt.

As a result of this campaign of treachery, a conscientious public servant has been shamefully wronged, and the people of Alabama have been deprived of the services of a good congressman.

It is not a pretty sight in this land of freedom and justice.

The New York *Times* looked to the immediate future in terms of what my defeat said about the political direction of the entire South:

The defeat this week of Representative Carl Elliott, Democrat of Alabama, is expected to cut into Administration support among Southern moderates and liberals. . . .

His defeat was attributed largely to his identification with both the Kennedy and Johnson Administrations and to his opposition to Gov. George C. Wallace of Alabama.

Some observers view Mr. Elliott's defeat as purely an Alabama matter, indicative of Governor Wallace's tightening grip on the state. . . .

But others see the Elliott defeat as evidence of a general swing to more militant conservatism throughout much of the South.

This has posed a problem for the relatively small band of Southern liberals and moderates: Is it worth the political risk to continue supporting programs that their more conservative colleagues oppose?

I took that risk, and it cost me dearly. I'd never thought much about what it would feel like to be leaving Congress. I'd always assumed that that day would be far in the future, and I'd always assumed *I'd* be the one to decide when that day had come.

So it felt strange to sit in the House chamber on a Saturday afternoon early that October and hear my colleagues, one by one, rise and give testament to my career. I can't say the occasion was a happy one, but the words I heard that afternoon, from foes as well as friends, from Republicans as well as Democrats, were ones I still treasure today.

There was Carl Albert, paying tribute to the one thing for which I would always want to be remembered:

"I thought of the first great legislative effort of Carl yesterday, when we were adopting the conference report on the amendments to the National Defense Education Act. . . .

"I was asked a few days ago what I considered to be three of the greatest pieces of legislation that I had had the opportunity to vote for during my years in Congress, and I put this down as one of the three. Any person who is associated with this legislation must be regarded as having had an illustrious career in the Congress of the

United States. Carl Elliott was the author of this bill, and in turn the bill which he authored has immortalized his name.

"Few people in our country have the opportunity of serving in Congress, and few who do serve in Congress have the opportunity to have such a major part in such an important piece of legislation as that.

"I am proud to have been a friend of Carl Elliott. He is a Congressman and a gentleman in every sense of both of those words. He has been one of the great Members of this House, sincere, kind, devoted, and dedicated to the principles in which he believes."

There was Claude Pepper, hardly able to contain his dismay at the forces that had brought this day about:

"I believe with my heart that one of the greatest tragedies that has ever befallen the great state of Alabama, America, and this House of Representatives is the passing from it for the present time of a man who has devoted 16 years of distinguished service to his district, his state and his country—Carl Elliott.

"Mr. Speaker, when Christ was being crucified, he said, 'Father, forgive them, for they know not what they do.' I venture to say, and to hope, that those who have removed Carl Elliott from their service and from the service of their country, will someday lament and repent the error of their way. . . .

"Carl Elliott is a man of shining courage. I believe that sometimes it is more rare to have political courage than to have personal courage, because to stand up against the winds of political hostility, to refuse to yield to forces that are ignoble and unworthy, to decline to turn one's back upon the people who need a champion as their spokesman and a warrior for their cause sometimes requires greater character and courage than is required of a man to face dangers of another sort. . . .

"I venture to say, Mr. Speaker, that the days are not distant when the great people of Alabama, who basically love Carl Elliott as he has loved them, will honor him with the highest office they can bestow upon him."

There were plenty of others with kind words to share—probably too many for anyone's comfort on the last of so many long afternoons that session. But it was Dick Bolling whose words struck closest to the heart of what had happened, and it was his words that struck the deepest chord inside me that afternoon—and many afternoons to come:

"It seems to me that one of the great tragedies of my experience in this House of Representatives is the fact that one of the ablest of its Members has been defeated by a people temporarily bereft of their reason. I am sure that the people of Alabama—and I think I can speak of Alabama with some conviction because I grew up there—will soon come to understand that in retiring Carl Elliott they retired one of their ablest spokesmen for several generations.

"His fault, if any, was foresight. His guilt, if any, was courage."

*In his hands people, like words, have become tools of the political trade;
and he has been a master at doing with them whatever he wished.*
From Watch Out for George Wallace,
by Wayne Greenhaw

THIRTEEN

<small>∽∾</small>

THE LAST STAND

I've never been one to worry as much about money as maybe I
should have. I've got plenty of friends—as well as foes—who
will attest to that fact. Personally speaking, I've never been much of
a businessman. Politically speaking, that was my strength as well as
my weakness.

The fact that the smell of money meant nothing to me allowed
me to keep a steady course through some pretty rough seas. I was
never confused by having to remember who I owed and how that
should affect my vote, because I didn't owe *anybody.* When I first
started out in politics, money didn't matter nearly as much as it did
by the time I was finished. Early on, I could afford to pretty much
disregard dollars, covering out of my own pocket whatever debt my
campaigns incurred. By the end of my career, however, that was
absolutely impossible.

Among the most pressing issues in American politics today is
the expense of campaigns and the question of who our politicians

are answerable to—the large mass of the voting public or the small
slivers of overly influential special-interest campaign contributors.
It's an issue whose particulars have hardly changed since my last
race for Congress. A fellow named Walter Pincus wrote a piece for
the Washington *Star* newspaper that described the financial fallout
of that 1964 campaign. I think it sheds a lot of light on the economic
squeeze men seeking public office face today. It also gives a pretty
good picture of where I stood as I decided which way to turn at the
end of that year:

Representative Carl Elliott of Alabama, 16 years in Congress
and for the last 4 years a member of the powerful House Rules
Committee, leaves office at the end of this session faced with
the problem of raising $20,000 to pay outstanding campaign
bills from his unsuccessful statewide primary race this past
June.

Though his situation may not be typical, Mr. Elliott's present dilemma is worth studying for it portrays a side of politics
that is little publicized.

Mr. Elliott's former district was a rural one—the largest
town having a population of 10,000. In 1948, when he first ran
for Congress, the Democratic nomination was—as it is now—
tantamount to election. His first primary race cost $12,000, of
which, he said recently, $7,500 was his own money.

Once he became the incumbent, finances were no problem. During the Eisenhower years he occasionally had a Republican opponent in the general election, but the State Democratic organization would help out with $1,000 and party
committees would put up advertising money.

Mr. Elliott's present plight was born in 1960. As a result of
that year's census, Alabama lost one of its nine congressional
seats. Its legislature failed to pass a redistricting bill, and in
1962 and again this year the Democratic primary candidates
had to run at large. . . .

Running at large in the 1962 Democratic primary, where
only eight of the nine incumbents could be selected, Mr. Elliott
had to raise a campaign war chest of nearly $100,000—an

amount almost unheard of among his rural constituency. He and his supporters decided upon two fund-raising devices—a mailed appeal for $10 contributions and a series of dinners.

The mailed appeal contained a personal message from the Congressman along with a blank check made out to his campaign committee. Mr. Elliott recalled recently that the cost of printing and mailing the appeal came to $3,000; the return on the effort was $3,400.

The dinners proved more successful. Ranging in price from $100—in the Congressman's hometown—to as little as $5, some $60,000 was raised.

When it was all over his deficit came to nearly $30,000. Mr. Elliott all but used up his savings to meet almost $20,000 of the bills with his own money.

This year, with the need as great, his close advisers decided the dinners had drained so much money from the district that they could not be repeated. Instead finance committees were established in each county to solicit directly. In rural areas, this type of solicitation—where the solicitor has to be reimbursed a day's pay and expenses—usually brings in little political money. Nonetheless, the Elliott campaign drew a respectable $40,000.

In addition, a reception was held in Washington one Sunday afternoon and about $7,500 was raised. Another $10,000 came from Alabamians outside his district, and members of the Elliott family put up $2,000.

That money would have been enough, Mr. Elliott said recently, had it not been for the United Conservative Coalition of Alabama.

Ten days before the Democratic primary, this group—which has among its members, according to Mr. Elliott, members of the White Citizens Council, Ku Klux Klan, John Birch Society and the state's growing Republican Party—met in Montgomery and decided to print cards for distribution around the state listing eight of the nine candidates. Mr. Elliott's name was left off. . . . He held a press conference the Saturday before the election, then decided the only effective thing he could do to combat the card was to appear on state-wide television on election eve.

His program, carried by half the stations in Alabama, cost him $15,000—all paid in advance the day before the election. He had to mortgage his car that day—for $3,100—to complete the payment. His TV appeal was not successful.

There were contributions in his last campaign which Mr. Elliott says he turned down, despite the fact that he sorely needed the money.

"I had an outfit offer me in Alabama," he related, "a substantial contribution provided I vote against wage and hour amendment proposals. I told them I always supported expansion of that act and didn't believe any new action was due in the coming Congress and I didn't believe I could take their contribution.

"I was told a fellow could arrange a $1,000 contribution if a certain person, not the fellow giving the money, was appointed postmaster. I told him I wasn't going to recommend that fellow and not to go any further.

"An Alabama group offered $500 to be given by their check. I turned them down twice because they were highly controversial. . . .

"There are stories told of people who have made money on campaigns, but it's hard for me to visualize. I don't know it any way but hand-to-mouth. The wonder of it all is that the vast majority (of Congressional candidates) do their best to play it honest."

As for the future of campaign fund raising: "It will be a high point in our civilization when, in a democracy, the people become so sophisticated they are willing to give $50 or $25 to candidates who need it."

In the meantime, Mr. Elliott's financial problems take a good part of each day's work. Three weeks' effort by friends brought in only $3,000.

"This business of campaign fund raising is awful hard even for a winner. For a loser . . ."

It was hard, awfully hard, to swallow the idea that I was a loser. I could work to pay off that debt, but the taste of defeat was not so easily erased, especially a defeat like that one. If I'd been whipped fair and square, that would have been one thing. I could have accepted that and gone on about my business. But there was so much that was just plain wrong about what had happened, about the way I'd been beaten and about the way Alabama was headed with the people who had come into power, that I couldn't just sit back and watch. I had to do something, but I wasn't sure just what it would be.

I couldn't imagine running for Congress again. My place on the Rules Committee was gone, filled in fact by the man I recommended when Speaker John McCormack called me in after my primary defeat and asked who I'd most like to take my place. I told him Claude Pepper, and Claude Pepper it was. I was pleased to see that, and I was tickled when Claude eventually became chairman of that committee. The first thing he did upon becoming chairman was to remove a portrait of Judge Howard Smith that was hanging in the committee's hearing room. When a staff member asked him where to put the picture, Pepper told him, "Under the front steps of the Capitol might be a suitable and safe place." Dick Bolling's portrait, by the way, was the only other picture hanging in that room, and it remained.

If I had come back to the House, I would have had to begin again as a freshman Congressman, working my way through the same process I had begun sixteen years earlier. I felt I had come too far and done too much to start all over again like that.

Meanwhile there had been a major shake-up in Alabama's Congressional delegation. Barry Goldwater's stand against civil rights in that year's presidential campaign made the Republican Party a suddenly formidable force in the South. In Alabama, it turned the entire state upside down. In the 1964 presidential election, nearly seventy percent of Alabama's voters chose Goldwater over Johnson. Beyond that, three Democratic House members—George Grant, George Huddleston and Kenneth Roberts—lost to Republican challengers. Albert Rains's empty House seat was filled by Jim Martin,

the man who had almost beaten Lister Hill in 1962. And Frank
Boykins' Mobile district also went to a Republican.

There was only one issue that mattered to Alabamians in that
election: race. That issue was wreaking havoc not only in the streets
but also within the political structure of the state. "There is a vast
Democratic vacuum in Alabama," proclaimed an editorial printed
that October in the Birmingham *News.*

That same editorial mentioned a "whisper" that I might be
running for governor in 1966. I don't know if I had made that
decision when that editorial was printed. But it wasn't long before I
figured out that was where I had to make my move. The way George
Wallace had seized power in this state, it was clear that the future of
Alabama lay in its governorship. I had been driven for sixteen years
in Congress by the goal of bettering the lives of poor people
throughout this nation. Now I saw that the lives of my own neighbors, rich, poor and in between, were in the hands of a man who
could only hurt them. The forces that had beaten me were now
totally steering the state of Alabama. The only way to stop what was
happening, as far as I could see, was to win the statehouse.

That would take some doing, but changes were afoot that
looked like they might make it possible. The very people Wallace
had worked so hard to suppress were now rising for the first time in
Alabama's history as a political force to be reckoned with. By the
end of 1964, with the passage that July of the Civil Rights Act and
with the awarding that December of the Nobel Peace Prize to Dr.
Martin Luther King, Jr., the civil rights movement was swelling. In
1965, it peaked.

First came Selma, where on a bright, breezy Sunday in March
some six hundred and fifty blacks left that city's Brown's Chapel
AME Church to begin a march toward Montgomery to secure their
voting rights. In a meeting with legislative leaders prior to the
planned march, George Wallace declared, "I'm not going to have a
bunch of niggers walking along a highway in this state as long as I'm
governor." I believe he did his best to keep his word.

As the marchers crossed Selma's Edmund Pettus Bridge,
named after a Confederate brigadier general, they could see a crowd
ahead of them. Waiting at the end of the bridge was an armed and

mounted civilian posse organized by Selma Sheriff Jim Clark, along with one hundred helmeted, gas-masked Alabama state troopers ordered to the scene by George Wallace.

When the protesters reached the end of the bridge, Major John Cloud of the state troopers ordered the blacks to disperse and go home. The marchers stopped, many kneeling to pray. Then Cloud ordered his men to attack. At the same time, Clark's men moved in. The protesters were surrounded, bombed with tear gas and whipped with chains, electric-shock cattle prods and rubber tubing wrapped with barbed wire.

Forty of the marchers were severely injured. Scenes of the massacre shot across the country like lightning. The Boston *Globe* asked, "What words can describe the depravity of the state troopers and mounted deputies who committed this outrage against America? And what can be said of Governor Wallace?" The New York *Times* said Wallace "has written another shameful page in his own record and in the history of Alabama."

Selma's "Bloody Sunday" became a national spectacle, staining Alabama just as Bull Connor had done with his dogs and hoses two years before in Birmingham. And it had the same effect, hastening rather than delaying the changes these protesters were out to make. President Lyndon Johnson's immediate reaction to the scene at Selma was to announce that he was submitting a Voting Rights bill to Congress.

Four months later, on August 6, 1965, he signed that bill into law.

As thousands of new black voters began to register in droves throughout the South, I believed that maybe, just maybe, the tide had turned. Maybe, just maybe, George Wallace had seen his day in Alabama. Maybe this state and the South were ready to turn over a new leaf.

That's what I had been hoping when I traveled up to Tufts University in Massachusetts in June of 1965 to receive an honorary degree. The speaker that day was Attorney General Nicholas Katzenbach, the same man who had faced George Wallace at the schoolhouse door in Tuscaloosa. A columnist named Ann Cottrell Free, writing in the Washington *Post,* used that image to begin a piece published the week of my honor from Tufts:

> The man who helped to open the "schoolhouse door" to 750,000 students has not been completely forgotten during these June days when universities are bestowing their accolades for excellence. But, ironically, when the President of Tufts University in Medford, Mass., handed an honorary degree of Doctor of Laws on Sunday to the tallest, gangliest political man since the days of Abraham Lincoln or "Kissin' Jim" Folsom, its recipient, Carl Elliott, accepted in the opinion of some, another political albatross.
>
> For the degree was for political courage as well as for his support of higher education while in Congress. The citation noted that the former Alabama Congressman "refused to campaign on a platform of racism when such a platform ran counter to his concept of responsible leadership."
>
> Being loved and admired by the folks in the land of Kennedys, Mrs. Peabody and Harriet Beecher Stowe will never win votes in the Alabama of Governor Wallace or Sheriff Jim Clark. And Mr. Elliott, his friends believe, will be seeking votes in Alabama again—perhaps for the governorship. They remind that other notable Elliott honors in the past—a seat on the powerful House Rules Committee and the friendship and admiration of the late John Kennedy—proved to be members of the albatross family.
>
> But Elliott is aware of all that. He is convinced that the albatross in this case is a better bird to swear by than the white rooster of white racial supremacy that adorns all ballots in Alabama. . . .
>
> He told the graduating class at Florence (Ala.) State College last week that most Alabama political speeches would be void of substance if a dozen words and phrases were removed. They are: "Segregation, integration, states' rights, Federal power, conservative, liberal, moderate, violence, law and order, central government, and sovereign state."

The class listened attentively. One of its members, Wendell Wilkie Gunn, was the second Negro student to graduate from a "white" Alabama college.

One June day in the future Carl Elliott may be able to tell an Alabama graduating class that the bird everyone thought was an albatross, in reality was a phoenix—arisen, live and kicking, from the ashes.

By then I had already decided. The people of Alabama deserved better than George Wallace. And I was prepared to give it to them.

Whether Wallace himself would be able to make a campaign was another matter. For more than sixty years, Alabama law had prohibited a governor from succeeding himself, but if you knew anything at all about George Wallace, you knew he wasn't going to let that get in his way. Sure enough, when the state legislature refused to approve an amendment changing that law during its regular session of 1965, Wallace called a special session that fall for the express purpose of pushing through the amendment.

As he so often did when blocked by the word of the law, Wallace turned to the will of the people. "I am willing to accept the judgment of the people," he lectured the legislature, urging them to turn their decision over to the voting public. The state House of Representatives heeded his call, approving the amendment, but the Senate resisted. There were enough men in the Senate fearful of the power Wallace had already collected to allow him any more. One of those men, a fellow from Dekalb County named Kenneth Hammond, delivered a speech to the Senate that pulled no punches:

"If the governor wins the succession fight it will make Huey P. Long look like a piker. He will have control of every string of federal money coming into the state. If he runs for president in 1968 the state will pay the bill. He will pit the white race against the minority the same way Hitler pitted his people against the Jews."

That sort of strong language was rarely heard in Montgomery in George Wallace's time. It helped beat the proposed amendment, which fell three votes shy of the number necessary to pass. But it also ensured that Hammond—along with almost every other man who had opposed Wallace in both the House and the Senate—was not in office when the smoke cleared after the 1966 elections.

I was hoping Wallace would win that fight. I wanted to meet him head on, to have it out once and for all on an open stage for all of Alabama to see. No longer bound by my obligations as a Congressman, I would be free this time around to speak my mind and my conscience more openly than ever before. As I told the New York *Times,* when I announced my candidacy in October of 1965, it was time to "clear the air and give the people of Alabama a clear-cut choice between a political moderate and an extremist."

I had the money I needed, with pledges of more than a hundred and fifty thousand dollars from a group of businessmen in Birmingham. And I had a broad enough base of support, with my farm background appealing to rural voters and my work in Congress attracting the votes of teachers, labor and, I hoped, blacks.

The Birmingham *News* responded to my announcement in terms I welcomed:

> Mr. Elliott is the man to whom one can look for the most unpolitical campaign of any who might wind up in this race. The former congressman has absolutely nothing to lose by being absolutely forthright, and he would look downright silly— as he well knows—by trying to cozy around any issues of sensitivity. . . .
>
> Mr. Elliott will be welcomed to the race by those who find politics fun, exciting, frustrating and monotonous alike. His presence is certain to be salubrious and he may safely be encouraged by all to speak his mind. That the viewpoint may shake some people or jar them uncomfortably will be good for Alabama, regardless of the campaigning's outcome.

That's the way I saw it, although the day I announced my candidacy I had no idea who I'd be campaigning against. The Alabama legislature had yet to decide George Wallace's reelection fate, and no one else had decided to run. But within a month things began to take shape.

First there was Wallace himself, whose immediate response to the legislative defeat was to hint that he might run for the U. S. Senate. Soon, however, there were rumors that he was thinking of running his wife Lurleen for governor. For the time being, that's all there was of that talk—rumors.

Meanwhile, other candidates for governor began to emerge. By January there was quite a menu for the voters to consider.

Jim Folsom was on the list, making what would be his last run for public office. There were some who said his candidacy was no more than a reflex action, an old fire horse heading for the stable door when he hears the clanging of the bell. But there were still enough elderly Alabamians around to give Big Jim some votes for old times' sake.

A retired office worker named Eunice Gore was on the list, too, carrying his Bible with him as he campaigned and claiming he had "the backing of the Lord."

Then there was A. W. "Nub" Todd, a former commissioner of agriculture who earned his nickname when he shot off his left arm hunting groundhogs as a boy. Todd grew up in Franklin County at the same time I did.

Charles Woods, a multimillionaire from Dothan, wore an eye-patch over his face, which was horribly burned from a World War II B-24 crash. Woods considered his scarred face an asset in the run for governor. "The first duty of a politician is to get attention," he said. "Nobody can ignore me."

Sherman Powell was a coon hunter, a lay preacher and a lawyer from Decatur who described himself as "just an ol' country boy" and used a miniskirted go-go girl dancing the Watusi to draw crowds to his speeches.

But by the time I officially launched my campaign in late January with a rally in Birmingham, the two candidates I was most concerned about were Ryan deGraffenried and John Patterson. Both had been through the governor's race before, and each, in his own way, had some strong support behind him.

DeGraffenried was a young, honest, handsome man who appealed to the well-heeled people in the business community not collared by George Wallace. His defeat in the previous governor's race set an encouraging tone—Alabama had a long history of gubernatorial candidates who lost their first go-around, then won on their second try. A poll in late 1965 showed deGraffenried favored by sixty-four percent of the voters.

Meanwhile, Patterson was back with the same message he had delivered to the state in 1958. He launched his campaign as a hardline segregationist, saying, "We will stand firm, no matter the odds," and calling Alabamians to rally around the slogan, "We Dare Defend Our Rights." Although Wallace had endorsed no one, Patterson was the obvious choice to inherit the votes George left behind.

No sooner did Patterson announce his candidacy, however, than a terrible tragedy altered the entire race.

Ryan deGraffenried was killed in an airplane crash.

He had just made a speech in the small north Alabama town of Fort Payne and was in a rush to get to his next appearance in Gadsden, thirty minutes away. The weather was awful, the winds were bad, and it would have been almost as quick to drive. But Ryan insisted on going by air. About four minutes after takeoff the twin-engine Cessna 310 in which he was flying slammed into the side of a place called Lookout Mountain. Both deGraffenried and his pilot were found dead.

That was in early February. The newspapers immediately boiled the governor's race down to a contest between me and John Patterson, but I knew better. DeGraffenried's death had left a void his supporters would move to fill. Sure enough, they came up with a replacement candidate, a state senator from Morgan County named Bob Gilchrist. I'd counted on that. But I hadn't counted on two other candidates who entered the race before the end of that month.

One was the state's current attorney general, Richmond Flowers.

The other was George Wallace's wife, Lurleen.

It had been a long, lonely winter for Wallace. His defeat by the state Senate was the first serious setback he'd suffered since becoming governor, and his silence throughout the ensuing several months set people to whispering that maybe George Wallace was finally starting to slip, that maybe his grip wasn't as tight as it used to be. But all that talk—as well as Wallace's silence—vanished as soon as it was announced that his wife would run for governor and, if elected, would have her husband on the payroll as a dollar-a-year "aide."

There was hardly any pretense at all about the charade, least of all from Wallace himself. "It's time for the people to show those mealymouthed politicians a thing or two," he said at the time of the announcement. "If the people want George Wallace, they'll vote for his wife."

Lurleen Wallace's candidacy was transparent. But Richmond Flowers' was harder to figure out.

Flowers came from a wealthy family down in Dothan and had been a member of the state Senate before becoming attorney general in 1963. He wasn't associated with any particular issues during his time in the legislature, but he was one of the most popular after-dinner speakers in Alabama, known primarily for the "nigger" stories he told, complete with black dialect.

After he was elected attorney general, Flowers suddenly turned over a new leaf, becoming a critic of George Wallace's racial policies. When he took over the prosecution of suspects in the civil rights murders of Viola Liuzzo and Jonathan Daniels, he was hailed as a liberal. And when he announced at the end of February 1966 that he was seeking the governorship, it was with the express intention of going after the newly registered black votes.

It's always been hard for me to figure out why Richmond Flowers made that governor's race. Some say he was put up by the Wallace people to take the black vote away from me, but I don't believe that. Others point to his subsequent indictment and conviction by the federal government for his part in an illegal stock offering. Their theory is that Flowers became aware early in his term as attorney general that the federal government was investigating him and that he tried to build a record as an anti-segregationist, hoping that the Johnson Justice Department would back off and be happy to have a liberal in Wallace territory.

In any event, Richmond Flowers had little hope of winning the

governor's race in 1966. But his pursuit of the black vote spelled
plenty of trouble for me. That was obvious to everyone, including
Washington *Post* columnists Evans and Novak, who devoted one of
their "Inside Report" columns to what was headlined THE ALABAMA
PUZZLE:

BIRMINGHAM

Secret soundings have now gone out from Washington to
anti-Wallace Democrats here to determine whether Carl Elliott,
a loyalist Democrat, has any real chance to win the Democratic
nomination for Governor this spring.

If the answer is yes, influential figures in the Johnson Administration trusted by Alabama Negro groups—Vice President Hubert Humphrey would be a natural—will quietly urge
leaders of more than 200,000 Negro voters to support Elliott in
the May 3 primary.

With a sizable bloc of Negro votes, Elliott, a 16-year veteran of Congress who lost in the 1964 Goldwater sweep, would
be in excellent position to get into the runoff primary on May
31. The runoff pits the two top runners in the first primary
against each other. Segregationist Gov. George Wallace, mas-
querading in the petticoat of his wife, Lurleen, is certain to be
one of the two.

But instead of voting for Elliott, a racial and political mod-
erate, the disorganized Negro vote may turn to state Attorney
General Richmond Flowers, an uncompromising champion of
Negro rights.

The problem with Flowers is that, even if he makes the
runoff and wins the vote of every single registered Negro, he
probably would lose in a landslide to Lurleen Wallace.

Out of an estimated 600,000 white voters, Flowers would
be lucky to capture 75,000. . . .

But Elliott might be able to beat Mrs. Wallace in the May
31 runoff. And if Elliott got into the general election against
Martin he would be assured of massive Negro support. With
the Negro vote now totalling 25 percent of the overall vote, it

could elect Elliott governor—and begin a new day for Alabama.

The question then is whether the Negro leaders, disorganized as they are, will have the foresight not to waste the Negro vote on Flowers.

I was hoping they would have that foresight. I was hoping they would understand the things I had already done for the education (with the LSA and the NDEA) and the health (with Medicare) of poor people, black and white alike, not just in Alabama but across the country. And I was hoping they would realize how much more could be done for them if I replaced George Wallace as governor.

Hope. I had an awful lot of it as February turned to March and the campaign kicked into high gear.

One of my favorite memories of that spring was the show we pulled together to put on the road. And there's no other word for it but a show. Jim Folsom had started the idea back in the 1940s with the Strawberry Pickers, the string band he brought up on stage to help draw crowds to his speeches and to entertain the folks once they got there. They'd warm the audience up with a few songs, just enough to whet the appetite. Then, with the promise that they'd be back after the speech, the musicians would leave the stage and Big Jim would come on and make his pitch. Finally, when he was done, the act would come back for a quick encore. Everyone went home entertained, maybe at least a little enlightened and hopefully ready to vote for Folsom.

Twenty years later every Alabama politician worth his salt was still putting the name of a musical act on the handbills advertising his next appearance—often with the name of the act printed in larger letters than the name of the candidate.

That 1966 primary race nearly drained Nashville dry as musical acts were brought south to sing for Alabama's would-be governors. Lurleen Wallace had a couple of boys who called themselves the Wilburn Brothers—Teddy and Doyle. Jim Folsom had an outfit named the Alabama Red Raiders, fronted by Ronald Johnson, who was also the mayor of Garden City. Nub Todd brought in the Butter Bean Pickers, as well as the nationally famous Carter Family. And Sherman Powell had the Johnny Whitley Trio, just in case folks got bored with his go-go girl.

But I have to say I had the biggest draw of them all: Hank Williams, Jr.

I'd gotten to know Hank, Sr., back when I was first in Congress and was making frequent trips down to Montgomery. His music had always meant something special to me. It touched something in my heart the first time I heard it, because it spoke to and about the common man. When he sang about longing to "scat right back to my pappy's farm," you knew he'd been there, and he had. He was born in a log cabin, just like me, on a sharecropper's farm, just like me. That was in south Alabama, in a place called Georgiana, some sixty miles south of Montgomery. They called him the "Hillbilly Shakespeare," and I think that's just about right.

I'll always remember one particular afternoon during my first term in Congress, when I was down in Montgomery and ran into Hank on the sidewalk. He'd been in town a day or two, performing. He was a pretty big star by then, but he didn't seem too impressed with himself. We stopped and talked for a while, and while we were standing there, a young boy, a black boy, about eight years old, came up and asked for a penny. He said he was supposed to get a penny box of matches for his father.

Hank reached into his pocket and pulled out a five-dollar bill and told him to go on. The boy walked away like he'd been hit with a brick.

I said, "A box of matches sure comes mighty high to you, Mr. Williams. I pay a penny for mine."

"Aww," he said, "I'd rather see the light in that boy's eye. That could be the first five-dollar bill he's ever held in his hands.

"With all the rest of this stuff together," he said, running his hands over his fine-tailored suit, *"that's* where I get my pay."

Hank Williams died before he was thirty, from what one writer said was "too much living, too much sorrow, too much love, and too much drink and drugs." When he was buried on January 4, 1953, they called his funeral in Montgomery the city's "biggest emotional plunge since the inauguration of Jefferson Davis."

He left behind a lot of sad admirers, he left behind a lot of beautiful songs, and he left behind a son, the little boy he called "Bocephus" but that his wife Audrey insisted on calling Hank, just like his daddy.

Hank, Jr., was only three when his father died, but his mother did all she could to make sure he picked up where his daddy left off. At eleven, Hank Williams, Jr., made his debut at the "Grand Ole Opry," singing his father's songs in his father's voice. At fourteen, he appeared on the Ed Sullivan show and signed a six-figure recording contract with MGM Records.

I was thinking about his father as much as him when I wrote Hank, Jr., a letter early in 1966 inviting him to be part of my campaign. He and his mother came down to Jasper to meet me, and I guess they liked what they saw, because they signed on for two hundred dollars a show—hardly a drop in the bucket compared to the money Hank was making in Nashville, but it was the best I could do.

They weren't with me all the time—I had a top-notch gospel quartet called Hovie Lister and the Statesmen traveling with me as well. But whenever Audrey and Hank and his group, The Cheatin' Hearts, joined our caravan, I noticed she held a pretty tight rein on young Hank, telling him what to do just about every time he turned around. I finally told her I thought maybe she ought to give him just a little more leeway.

"Yeah, you can say that," she said, "but you've never had the job of raising a genius. And I've raised *two.*"

My best memory of Hank, Jr., came late in that campaign. We were going over Sand Mountain near Huntsville when I found out Hank turned seventeen that day. I told him we'd stop at the next little roadside restaurant and buy him a birthday lunch. Of course he thought that'd be all right.

We stopped, ate lunch, and just about then the schools around there started letting out. All these teenagers came pouring into that little restaurant, the way they did every day, and when they found out Hank Williams, Jr., was there, they came flocking over for auto-graphs.

I took one look at the signature he was putting on those pieces of paper, and I was stunned. It was a horrible scrawl. I could see this boy hadn't spent enough time in school. And I mentioned it, how it didn't pay to grow up ignorant.

We talked some, then he said, "Mr. Elliott, how much do you reckon the president of one of these little colleges around here makes in a year?"

I said about twenty-five thousand dollars, which was about the going rate at that time.

He did a little bit of figuring, then he said, "Well, I make a hundred and seventy-five thousand dollars a year just selling my records. That's seven times what you just told me."

I said, "Maybe so, but none of that makes any difference. A fellow *needs* an education, whether he picks a guitar or teaches school."

I said, "You're not going to be in demand forever. Things change, you know. But an education is something that stays with you no matter what."

I don't think my little speech made much difference to young Hank. He had some pretty hard times later on, turned into quite a hell-raiser, and took an awful spill off a mountain out in Montana, nearly killing himself. But he came back after that, and was more in demand than ever. Still is. So maybe he was right after all.

That campaign turned pretty ugly pretty fast.

I started off strong, telling a crowd in Birmingham, "We must have racial peace. We must seize the leadership from the self-serving extremists on both sides who use the race issue as a whipsaw for political gain or momentary personal gain."

In Gadsden, I chided the Wallace crowd for "cussing Uncle Sam" and said, "It might have served my political well-being in the past, and it might serve it today for me to curse the federal government and shout 'Never' at the top of my voice. But I'm not going to do it. I'm not going to do it today, tomorrow or ever."

In Talladega, I told them, "The smear artists are saying that if you lift my shirt you'll find the words 'U. S. Government Approved' stamped on my back. What the words read in fact are: 'My Country Right or Wrong, My Country!' And they are imprinted in my heart, mind and soul, not on my back."

Every place I stopped, the crowds seemed to get bigger. Fifteen hundred in Talladega. Two thousand in Tuscaloosa. Three thousand at Auburn. Six thousand in Huntsville. Lord God, that first month it was looking like I'd win this thing.

Almost immediately the Klan took the battle beyond words. I spent more than fifty thousand dollars for billboard space across the state, putting my name and face up where people could see them. Soon my face was being torn away, and the words "NEVER! NEVER! NEVER!" were scrawled across my name.

"That's the kind of thing that has become encouraged to be part of Alabama life," I told a crowd in Mobile. "The Kluxers can tear down every sign I've got, every one of them, and they can tear up every piece of literature I've got, but that will not alter the fact that Carl Elliott continues to lead the crusade for a better Alabama."

It got worse. Wherever my people went, they were watched. Some of my campaign workers' cars were run off the road by drivers who then disappeared into the night. Others would come over a hill in the northern counties and find Coca-Cola crates dropped in the road like land mines, busting their tires and endangering their lives. Some were shot at.

The campaign hadn't been going long when one of the fellows working for me, a big old boy named Ernie Thompson, from up in Franklin County, told me he was taking an afternoon off to go down to Birmingham. I asked him why.

"To buy me a pistol," he said.

"Oh no, you're not," I told him. "The only people that carry pistols in these parts are the Wallace people. But *my* folks are not going to carry them. I won't have it."

I understood Ernie's feelings, though. He'd gotten shot at up near a place called Center Point, and he was not one to back down from a battle.

And it did start to seem like a battle.

In Midfield, at a shopping center where George Wallace had delivered a speech two weeks earlier, I was told my rally had to be canceled because it would "disrupt business activities."

In Tuscaloosa, where I was scheduled to give a nighttime talk outside the courthouse, the lights went out just before I began my speech. No one could get the power back on, so I got hold of a flashlight and addressed the crowd anyway, from the back of a flatbed truck. When reporters asked the probate judge about the mysterious power loss, he shrugged: "I think it was just one of those things that will occur."

There were plenty of occurrences wherever I went. In Bessemer, a bunch of hooligans physically pushed us off a stage. I was threatened with arrest for speaking without a license, based on an ordinance that had just been passed a day or two before.

Then there were bomb threats. Those were a pretty effective tactic. You get an auditorium full of people waiting for a speech, and a bomb threat clears them out, not many of them are going to come back when the all clear is given.

We got one of those threats in Oneonta one night, up at the Blount County Courthouse. It was raining pretty hard, and about half the crowd was still around when the alarm was called off. We got started real late, and by the time I finished speaking, the rain was coming down even harder, too hard to go back out. So I got Hovie Lister and his band to come back on, the crowd settled back and joined in, and we had ourselves an all-night singing that went well beyond midnight.

My wife Jane joined the campaign as well, pinch-hitting for me time and again, when I had to be two places at once. One newspaper made a pointed reference to Lurleen Wallace by observing that "Mrs. Elliott will be speaking in behalf of her husband's candidacy and not vice versa." But we weren't out to attack Lurleen. Far from it. The way I saw it then, and the way I still see it, is that she was a victim of circumstances more than anything else.

The most tragic of those circumstances is she was dying when she made that campaign. George knew it, and that raises a lot of questions.

Lurleen and George had been together a long time. She was a

clerk in a Tuscaloosa five-and-ten-cent store when she met George fresh out of law school and married him in 1943. She gave birth to all four of George's children and stayed at his side from the beginning of his career in politics, through thick and thin. When he asked her to run for governor, she balked at first, according to Lurleen herself, who described her hesitation in an interview with a reporter following that election.

"I doubted whether I would really be governor," she said, "whether George was just playing some kind of political trick just to see whether it would work or not, or whether it was the way he explained it: to keep 'our' power base, 'we' had to keep running and winning. I figured that he knew more about politics than anybody else I had ever seen or heard in the world.

"When I was a little girl I used to listen to Franklin Delano Roosevelt on the radio; he had the most pleasant voice, and he was the most wonderful man to me. Somehow I figured George knew about as much about politics as Franklin Delano Roosevelt. I figured he knew I could win or he wouldn't want me to run. If I lost, I thought, it'd be just like him losing. He never liked to lose.

"The worst I ever saw him act was after he lost the governor's election in 1958. He went sour all over. I thought we were going to have to split up. It came almost to that. He just wasn't himself for nearly a year. Finally he came back around and started running for governor again, and he was all right.

"When I took on the job of running, I decided he knew exactly what he was doing."

It's that very fact—that George Wallace knew exactly what he was doing—that raised some pretty serious questions when he announced Lurleen's candidacy hardly a month after she had undergone extensive surgery for what they said was uterine cancer, which her doctors had detected late in 1965. Wallace had announced how "shocked" he was at the time that cancer was detected, and that's where some people have a problem with his story—and his sincerity.

The fact, according to people close to Wallace and to reporters who later investigated the story, is that Lurleen's cancer was actually first detected in 1961 during the birth of her last child. When doctors told George some "suspicious" tissue had been found in

Lurleen's abdomen during the caesarean birth, he chose not to tell her. But, according to Montgomery newspaper publisher Harold Martin, Wallace was well aware of the seriousness of his wife's condition, and while he might have kept it from her, he wasn't keeping it from everyone.

"Wallace told people when he was first inaugurated as governor [in 1963] that he doubted Lurleen would live out his term," Martin told a reporter named Michael Dorman, who wrote a book called *The George Wallace Myth*. According to Martin, Wallace's reaction to the 1965 "discovery" of Lurleen's cancer was a sham.

"The significance of this was that, when uterine cancer appears for a second time in a patient, it almost always eventually becomes fatal," said Martin. "Wallace was telling people at the time how shocked he was to learn Lurleen had cancer. I knew he couldn't be shocked because she'd had it before. I sent word to him that, if he didn't stop talking about the shock, I'd make the true story public. He sent word back to me that he really wasn't surprised at all, and he stopped talking about the shock. Later on, even though he knew how serious Lurleen's condition was, he had her go ahead and run for governor. He even had her campaigning out in California six weeks after one of her operations."

There is no doubt Lurleen Wallace was nervous and tired during that governor's campaign. I saw her many times, and she looked awfully bad. How much was her illness I can't say. There were times you could see it was all she could do to force a smile and wave from the back seat of her limousine. Most of her speeches consisted of hardly more than a wave and a few words. Then George would take the microphone and give the crowd what they came for.

Every time the stories about Lurleen's health are told—and they've been told time and time again in newspapers, magazines and books—George and his people deny them. Documented facts apparently don't mean as much to the people who follow George Wallace as Wallace's own word. That's the only way to explain the final question raised by a close friend of Lurleen Wallace's who talked about that 1966 campaign in Wayne Greenhaw's book, *Watch Out for George Wallace:*

"I don't care what George Wallace says, he made her run, and he caused her death. If she had not run, maybe she could have relaxed and enjoyed her last year on earth. That kind of strenuous work—getting up early, traveling all over the state, speaking four and five times a day, ending up late at night in some little town God knows where—it had to use up her energy. I was her friend up to the end, but I don't care about seeing George Wallace again. It's just awful, the way he put her up to politics to further his own career. And that's exactly what he did. I don't understand how people could go on voting for him after they saw what he did to her."

It wasn't the Wallaces I worried about as that campaign hit full tilt in April. It was Richmond Flowers. By that time, everyone knew Lurleen was going to finish first in the primary. A vote for her was a vote for George, and there were more votes for George than anyone else in Alabama. The real race was to finish a strong enough second to force a runoff. To finish that strongly, I knew I had to have the black vote.

Flowers was going all out into the black communities. In fact, he was campaigning there almost exclusively. It was obvious that tactic would not get him near enough votes for a runoff. But while he couldn't hurt Wallace, he could sure as hell hurt me.

Meanwhile I went about courting blacks and whites alike, refusing to go to either extreme for the votes of one or the other. I summarized my stance in a speech in Selma: "I have not come to Selma tonight to stand on the Edmund Pettus Bridge and shout 'Never!' Nor have I come to stand in the Brown's Chapel AME Church and sing 'We Shall Overcome.' There *must* be a middle ground for Alabamians."

In the middle is just where I found myself as the black political organizations in the state moved toward endorsing a candidate. Richmond Flowers had done exactly what I'd mentioned in my speech, joining hands with black leaders in the Brown's Chapel Church and singing "We Shall Overcome" with them. And they were responding to him as the alternative to George Wallace.

Meanwhile I approached the black audiences as I did the

whites, honestly and straightforwardly. I didn't cozy up to them, but I didn't back away either. When I made a speech in the town square of a place called Greenville, three times as many black people were in the crowd as white. When my talk was done, I shook hands with the crowd, black and white alike. Then I went inside to pay my respects to the probate judge, who hadn't come out to hear my speech. I began to thank him for the privilege of speaking at his courthouse when he suddenly cut me off.

"You," he said, as if pronouncing judgment from the bench, "have violated Southern tradition, shaking hands with those niggers."

"Now you hold it right the hell there," I said. "Don't you tell me about Southern tradition, by God. I'm a mountain man, and you're a Black Belt fellow, but I'm as much a Southerner as you are.

"Don't you *worry* about Southern tradition," I told him. Then I bade him good day, and left.

As I was walking away, this judge came out and hollered right there in front of the crowd, "You've gone around and shaken hands with these *niggers!* No white man's ever done that around here before."

I turned and said, "Well, this is a new kind of day, and I'm a new kind of white man."

But it began to look like I wasn't new enough. The traditional black establishment in the state, led by men like Arthur Shores—who had been Autherine Lucy's attorney at the University of Alabama and whose Birmingham home had been bombed so often people took to calling his neighborhood "Dynamite Hill"—and Joe Reed—who was part of a newly formed black organization called the Alabama Democratic Conference—were with me in the beginning, trying to convince their colleagues that I stood the best chance of any candidate in the race of attracting liberal and moderate white support. But as the momentum among the younger black community moved toward Flowers, it was clear their support was slipping away from me. When word spread that Martin Luther King, Jr., was getting set to endorse Flowers, I knew it was time to act.

Before that campaign began, I assumed I *had* the black vote. I assumed actions counted for more than words or mere gestures.

And I assumed my actions—the color-blind education and health bills I had pushed through Congress and the support I had given John Kennedy—spoke for themselves.

But I was wrong. I could see I was wrong, and the last thing left for me to do was turn to King himself.

The second week in April I sent Garve Ivey and my friend Barney Weeks, who was head of the Alabama AFL-CIO, to Washington, D. C., to meet with King and see what he might do to help us. The best Garve and Barney could get was a meeting with a King aide, but at that meeting the aide relayed King's word that, if King gave his endorsement to anyone in the Alabama race, it would be to me. At worst, he said, King would stay out of it and endorse no one.

At the same time, Garve and Barney got one of Lyndon Johnson's staff members to ask the President to speak to King about my situation. Word came back that King had checked up on things down here and had decided it had gone too far for Flowers.

"All it's going to do is hurt me if I try to turn them around," King told the President. "I've got to walk in front and let them push. There is nothing I can do about it."

Garve and Barney flew back that day from Washington to Huntsville, where I was making a speech. They met me at my motel afterward.

"What's the situation, Garve?" I asked.

"By God," he said, "we've lost the election."

"What are you talking about?"

"Lyndon Johnson can't turn him around."

"The hell he can't," I said. "He can't turn Martin Luther King around?"

"Sure as hell can't," said Garve. "Because King can't turn his people down here around."

I couldn't believe that was true. When I got word that King was coming to Birmingham later that week, I met him at the airport. We sat down for what turned out to be a quick discussion.

"I understand the pressure you've got on you," I told King. "But I also understand that you gave your word to my people that you'd stay out of this."

"A word means different things at different times," King answered. "I'm sorry about this. I understand your situation. But you must understand mine."

With that he left. By the time his motorcade got to Selma, King had publicly come out with an endorsement of Richmond Flowers for governor of Alabama, prompting both the Confederation of Alabama Political Organizations and the Alabama Democratic Conference—the state's two leading black political groups—to follow suit. And writers like Jack Nelson of the Los Angeles *Times,* an Alabama native himself, had their stories for the next day.

"The endorsements," wrote Nelson, filing his story from Atlanta, "will virtually eliminate Congressman Carl Elliott."

It was true. I didn't stand a ghost's chance in hell after that day. Looking back, I'm not sure I had a chance before it. But there was also no way I was going to quit. It was no longer a question of winning anymore, but of being heard. I didn't want my voice and my message to die in the dust. If people wouldn't wake up and listen right then, I had faith they'd listen *someday.*

So I kept at it, plowing across the state, from Eufaula, to Tuskegee, to Sylacauga, to Cottondale, to Eutaw. The crowds got thinner, and the money dried up. When they saw I couldn't win, the people down in Birmingham who had promised me some pretty big checks pulled back their pledges. I'd taken a bank loan on their word, and now I had that loan to settle myself.

Still we went on, my group of friends and me. That's what they were to me now, more than anything else—friends. I gathered them all together before the last stretch drive and told them they should go ahead and quit now, that they'd be wasting their time with me from here on in and that I'd hold it against none of them if they just packed up and moved on. But they didn't do that. They stayed with me to the end, Garve, Mary, Julian, Elise Lowery and all the rest. I guess it was a matter of faith, and they showed theirs.

In the last week of the campaign, I went through with a half hour of television time I'd bought in Birmingham. That bill alone was thirty-eight thousand dollars—thirty thousand for the time and eight thousand for the production. It had been a rough day as it was

—I had a pretty good portable public address system we'd used for most of the campaign and it was stolen that afternoon in Bessemer. Then, one after the other late that afternoon, I got telegrams from three people who had promised to pay for the broadcast that night. Each of them was pulling out. So I called John McCormack in Washington and told him I wanted to cash in my Congressional pension.

"Carl," he said, "that's crazy. I don't care what's happened down there, you can't do this. The time will come when you'll need this money to live on."

But I told him I had to have it. I'd given my word to a lot of people, and that was it.

The money came. I went on the air that night. Then I went home to Jasper for election day. The whole nation was watching Alabama that day. More than two hundred federal observers were dispatched by the Justice Department to make sure the newly registered blacks were allowed to vote without obstruction. One hundred twenty-two thousand blacks had registered since the Voting Rights Act the year before, nearly doubling the number of registered black voters in the state.

I stayed up late that night to hear the results. It didn't take long to see that I was nowhere within reach of a runoff with the Wallaces. At that point I got together my little gang around here. They wanted me to meet with them one last time, particularly the young folks. I guess I'd sort of become their hero for a while. Some of them were crying and carrying on, but I calmed them down with a little speech about the fact that we hadn't really lost, and that this fight would be won someday by someone else. That was one of the saddest nights of my life, but I didn't show it to them.

Then, about one o'clock that morning, I told them goodbye and went home to fix myself a little supper.

There was no runoff for that election.

Lurleen Wallace got more votes than the other ten candidates combined. I finished third, behind Richmond Flowers.

I was more than half a million dollars in debt. I wasn't sure exactly what I was going to do next, but I knew my political career had been spent.

For right or for wrong, it was gone.

"I'll Never Get Out of This World Alive"

Hank Williams, 1952

FOURTEEN

∾

THE AFTERMATH

S ome time back, a fellow came to my front door, the way so many have in the twenty-five years since that 1966 campaign— my last campaign.

I've talked to more of these people than I can count, men and women alike, some of them college students working on a thesis or a dissertation, some of them historians writing a book or a paper on Alabama history or politics, some of them journalists trying to sort out and make sense of what happened to this state and the rest of the Deep South in the 1950s and sixties. They all want to talk to someone who was in the middle of it all, they come across my name, and eventually they wind up here in Jasper, on my front porch.

I give them an afternoon, maybe a day, sometimes more, listening to their questions and trying my best to give them answers that might help, although Lord knows there are plenty of questions I gave up trying to answer a long time ago.

But this fellow was different. His name was William Bradford

Huie, from over in Hartselle, an hour or so east of Jasper. He'd written a few novels, including a couple of national best-sellers that had made him pretty rich. But it was his newspaper and magazine writing that had made Huie most famous—or infamous—in Alabama. Writing for magazines like *Look* and newspapers like the New York *Herald-Tribune,* he had spent a large part of his career investigating the troubles and peculiarities of the South and describing them to readers in the rest of the country. Huie was the man who first reported Jim Folsom's illegitimate son back in the late 1940s. Twenty years later he shadowed George Wallace throughout Wallace's 1968 presidential primary campaign. Two years before that, just as I was launching my 1966 campaign for governor, Huie came to my door to talk about an idea for a new book.

He wasn't interested in writing this one himself, Huie said. He wanted *me* to write it, a book about George Wallace. He said he'd read all the other books about George—and God knows there have been enough of them in the past two decades. But none of them had told the story the way it ought to be told, he said.

I asked him how it ought to be told.

"I can tell you exactly how it ought to *begin*," he said.

"And how's that?" I asked.

"I'd start it with one sentence," said Huie. *"I hate George Wallace."*

That really tickled me. I sat there smiling and shaking my head. And Huie, he was real puzzled. He figured, if there was any man in the world who had a right to hate George Wallace, it was me. Yet here I was, waving that idea away. He wanted to know why.

"Well," I finally told him, "I've definitely got feelings about George Wallace, real strong feelings. But how can a fellow who wants to leave behind him a message that hate just doesn't work, that it reaps nothing but trouble and terror, how can he begin a book with a statement like that?"

And it's true. I've got plenty of feelings about George Wallace, but hate is not one of them. I don't think I've ever felt hate for anyone in my life. Anger, yes. Even rage. But not hate, not since I stood in that crowd as a little boy, watching Tom Heflin cast his spell over the people standing around me. I was frightened by what

I saw and felt that day. I sensed something dangerous in the air, and I guess I just resolved to steer clear of that danger the rest of my life. Of course I finally found out no matter how hard you try to keep hatred out of yourself, there's no way you can control it in others. And it's awfully hard to steer clear when the people around you are simmering with it.

I used to spend a lot of time thinking about these sorts of things, about what they had to do with what finally happened to me. But after a while that kind of thinking can wear a fellow out, especially when no answers come. And the days go by. And life goes on. After a while you learn to just put it aside, to let it be and try to move on.

Of course, the idea of moving on takes on a whole different meaning when you're seventy-seven years old, when you're bound to a wheelchair and living alone, the way I am today. I used to always think of myself as a man in a hurry. There were never enough hours in the day for me. But now things have really slowed down. The days pass pretty slowly when they're spent in one spot, sitting still. My telephone rings now and then, but it takes me a while to get to it, what with this wheelchair. Sometimes I answer in time, but just as often no one's on the line when I finally pick up. Just a dial tone. It's the same with the doorbell, but then that's usually the nurse who comes by three times a week to give me a checkup and a shave. She's patient enough to wait when she rings. She knows I'm coming.

I don't get out much. It's too much trouble to get myself packed up and loaded into a car. And to tell the truth, it hurts. My legs are numb to the touch, but they still get to aching deep inside sometimes, so it's best for me to stay put. Most of my days are spent right here, in the house where my family grew up. Of course the difference now is they're all gone. Jane's passed away, and the children, they're off raising families of their own. It's just me here now, me and John Williams, an old Army cook who drives down five mornings a week from the trailer where he lives in Cullman County. John fixes breakfast and lunch for me and keeps house a bit. Sometimes it gets a little tight scraping together the money to write him his paycheck, but so far I've managed. If the porch out front is rotting, or the roof upstairs is leaking, I just let those things go and take care of the more pressing things first, like groceries and rent. I've never had a lot of extravagant needs, and that's served me well in recent years.

Mostly I stay at the dining-room table, going through the mail, writing letters and reading the newspapers, although the headlines are just about all I can make out lately. The diabetes that put me in this wheelchair three years ago is working on my eyes now. Reading has always been like a religion for me, so it's easy to understand why the loss of my sight hurts a lot more than the loss of my legs. I'm thankful for the friends who stop in now and then to read to me.

I don't pay as much attention to time as I used to. One day pretty much blends into the next. But then along comes a call like the one I got the other afternoon, and it reminds me how the years have drifted by. This call was my friend Red Cox, from Cox's Mountain, telling me that Albert Rains had died the night before. Albert had just turned eighty-nine. He was born in 1902. They were having the funeral in a few days, and his wife was inviting me to sit near her and other friends at the funeral. I greatly regretted that I was physically unable to attend. I was one of Albert's sincere friends and admirers.

Yes, time surely has gone by. Tom Bevill has been the Congressman from this district for twenty-five years now. While I was losing that race for governor in 1966, he was back in Jasper, running again for Congress and winning this time. He's been there ever since. Tom's on the House Appropriations Committee now, a sign of the seniority he's secured. They don't let just anyone get their hands on the purse strings up there, and the people down here are happy to have their own man in Washington in such a powerful position.

It's a two-hour drive to Gadsden, where Rains's funeral was to be held. I decided I couldn't stand the trip. I sent my regrets, and I've spent some time since then thinking about Albert being gone.

So many are gone now: Lister Hill, John Sparkman, Jim Folsom, Hugo Black, Lecil Gray, Roy Mayhall.

Gone.

And those beyond Alabama, friends and foes alike: Sam Rayburn, John Kennedy, John McCormack, Adam Clayton Powell, Graham Barden, Howard Smith, Claude Pepper.

All gone.

I tried to stay in touch with most of them after that 1966 defeat, but there was no getting around the fact that I was on the outside now, looking in. Lyndon Johnson did his best to help, appointing me to a national commission on libraries. I also set up a law practice in Washington, taking on clients that included the American Publishing Association and the American Vocational Education Association. Lobbying work is what it was, and I was pretty fair at it, though I didn't really like doing it. It was demeaning, to tell the truth, but I was facing some pretty hard reality by that time. Half a million dollars of debt is about as hard as reality can get.

I did all right for a year or two, lobbying for the same causes I'd championed in Congress, but then Richard Nixon was elected President in 1968, the Republicans moved into Washington, and there was not much need anymore for a lobbyist with my particular credentials.

So I came home, swallowed some more of my pride and began knocking on college doors, asking my alma mater and a dozen other universities and junior colleges in the state if they could use a history or English or political science instructor with some pretty extensive personal experience behind him. The responses were all the same. They said, no, they couldn't do that. They told me I'd become a controversial fellow, pretty much an untouchable as far as state institutions went. They all had to depend on George Wallace and his people for funds to keep them going, and George would not appreciate seeing Carl Elliott's name on the payroll.

Now that kind of broke my spirit a little bit. Colleges, education, those things always meant so much to me, more than anything else in the world when you got right down to it. I'd aimed a lot of my work, a lot of my life, in those directions. So when those doors were closed to me, well, I felt awfully bad about that.

Still, there was no time to feel sorry for myself. That wouldn't help my family, and it wouldn't satisfy my creditors. I needed work, and if no one else would give it to me, I'd make it myself, which I did, going back to lawyering and building a base among the same clients I'd had thirty years earlier—the poor and the disadvantaged. It wasn't easy stepping back into the world of cold calls and wooing clients at age sixty. It was hard to swallow, being back in the same place, doing the same thing I'd done when I was twenty-five. It was hard seeing the lawyers around me who were my age, with their careers built up so big, with their houses and their land and all their possessions. They had carved out their place, and here I was, again looking for mine.

I know it wasn't easy for my family. Jane never said a word, never complained when she went back to work herself, opening up a little bookstore down in town. But I know it was awfully tough for my children to see us having to work hard to make ends meet, and to see people point at me as I walked down the street, saying, "There's that old son of a bitch that didn't have sense enough to keep after his business, the bastard that turned his back on us. He'd of been up yonder if he'd had any sense."

"Up yonder" is what folks around here call Washington. They'll send a fellow back there until his twilight years, then bring him home to die in comfort and security, as long as he does well enough by them. Me, I had become pretty much a political cast-away, an untouchable, and I know that had to be hard for my children to see, no matter how much they believed in me and the things I stood for. It would have been so much easier for them to proudly point to their father as a more typical former United States Congressman.

I was looking for my place, and I found it with my son Carl. We went into a law partnership together with Caine O'Rear, Jr., and Joel P. Robinson, the latter of whom, as this is written, is chairman of the Walker County Democratic Committee. This partnership was formed in the late 1960s. This was just about the time the federal government had started paying damages to coal miners with black lung disease. I built up a pretty good practice at that, and a pretty good reputation as well. Folks—coal miners—came from all over, from Florida, Kentucky, West Virginia, to see me about their cases. If you could prove they had it, prove it in court and make it stick, it was worth about fifteen to twenty thousand dollars to each appli- cant, which might not seem like much to some people but can mean a whole lot to a person who needs it. And along with that money, the government paid me a fee of about ten percent for each case I won—*if* I won.

I won quite a few, handling as many as thirty-six cases in a year, and paying my creditors about half of every dollar I earned. Over the course of ten years, I was able to cut my debt in half, but by the mid-1980s, with the Reagan administration slicing black lung benefits, that business shrank to almost nothing.

There was other law work I did during that time that I was awfully proud of, including representing the Creek Indian nation east of the Mississippi against the United States of America—yes, the same Creek Indians who had been brutalized a century and a half earlier by Andrew Jackson. This was in 1974, when the descendants of the Creeks who had been driven into Florida after the Battle of Horseshoe Bend were continuing a court fight over a claim they had first filed in 1951 for three million acres of land they had been promised under a treaty written in 1814. The modern Creeks had now merged with the Florida Seminoles, and the government was using this fact to resist the Creek claim. We were making good headway with that case, until I had a heart attack that summer. By the time I recovered, the case had stalled and was eventually dismissed.

That heart attack was just the sort of thing that has seemed to rise up and snap at me at just the wrong time, time and time again over the past twenty-five years. When things are going good for a fellow, it's pretty easy for him to get to thinking he's just as smart as hell, that he can do just about anything. But the one thing he forgets to figure on is calamity. And it comes. You never know when, you never know how, and rarely do you know why, but it comes. And when it does, it can pull everything you've got out from under your feet.

Just about the time I left Congress, I helped bankroll my brothers in a chicken farm operation. It seemed like a safe investment at the time. Who could have known egg prices would start falling the next year and keep sinking until it got so bad it finally busted us? That pushed my debt a little deeper.

Who could have known the worst tornado of the century

would rip through the heart of Jasper in 1974, tearing open the back half of my house at a time when I hadn't had the money to keep up my home insurance payments?

But the money matters meant nothing next to my son Carl's death in 1977.

We'd known Carl was diabetic ever since he'd been bitten by a squirrel when he was nine and Dr. T. B. Payne, Jr., had discovered the condition while performing routine tests related to the bite. He'd been on insulin ever since and, except for his pack-a-day smoking habit, had taken real good care of himself. So I was worried when his wife called in the middle of the night early that year to say Carl was having some pretty severe chest pains. We got him in an ambulance, and the hospital in Jasper sent him on to Birmingham. The doctors in the cardiac unit down there stabilized him and said he'd be all right, and he was, for the next several days. But on a Thursday afternoon, as I was down in the hospital cafeteria getting a sandwich and Jane was on her way back to Jasper to pick up a change of clothes, a nurse rushed in and told me I better get back upstairs. When I got to Carl's floor, two doctors and a chaplain met me. I knew then my boy was dying. They didn't have to tell me.

He was still alive when I came in his room, but he was unconscious. Five minutes after that, Carl was dead. He was thirty-five years old. When Jane got to the hospital an hour later, I met her with the news. Our son's body had already been sent to the morgue.

I can't describe how hard Carl's death hit us, all of us. Jane and me, John and Martha and Lenora. Any family who has gone through something like that knows what I mean. And those that haven't, well, there's no way they can ever know. And they should be thankful that's so.

I found out I was diabetic in 1975 and began taking insulin that year, giving myself the same shots Carl had since he was nine. Even with that medication, a person has spells now and then. You feel dizzy, sometimes you even pass out. It's hard to tell when they'll come on. One day, a few years after Carl passed away, I was driving up near Gober Ridge and decided to stop by the old house where I'd been raised, to muse a little bit. I was parked there for a short while and began feeling lightheaded. It quickly got to the point where I couldn't stay awake. So I locked the car doors and laid back to rest.

Next thing I knew, I was wakened by the sound of someone tapping on the window. There stood this big fellow shaking his head and telling me I couldn't be there, that I had to move my car, that this was private property. Half awake, I told him this was where I'd been raised, that I'd played in this yard right here when I was a boy.

He wasn't much impressed by that. I still had to move, he said. As I was leaving, I asked him who he was, anyway. He told me he was the caretaker for the cemetery across the road. I told him I meant what was his *name*. I knew just about every family name in those parts, and sure enough I recognized his when he told me. His grandmother and my mother were first cousins, as were his grandfather and my father.

None of that meant much to him, and neither did my name. As I was driving away, I thought it was pretty funny that I'd go back to the place I grew up and be driven out by a man who had never heard of me—of my name, or who I was, or what I'd done. I thought that was a strange thing, but really it isn't. It happens often to me now.

That visit to Gober Ridge took place in 1984. A year later, Jane came down with what we thought was the flu. She was walking unsteadily and had a severe headache. Jane was never one to take sick, but this thing stayed with her for several days. Finally we got her to the hospital in Jasper, and just as they had done with Carl, they sent Jane down to Birmingham, where tests revealed an abscess on her brain. Surgery was performed immediately. The doctors said it looked pretty bad, but not fatal. After the operation, the surgeon came out and told me I was a mighty lucky man. "Your wife's going to be all right," he told me.

That was on a Thursday afternoon. I was back at home on Saturday morning when the phone rang at 2 A.M. Something was wrong with Jane, they said, and I should get right there. At 4 A.M. I was at Jane's bedside. At 9 P.M. Harold Benson, a minister from Jasper, arrived. At ten, Jane died.

More than five hundred people came to Jane's funeral at the

First United Methodist Church, the same church where Franklin Roosevelt had come when William Bankhead died.

It wasn't far from there to the Oak Hill Cemetery, where Jane was buried, in a plot beside our son.

Loneliness is not something I ever paid much attention to. It's not something I ever had time for. But when Jane died, for the first time in my life I felt lonely. It wouldn't hit me too hard during the daytime, but at night, that's when I'd start to feel it. Suddenly finding yourself at home alone, with your wife gone, your children gone, knowing they're gone for good, that no one's coming back, that takes some getting used to. That takes a lot of getting used to.

Things were only compounded by the fact that my circle of friends had grown so much smaller over the years, that my career and business had shrunk to almost nothing and that I still had the burden of debt pressing hard on my shoulders—and on my soul. It was torture to know I owed any man something I was unable to pay. And that torture only got worse when my condition developed into diabetic neuropathy, numbing the nerves in my legs, deadening the muscles and putting me in a wheelchair in 1988. Things had been slowing down for me for some time, but that brought everything to just about a standstill. For more than twenty years my world had been shrinking pretty steadily, my life closing in to a tighter and tighter circle. Now it had finally pulled pretty much inside the walls of my home, which is where I have stayed almost entirely since then.

I'd talk to Garve every week, but he had his own life, his business interests and his own family to tend to. My children were there for me if I needed them, but no man wants to be a burden, especially on his own family. I certainly wasn't seeking, nor would I accept, pity. I still had work to keep my busy, researching and writing a series of books I had begun in the 1950s on the history of northwest Alabama. I had a secretary from Red Bay named Barbara Cashion to help me with the latest of those books, and she became a good friend as well, someone I could count on in a pinch. And if I needed them, there was always Mary Allen Jolley down in Tuscaloosa and Julian Butler in Huntsville, good friends to the end.

That pretty much summed up the boundaries of my world in early 1989, when I got a phone call out of the blue from a fellow who said he was a reporter for the Boston *Globe*. Said his name was Wil Haygood and he was writing a book about Adam Clayton Powell. He wanted to know if he could come talk to me about Powell, which he did. Not long after, he called again, and this time he said he wanted to talk to me about myself, for a story in his newspaper. I didn't see why anyone in Boston would care about Carl Elliott, but I was willing, and Wil came on down. He spent a few days, talking to me and hunting up some of my old friends. Then he left, and not long after I got a copy of his story in the mail. It was headlined TWILIGHT OF A SOUTHERN LIBERAL—CARL ELLIOTT: FLAT BROKE AND NEARLY FORGOTTEN:

JASPER ALA.—His creditors, like wild geese, have come and gone, and come again. Sometimes, knowing it is them, he just lets the phone ring; damn the debt. Dead leaves circle the yard and the weeds need cutting. The other day a couple of boys came by, wanting to clean the place up and make a few bucks. The old congressman is flat broke. He waved them off.

Books, literary books, are everywhere in the house. He reads by a naked lightbulb. After supper he grabs a piece of his stomach flesh and sticks himself with a needle's worth of insulin. He was in the kitchen one morning, frying something Southern and fell like timber. It wasn't just the diabetes anymore. A muscle disorder popped up out of the blue. He needs a walker to walk. His personal papers are in boxes nudged against the living room wall. Somewhere there's an honorary degree from Tufts University, for his sponsoring "numerous bills in Congress affecting education and welfare of the disadvantaged." He is trying to press the life together now and ship it off to the university in Tuscaloosa. "There is enough," he is saying about his papers, "to keep my friends and enemies busy for a long time."

For much of his 16 years in Congress, Carl Elliott was one of the most powerful legislators in America. In 1958 he pushed the historic National Defense Education Act through Congress,

a furious and eloquent reaction against the Russians' launch of
Sputnik. The act enabled millions to attend college on student
loans. Even in the 1950s Elliott had 1960s passions. He got on
the House Rules Committee in 1961 because they needed a
Southerner willing to go against other Southerners who were
holding up John F. Kennedy's bills. With Kennedy, everything
was jets taking off. With Kennedy in the White House, Carl
Elliott was in the White House.

But Elliott would attract the kind of hate in Alabama that
Kennedy did when he took on George Wallace. Alabamians
voted Elliott out of office in 1964. He sat idle for a while, then,
sensing victory hissing from the State House door in Montgomery, or something approaching victory, he returned to Alabama
in 1966 and took on George Wallace for the governorship,
flinging his big brooding body at Wallace and all that Wallace
stood for.

It was a brutal campaign, of gunfire and bomb threats, of
tiny desperation and loud hopes. When his campaign ran out of
money, Elliott told everyone to hold on, he'd get more. He
withdrew every red cent from his congressional pension. Tilt at
windmills and they sometimes tilt back. He lost.

A kind of darkness has spread over his life since then.
Right in front of his eyes they took his house. He couldn't meet
the mortgage. The family farm has also been yanked. The car
was repossessed, and that wasn't too long ago. He had been
driving around without insurance anyway. Folks do gossip,
here and everywhere. It has been hard to stay. "Nearly starved
to death," he says. Little wonder he reads poetry, and anything
he can get his hands on about Thomas Jefferson. "Jefferson lost
his farm. He sold his library to the Library of Congress. He had
a lot of the same problems I had. Makes a fella feel kind of kin
to him," says Elliott.

You can get here by taking the John Hollis Bankhead
highway out from Birmingham. John Hollis was Tallulah Bankhead's granddaddy. She left Jasper for the London stage and
became, as they called it in those days, a smash.

The sign in the yard reads "Carl Elliott Sr., Attorney at Law." The sign is as big as a door.

. . . His clients, says Garve Ivey, "were people who worked in the campaigns who couldn't afford to pay him. These poor folks kept continuing to trip up and down his steps."

. . . With no one at home except himself, mail piled up, so did bills. There was no congressional pension coming in because he had taken it out for the Wallace campaign, which mystified many. "Elliott is quixotic. He's not shrewd and careful. He's restless," says Virginia Van der Veer Hamilton, a retired professor of history from the University of Alabama at Birmingham.

They turned his phone off. He was sued 39 times by creditors. "His life became an absolute economic nightmare," says Julian Butler, a Huntsville lawyer who has handled Elliott's legal woes. They were hounded by courts. "We would string it out in court," says Butler. "Sometimes we had a friendly judge who would not set cases."

There have been fund-raisers. "We have appreciation dinners for him," says Garve Ivey. "Well, people get appreciated out."

Sometimes a storm gathered without warning. There was a move afoot to take Carl Elliott's name off the street named for him here because of a spat with a local official. Garve Ivey still has his teeth in his head. He picked up the phone and made some calls and stopped that movement in its tracks.

Elliott always has loved books. When he was in Congress he'd return almost every weekend and go into the hills giving books away to school libraries. His wife had a bookstore here, but couldn't make a go of it. Elliott would come in the bookstore like the wind, grab books, put them under his arms and then go give them away.

It is strange the way history goes, vertically sometimes, sometimes in circles. George Wallace is in a wheelchair. Carl Elliott is in a wheelchair. One put there by a lunatic gunman, the other by the gift of time. And time is nothing if not a gift.

Poverty has circled up to the congressman again like in youth, when it laid at his chest like a rock. But it is almost a glorious existence now, the way he has been pushed into the blasted history of this state, of schoolgirls dead in church bombings, of Bull Connor, of bullets, of some blacks forgiving George Wallace, of Birmingham's black mayor, of Alabama's good morning light. "When but for the truth," Carl Elliott says, "man ought to die."

Wil Haygood said this story meant a lot to him, personally as well as professionally. He's not from Alabama, but he has grandparents who are. They were sharecroppers, down near Selma, who moved north in the 1930s to make a new life for themselves. They were black, as is their grandson, who now roams the country writing stories for one of the nation's largest newspapers.

A lot of newspapers reprinted Wil Haygood's story about me, and I started getting phone calls and letters from people I'd never met, some who wanted to thank me for the work I'd done in Congress, others congratulating me for what they called my courage, a few offering help in the form of a few dollars.

That gave me a lot of letter writing to do, responding to all this mail. It was good to hear from these strangers, nice to know there were people out there who cared about some of the things that had meant so much to me.

But that mail and those phone calls were nothing compared with what came after it was announced in the spring of 1990 that I had been named the first recipient of the John F. Kennedy Profile in Courage Award. It had been created by the John F. Kennedy Library Foundation to encourage elected officials to show courage in their politics. More than five thousand people were nominated, but I didn't know I was among them until Julian Butler and Mary Allen Jolley let me know they had put together a package about me and sent it to Boston. When word came in late May from the Kennedy Foundation in Boston that I was the winner, the phone began ringing off the hook and it didn't stop for two months.

The trip to Boston was a pretty large affair. More than thirty of my family and friends flew up together. My children were there, of course, and some of my sisters and brothers, and Barbara, and Julian and Mary and Garve. Wil Haygood came. And the Kennedys. And the reporters. To tell the truth, it was hard for me to make it through the day. As much as I wanted to see and do all they had scheduled for me, I had to rest in the middle of the afternoon and miss some of the ceremonies. I made sure, however, that I made it into the Library itself. I'd heard there was a particular display inside, and I wanted to see it for myself. Sure enough it was there, an exhibit on the civil rights movement—including a photo of George Wallace's stand in the schoolhouse door, above an excerpt from a speech John Kennedy made at the time of that showdown. Kennedy's words, though spoken nearly thirty years before, could have been delivered yesterday, as I and just about everyone else in this country watched a videotape of members of the Los Angeles Police Department beating a black man within an inch of his life. News programs showed demonstrations across the country against racism and police brutality. And John Kennedy's words are frozen up on that wall:

"... We face therefore a moral crisis as a country and a people. It cannot be met by repressive police action. It cannot be left to increased demonstrations in the streets. It cannot be quieted by token moves or talk. It is a time to act in the Congress, in your state and local legislative body, and, above all, in all of our daily lives."

Whether it's Bull Connor in 1963 or those L. A. policemen in 1991, the crisis remains.

They gave me twenty-five thousand dollars with the Profile in Courage award, which I've passed on to some of the people I owe. They also gave me a nice trophy, an inscribed silver and glass lantern, that I've donated to the Carl Elliott Regional Library here in Jasper. The folks right here are the ones who first sent me to Congress, so I think it's only right that this award should belong to them.

As for the phone calls and letters, they came fast and furious for a while, from people across the country as well as from friends and former foes right here in Alabama. More than a few letters came from people telling me they'd worked against me during my last campaigns and that they were sorry now for that fact. One fellow apologized and included a hundred-dollar check, "for groceries."

One letter that stood out among the bunch came from a man I hadn't heard from in a long, long time: George Wallace. It began with congratulations for the award, but he quickly turned it around to himself, talking about the subject of civil rights and the good work he'd done for that cause in the years following the 1960s. The letter was typed, but George scribbled a postscript below his signature, reciting the percentages of blacks who had voted for him in his last election. Votes apparently still matter most to George.

That's just like him, always positioning himself, always adjusting and arranging the facts to suit his situation, always gauging the wind and trying to get himself out in front of it. George Wallace spent his whole political career consumed with defining and redefining himself, suiting himself to whatever the times demanded. Judging by the letter he sent me, he's still doing it.

So what does it all mean? What has it all come to? Why should anyone care about an old one-gallused hillbilly's memories of things that happened more than twenty-five years ago? What does my story matter now?

Maybe it doesn't matter much at all. But I look around me, at the nation as a whole, and at Alabama in particular, and I see echoes of the past that convince me my story is more than mere nostalgia.

I see the educational system of our nation in crisis, with alarms that foreign students' test scores are outdistancing those of our own, with reports on education from the federal government calling us "a nation at risk," and I don't see much difference between the situation today and the situation thirty-three years ago, when the National Defense Education Act was passed. A national magazine contacted me after I won the Kennedy Award and asked me to write a piece on what I think should be done about America's educational crisis today. I told them to look up the testimonies, suggestions and programs spelled out in the NDEA, and they'd find some pretty good answers. Not much has changed. Schools, teachers and the entire educational system need money and resources, and the federal government must give it to them.

I see racism bursting out anew in cities and schools across the country, and on college campuses as never before. It's fear and resentment that breed racism, that make people ripe to seek out targets for their anger. That fear is what George Wallace seized on thirty years ago, and it's crept into colleges and into the workplace today, with blacks now challenging white people in places they weren't challenged before. That kind of confrontation can create racism, and we've got to recognize and understand it before we can do anything about it. The struggle for civil rights is far from finished. It's subtler now, it's not being played out in the streets, there are no more Bull Connors around to use as easy symbols. But racism is still there, and our only weapons are awareness and education.

I see Congress, reformed in many ways since the days when men like Howard Smith could choke it with their inordinate behind-the-scenes power, but still struggling with the issue of financial influence and political independence, with the investigation of the so-called Keating Five making headlines in the newspapers every day, with people debating how in the world we can restructure the political process to make elections and campaigns less enormously expensive. The same financial pressures that helped push me out of office and into debt twenty-five years ago are even worse today. Every politician feels them. Somehow we have to insulate our representatives from the tug of money.

I see Alabama still mired in the same fear and anger and resistance that were holding it back thirty years ago. The same forces I wound up helpless against are pretty much still in control of this state today. Alabama has a long history of turning out expatriated journalists who left the state to make their careers elsewhere. One of those writers is a fellow named Howell Raines, whose roots are in Walker and Cullman counties. Raines is now Washington bureau chief for the New York *Times.* Little more than a week after I received the Kennedy Award, the New York *Times Magazine* ran a cover story by Raines about Alabama's ongoing 1990 primary election campaigns and about its historical legacy. The headline described a state "in a Wallace-era time warp, dirt-poor and back-ward." What Raines saw and felt didn't surprise me at all:

> . . . what I found in a series of visits to Alabama was an aston-ishing unanimity of shame and rage that while the New South awakening has energized every other state in the region, Ala-bama remains in what one statewide magazine called "a sleeper hold." . . .

In the early 1800s, the land rush known as Alabama Fever peopled the state's mineral-rich hills and fertile coastal plain with a rough mix of planters, horse-traders, horny-handed woodsmen and enslaved blacks. The state's love of confronta-tion and shady dealing—and the outsider mentality that was marketed as a national political attitude by George C. Wallace —are rooted in that period. Its feelings of aggrievement intensi-fied after the turn of the century, when J. P. Morgan and other capitalists used Alabama iron and coal to fatten bank accounts in Pittsburgh and New York.

These corporations probably deserve as much credit as the Ku Klux Klan for institutionalizing violence as a way of settling social disputes. They used their political influence to convert the Alabama National Guard into a union-busting army. Hav-ing watched bullets, dynamite and horsewhips used against whites eager to claim their economic rights during the 1920's, the state had a model for deadly behavior when its black citi-zens tried to claim their Constitutional rights in the 50's and 60's.

It is impossible to understand what Professor [William] Barnard calls the "retardation of Alabama politics" without mastering this capsule history. Against this backdrop, two other forces come into play—bad luck and an astonishing tolerance for corruption. . . .

Every time the Alabama electorate has risen up and voted for change, something has happened to thwart the process of reform that began more than 20 years ago in the bellwether states of the New South transformation—North Carolina,

Georgia and Florida—and then spread throughout the region, skipping Alabama as if its wells had been poisoned.

Alabama's ship of state "is dead in the water, sort of rocking back and forth, while the flagships of our sister states are steaming steadily past us," says Attorney General Don Siegelman, another Democratic gubernatorial candidate. "Every other state in the South has elected at least one New South governor."

Alabamians appeared ready to vote for a New South progressive in 1966 when Ryan de Graffenried, a racial moderate from Tuscaloosa, was leading the race for governor. His death in a plane crash cleared the way for Wallace, who was barred by law from seeking a second consecutive term, to run his wife, Lurleen, for governor.

In 1970, another progressive, Albert P. Brewer, was leading George Wallace in the polls. Then the Wallace claque unleashed the dirtiest campaign in Alabama history, using the Klan to paper the state with leaflets falsely depicting the clean-living Brewer and his family as sexual deviants, alcoholics and miscegenists. . . .

For years Alabamians comforted themselves by making fun of their backward neighbors. But Louisiana and Arkansas elected polished young Ivy Leaguers as governors while Alabama wallowed along with Gov. Guy Hunt, a former Amway salesman, who is running for another term. Now, even the habit of scoffing at Mississippi, the regional scapegoat, is threatened. Ray Mabus, that state's Harvard-educated governor, has begun an education program that seems likely to lift his state, currently 49th in spending on schools, past Alabama, which is 47th.

The big question in the 1990 election is whether corrupt money, dirty campaign tactics or weak candidates will once again conspire to keep Alabama, in Ray Scott's phrase, "down below the salt in the pickle barrel."

I guess that question was answered when Guy Hunt, using campaign ads with racist and homophobic overtones against his opponent, won that election. He's governor now. And George Wallace's son is treasurer. And Jim Folsom's son is lieutenant governor. And Ryan de Graffenried's son is in the state senate.

Echoes. They're everywhere.

I've gotten to reading the book of Job lately, and I feel good about the fact that I've never lost faith. I've lost no more faith in the idea that doing what seems like the right thing is the only thing you *can* do than I have in the belief that this country is made for a good man and that it has plenty of good men in it. It just might be that I have more faith in America than any man alive. Lord knows, my faith's been tested.

There's been damage, no doubt about it. And not just to me. I can't think of anything worse than what happened to this state, to have it demeaned as George Wallace and the people around him demeaned it. They did Alabama at least one generation of damage, just wiped out one entire generation.

And I'm not fool enough to think it can't happen again, or that it's not still happening right now. It's not dead at all, not at all, the hate and hysteria and fear that lives somewhere in men's minds and in their souls. It's there, like a poison, doing battle with whatever sense of decency each of us might have. That's a struggle that I guess goes on forever, within every one of us.

They asked me to make a speech in Boston when I went up last spring for that award. The words I said then delivered the same message I've tried to share most all my life:

". . . early in my life I became aware that brains and ability knew no economic, racial or other distinctions. When the good Lord distributed intellectual ability, I am sure he did so without regard to the color or station in life of the recipient.

"In my case I dedicated my public life to ensuring in every way possible that the sons and daughters of the working men and women of this nation would have the opportunity to achieve the highest level of education commensurate with their ability, unfettered by economic, racial or other artificial barriers. I am proud of the accomplishments that have been made to that end. But our work is not yet finished.

"As long as we have overcrowded classrooms, underpaid teachers, schools with inadequate libraries and young men and women who are denied an education because they do not have the resources, our work is not yet finished.

"John F. Kennedy's vision for America will not be fully accomplished until all our young people have the opportunity to obtain the quality of education which is their birthright. Such educated young people engaged in public service are essential to meeting the challenges of each new frontier.

"There were those who said I was ahead of my time. But they were wrong. I believe that I was always behind the times that ought to be."

I still have no doubt that education is the answer to almost every problem this nation has. The fact that schooling remains so neglected in my own state breaks my heart. The thing I cherish today, more than any award or honor, is the National Defense Education Act. It is still putting equipment into schools, still training teachers and still giving good students an opportunity to go to college. More than twenty million students have taken that opportunity, and I consider them my family in a way, sort of like my own children.

That's something no one can take away from me. It's kind of like faith, and what a man believes in, and the things he has to live with when he's finally alone with himself and answering to nothing but what's inside him.

When everything's said and done, when all the shouting and the hullabaloo are over, when there are no postscripts left to write, all you've got is yourself and the way you lived your life, the things you stood for or didn't stand for. If you can live with that, you're all right.

And me, I can live with that.

INDEX